LABELING THEORY

LABELING THEORY

Empirical Tests

Advances in Criminological Theory

Volume 18

David P. Farrington
Joseph Murray
editors

Transaction Publishers
New Brunswick (U.S.A.) and London (U.K.)

Library of Congress Catalog Number: 2013012464
ISBN: 978-1-4128-4246-4
Printed in the United States of America

Library of Congress Cataloging-in-Publication Data

Labeling theory : empirical tests / David P. Farrington and Joseph Murray, editors.
    pages cm. — (Advances in criminological theory ; volume 18)
  Includes bibliographical references and index.
  ISBN 978-1-4128-4246-4
  1. Criminology. 2. Deviant behavior—Labeling theory. 3. Criminal behavior. I. Farrington, David P.
  HV6025.L23 2013
  364.3—dc23
                                                    2013012464

Contents

Part III: Specific Empirical Tests

Preface

Labeling theory has been an extremely important and influential theory in criminology, but it has recently been rather neglected. There have been no books on empirical tests of the theory since the second edition of *The Labeling of Deviance: Evaluating a Perspective* in 1980 (edited by Walter Gove). This book aims to reinvigorate labeling theory by presenting a comprehensive range of modern tests of the theory, especially focusing on the effects of official processing on offending.

In the first section on expositions of labeling theory, Ross Matsueda chronicles the early history and development of the theory, highlighting its origins in symbolic interactionist theory and the contributions of the early pioneers. This is followed by Fred Markowitz's review of research on labeling theory as applied to mental illness. Francis Cullen and Cheryl Jonson then discuss the relationship between labeling theory and correctional rehabilitation, concluding that the two paradigms can be reconciled and are not incompatible.

The second section, on previous tests of labeling theory, begins with a review of prior empirical tests by Kelle Barrick. Anthony Petrosino and his colleagues then summarize their systematic review on the impact of juvenile system processing on delinquency. Based on results from twenty-nine randomized controlled trials, and in agreement with labeling theory, they conclude that juvenile system processing has an undesirable effect on offending. Lawrence Sherman then discusses experiments on criminal sanctions, focusing on the relationship between labeling and deterrence, defiance, and restorative justice.

The third section on specific empirical tests of labeling theory begins with a chapter by Marvin Krohn and his colleagues on the effects of official intervention on later offending in the Rochester Youth Development Study.

Joseph Murray and his colleagues then investigate the long-term effects of conviction and incarceration on offending in the Cambridge Study in Delinquent Development. Generally, the results of these analyses of major prospective longitudinal surveys tend to confirm the predictions of labeling theory. Finally, Steven Raphael reviews the effects of convictions and incarceration on future employment outcomes.

We believe that this book presents the best available comprehensive and up-to-date knowledge about labeling theory, and we hope that it will make criminologists even more aware of the importance of this theory.

David P. Farrington and Joseph Murray
Cambridge, U.K.
February 2013

1

Empirical Tests of Labeling Theory in Criminology

David P. Farrington and Joseph Murray

Labeling theory has been very important and influential in the history of criminology, as shown in Chapter 2 by Matsueda. In books on criminological theory (e.g., Cullen and Wilcox, 2010; Lilly et al., 2011), it is always included. However, there have been very few books on labeling theory itself. The most important criminological book was edited by Walter Gove (1980). The present volume is, therefore, the first book on labeling theory in criminology for more than thirty years.

Labeling theory was particularly important in the 1960s and 1970s. The books by Howard Becker (1963) and Edwin Lemert (1967) were very influential and very highly cited. As Cullen and Jonson point out in Chapter 4, the citation analysis by Stephen Cole (1975) showed that labeling theory emerged as a popular perspective in the late 1960s and then became the dominant criminological paradigm in the early 1970s. (For more recent citation analyses, see Cohn and Farrington, 2012.)

Labeling theory was originally presented as a "perspective" rather than a scientific theory with falsifiable empirical hypotheses. However, it focused particularly on two important questions: Why are some people rather than others chosen for official labeling? And what is the effect of official labeling on future behavior? There have been many attempts to investigate the first question, and especially to study possible gender and racial biases in official processing (e.g., Farrington et al., 2003, 2010). However, this book focuses mainly on the second of these questions.

While these questions can certainly be tested empirically, the early researchers on labeling theory were often hostile to traditional scientific research methods. As Gove (1980: 13–14) pointed out, "the labeling perspective is rooted in the symbolic interaction tradition which has been much more concerned with developing insight and sensitizing concepts than with developing sets of testable propositions." In some ways the early researchers often regarded themselves as part of a messianic movement to criticize the evils of state power and the biases against the powerless in official processing. When one of us (David Farrington) submitted an empirical test of labeling theory (that was eventually published as Farrington, 1977) to *Social Forces*, one reviewer basically said that the article should not be published because its scientific approach went against everything that labeling theorists had been fighting for! However, Becker (1963: 179) argued that:

> Labeling places the actor in circumstances which make it harder for him to continue the normal routines of everyday life and thus provoke him to "abnormal" actions . . . The degree to which labeling has such effects is, however, an empirical one, to be settled by research into specific cases rather than theoretical fiat.

This book is based on the assumption that the main hypothesis derived from labeling theory (concerning the effects of official labeling on subsequent behavior) can and should be tested empirically. Ideally, quantitative predictions should be made and tested, for example, specifying how much increase in offending is caused by different types of labeling with different types of people. These quantitative predictions could be based on simple models of offending, such as those proposed and tested by John MacLeod et al. (2012). However, at present, criminological theories rarely make such quantitative predictions.

After its heyday in the 1960s and 1970s, interest in labeling theory declined. As Frances Palamara et al. (1986: 90) pointed out:

> Since the mid-1970s, disenchantment with labeling theory has spread rapidly. Critics have observed that stable patterns of deviance can arise in the absence of societal reaction, and that formal sanctions are typically invoked only after deviance has become serious and stabilized. To support these claims, they have marshalled data indicating that state intervention has "no effect" on recidivism rates or on commitment to deviant careers.

In his influential book, Gove (1980: 268) concluded that:

> By now I think the evidence is quite clear regarding the labeling explanation of crime. Briefly put, labeling theory points to processes that exist but their overall impact is small.

Later Developments

After the initial enthusiasm followed by the disillusionment, the key postulate of labeling theory is now included in several of the most influential criminological theories. For example, Farrington (2006) systematically compared the assumptions of eight major developmental and life-course theories, and found that six explicitly assumed that official processing caused an increase in later offending. For example, Terrie Moffitt (1993) proposed that "snares" such as conviction and incarceration amplified antisocial behavior, and Robert Sampson and John Laub (2005) argued that incarceration could cause labeling and poor job stability, which in turn predicted continued offending.

The effects of official processing on subsequent offending and antisocial behavior is a crucially important topic in criminology, for both theory and policy. Labeling theory is often contrasted with ideas of deterrence and rehabilitation (see Chapter 4 by Cullen and Jonson). It has also been contrasted with defiance theory and reintegrative shaming (see Chapter 7 by Lawrence Sherman).

While this book focuses mainly on offending, there are chapters on labeling theory as applied to mental illness (Chapter 3 by Fred Markowitz) and on the effects of labeling on employment outcomes (Chapter 10 by Steven Raphael). We do not focus on other effects of labeling, for example, on marriage (e.g., Huebner, 2005); on other types of labeling, for example, by parents (e.g., Liu, 2000); or on the effects of labeling communities (e.g., Clear, 2007; Hirschfield, 2008).

There have been many studies on the effects of sanctions on offending. Daniel Nagin et al. (2009) completed an extensive review of the deterrent effects of imprisonment and generally found that (compared with alternative sentences) it was followed by an increase rather than a decrease in reoffending. Similarly, a systematic review by Patrice Villettaz et al. (2006) reported that reoffending rates were lower after non-custodial sentences as compared with custodial sentences in eleven out of thirteen significant comparisons. Another systematic review by Anthony Petrosino et al. (forthcoming) concluded that reoffending rates were greater after a deterrent intervention in institutions ("Scared Straight") than in control conditions. Also, a systematic review of the effects of boot camps by David Wilson and Doris MacKenzie (2006) found very variable effects but overall no evidence of any consistent impact on reoffending. In criminology, generally, there is a widespread belief that punitive interventions are likely to lead to more, rather than less, offending.

Investigating the Effects of Labeling

In investigating the effects of labeling, it is important to control for selection effects in order to maximize the internal validity of the conclusions (Farrington, 2003; Murray et al., 2009). For example, if we investigated the effects of labeling by comparing the self-reported offending of convicted versus unconvicted youth, a major problem is that the convicted youth were different from the unconvicted youth before the conviction, making it difficult to disentangle the effects of the conviction from pre-existing differences. Selection effects can be controlled either experimentally (in a randomized experiment) or statistically (in a quasi-experiment). The randomized experiment is more convincing because the randomization ensures that the labeled youth are equivalent to the unlabeled youth on all measured and unmeasured variables in advance of the labeling. The quasi-experiment typically has problems in fully equating the labeled and unlabeled youth (because of unmeasured variables) and also in determining causal order (e.g., establishing that the increase in offending occurred after the labeling).

Several randomized experiments have been carried out to investigate either the effects of diversion from the juvenile justice system as compared to court processing or the effect of imprisonment (Farrington and Welsh, 2006). Generally, the experiments show either no difference in subsequent offending (e.g., Empey and Lubeck, 1971; Barton and Butts, 1990; Killias et al., 2010) or greater offending after a more punitive disposal (e.g., Palmer, 1974; Klein, 1986). Several experiments on restorative justice and spouse assault are reviewed in Chapter 7 by Lawrence Sherman. The experiment of Malcolm Klein (1986) was explicitly intended as a test of labeling theory and generally the results were concordant with the predictions of the theory.

Quasi-experimental tests of labeling theory are most convincing if they are carried out in longitudinal studies (to establish causal order), if labeling is measured by official records and offending is measured by self-reports, and if selection effects are controlled by matching or regression methods. The first cross-sectional tests, using matching, were carried out by Martin Gold and Jay Williams (1969) and Gold (1970). They found that, in most cases, self-reported offending increased after youths were apprehended by the police. The first longitudinal test was carried out by Farrington (1977) in the Cambridge Study in Delinquent Development, which is a prospective longitudinal survey of London males from age eight to fifty-six (Farrington et al., 2013). A later test in the same study is described in Chapter 9 by Murray, Blokland, Farrington, and Theobald.

Farrington (1977) matched boys who were first convicted between ages fourteen and eighteen with boys who were not convicted up to age eighteen on self-reported delinquency at age fourteen, troublesomeness at age ten, and five important risk factors measured at age eight to ten. He found that the self-reported offending of the convicted boys increased by age eighteen, whereas the self-reported offending of the matched unconvicted boys decreased. By studying self-reported offending at age sixteen, he further showed that the increase did not occur until after the conviction. He also tested mediating processes and found that the convicted youths became more hostile to the police after the conviction, but they did not increase their association with delinquent peers. Farrington et al. (1978) then discovered that similar results were obtained for first convictions between ages eighteen and twenty-one.

John Hagan and Alberto Palloni (1990) analyzed the same data but used regression techniques rather than matching. They found that convictions predicted self-reported offending (at ages sixteen, eighteen, and twenty-one) after controlling for prior self-reported offending and key risk factors. In the Montreal longitudinal–experimental study, Uberto Gatti et al. (2009) showed that juvenile justice intervention (especially placement) predicted adult official offending (in a regression analysis) after controlling for juvenile self-reported offending and key risk factors. And in the Edinburgh Study of Youth Transitions and Crime, Leslie McAra and Susan McVie (2007) used propensity score matching to demonstrate that juvenile justice interventions were followed by an increase in self-reported offending. The important analyses in the Rochester Youth Development Study by Jón Bernburg and Krohn (2003) and Bernburg et al. (2006) are discussed in detail in Chapter 8 by Krohn, Lopes, and Ward. They also concluded that official processing was followed by an increase in self-reported offending.

One of the most important recent literature reviews, of the effects of arrests and sanctions on subsequent behavior, was completed by Huizinga and Henry (2008). Based on counting amplifying, suppressing, and null results, they concluded (p. 245) that "the weight of evidence suggests that arrest and sanctions either do not have much effect or increase subsequent delinquent behavior." In Chapter 4, Kelle Barrick reviews empirical tests of labeling theory, focusing on significant results, while in Chapter 5 Petrosino, Turpin-Petrosino, and Guckenburg report on a meta-analysis of the impact of juvenile system processing on delinquency. Both conclude that the preponderance of evidence suggests that official labeling tends to be followed by an increase in offending.

Future Developments

We hope that this book describes the "state-of-the-art" of current empirical research on labeling theory and the effects of official processing on offending. In order to carry out even better tests of the main hypothesis, new randomized experiments on sanctions are needed, and new longitudinal studies should be carried out, beginning in childhood, with frequent repeated measures of both official processing and self-reported offending. These latter studies could investigate how changes in offending cause official processing and how official processing causes changes in offending. One of the best existing longitudinal studies for this purpose is the Pittsburgh Youth Study. Farrington et al. (2002) used the repeated assessments to show that changes within individuals in parenting factors were followed by changes within individuals in self-reported offending. It is also desirable to implement randomized experiments within prospective longitudinal studies (Farrington, forthcoming).

In future research on labeling, it is important to investigate mediators and moderators, as recommended by Raymond Paternoster and LeeAnn Iovanni (1989), following the methods pioneered by Reuben Baron and David Kenny (1986; see, e.g., Theobald et al., 2013). Labeling theory suggests that a deviant self-concept is an important mediating factor (e.g., Adams et al., 2003; Cechaviciute and Kenny, 2007), but this has rarely been studied in experimental or longitudinal tests of the theory. Similarly, the effects of labeling may vary with gender (e.g., Lanctôt et al., 2007) or race (e.g., Harris, 1976), but these kinds of moderating factors have also rarely been investigated in the major experimental and longitudinal (community) studies.

Research on labeling theory has important implications for policy and practice. The current findings showing that official processing is often followed by an increase (or at least no decrease) in offending are very worrying. More research is needed to specify the types of sanctions that are most effective with different types of people. It is to be expected that, depending on types of sanctions, types of people, and other boundary conditions or moderating factors, official processing might increase, decrease, or have no effect on offending. Future research on labeling theory (and on associated topics such as deterrence, rehabilitation, defiance, and restorative justice) should lead to recommendations about how to decrease offending. That would be in everyone's interests.

References

Adams, M. S., C. Y. Robertson, P. Gray-Ray, and M. C. Ray. "Labeling and Delinquency." *Adolescence* 38 (2003): 171–86.

Baron, R. M. and D. A. Kenny. "The Moderator–Mediator Variable Distinction in Social Psychological Research: Conceptual, Strategic, and Statistical Considerations." *Journal of Personality and Social Psychology* 51 (1986): 1173–82.

Barton, W. H. and J. A. Butts. "Viable Options: Intensive Supervision Programs for Juvenile Delinquents." *Crime and Delinquency* 36 (1990): 238–56.

Becker, H. S. *Outsiders: Studies in the Sociology of Deviance*. New York: Free Press, 1963.

Bernburg, J. G. and M. D. Krohn. "Labeling, Life Chances, and Adult Crime: The Direct and Indirect Effects of Official Intervention in Adolescence on Crime in Early Adulthood." *Criminology* 41 (2003): 1287–318.

Bernburg, J. G., M. D. Krohn, and C. J. Rivera. "Official Labeling, Criminal Embeddedness, and Subsequent Delinquency: A Longitudinal Test of Labeling Theory." *Journal of Research in Crime and Delinquency* 43 (2006): 67–88.

Cechaviciute, I. and D. T. Kenny. "The Relationship between Neutralizations and Perceived Delinquent Labeling on Criminal History in Young Offenders Serving Community Orders." *Criminal Justice and Behavior* 34 (2007): 816–29.

Clear, T. R. *Imprisoning Communities: How Mass Incarceration Makes Disadvantaged Neighborhoods Worse*. New York: Oxford University Press, 2007.

Cohn, E. G. and D. P. Farrington. *Scholarly Influence in Criminology and Criminal Justice*. Hauppage, NY: Nova Science Publishers, 2012.

Cole, S. "The Growth of Scientific Knowledge: Theories of Deviance as a Case Study." In *The Idea of Social Structure: Papers in Honor of Robert K. Merton*, edited by L. A. Coser, 175–220. New York: Harcourt Brace Jovanovich, 1975.

Cullen, F. T. and P. Wilcox, eds. *Encyclopedia of Criminological Theory*, 2 vols. Thousand Oaks, CA: Sage, 2010.

Empey, L. T. and S. G. Lubeck. *The Silverlake Experiment: Testing Delinquency Theory and Community Intervention*. Chicago: Aldine, 1971.

Farrington, D. P. "The Effects of Public Labelling." *British Journal of Criminology* 17 (1977): 112–25.

——. "Methodological Quality Standards for Evaluation Research." *Annals of the American Academy of Political and Social Science* 587 (2003): 49–68.

——. "Building Developmental and Life-Course Theories of Offending." In *Taking Stock: The Status of Criminological Theory*, edited by F. T. Cullen, J. P. Wright, and K. R. Blevins, 335–64. New Brunswick, NJ: Transaction, 2006.

——. "Longitudinal and Experimental Research in Criminology." In *Crime and Justice, 1975–2025*, edited by M. Tonry. Chicago: University of Chicago Press, forthcoming.

Farrington, D. P., D. Jolliffe, J. D. Hawkins, R. F. Catalano, K. G. Hill, and R. Kosterman. "Why Are Boys More Likely to Be Referred to Juvenile Court? Gender Differences in Official and Self-Reported Delinquency." *Victims and Offenders* 5 (2010): 25–44.

Farrington, D. P., R. Loeber, and M. Stouthamer-Loeber. "How Can the Relationship between Race and Violence Be Explained?" In *Violent Crime: Assessing Race and Ethnic Differences*, edited by D. F. Hawkins, 213–37. Cambridge: Cambridge University Press, 2003.

Farrington, D. P., R. Loeber, Y. Yin, and S. J. Anderson. "Are Within-Individual Causes of Delinquency the Same as Between-Individual Causes?" *Criminal Behaviour and Mental Health* 12 (2002): 53–68.

Farrington, D. P., S. G. Osborn, and D. J. West. "The Persistence of Labelling Effects." *British Journal of Criminology* 18 (1978): 277–84.

Farrington, D. P., A. R. Piquero, and W. G. Jennings. *Offending from Childhood to Late Middle Age: Recent Results from the Cambridge Study in Delinquent Development.* New York: Springer, 2013.

Farrington, D. P. and B. C. Welsh. "A Half-Century of Randomized Experiments on Crime and Justice." In *Crime and Justice*, edited by M. Tonry, vol. 34, 55–132. Chicago: University of Chicago Press, 2006.

Gatti, U., R. E. Tremblay, and F. Vitaro. "Iatrogenic Effect of Juvenile Justice." *Journal of Child Psychology and Psychiatry* 50 (2009): 991–98.

Gold, M. *Delinquent Behavior in an American City.* Belmont, CA: Brooks/Cole, 1970.

Gold, M. and J. R. Williams. "National Study of the Aftermath of Apprehension." *Prospectus: A Journal of Law Reform* 3 (1969): 3–12.

Gove, W. R., ed. *The Labeling of Deviance: Evaluating a Perspective.* 2nd ed. Beverly Hills, CA: Sage, 1980.

Hagan, J. and A. Palloni. "The Social Reproduction of a Criminal Class in Working-Class London, Circa 1950–1980." *American Journal of Sociology* 96 (1990): 265–99.

Harris, A. R. "Race, Commitment to Deviance, and Spoiled Identity." *American Sociological Review* 41 (1976): 432–42.

Hirschfield, P. J. "The Declining Significance of Delinquent Labels in Disadvantaged Urban Communities." *Sociological Forum* 23 (2008): 575–601.

Huebner, B. "The Effect of Incarceration on Marriage and Work over the Life Course." *Justice Quarterly* 22 (2005): 281–303.

Huizinga, D. and K. L. Henry. "The Effect of Arrest and Justice System Sanctions on Subsequent Behavior: Findings from Longitudinal and Other Studies." In *The Long View of Crime: A Synthesis of Longitudinal Research*, edited by A. M. Liberman, 220–54. New York: Springer, 2008.

Killias, M., G. Gillieron, F. Villard, and C. Poglia. "How Damaging Is Imprisonment in the Long-Term? A Controlled Experiment Comparing Long-Term Effects of Community Service and Short Custodial Sentences on Reoffending and Social Integration." *Journal of Experimental Criminology* 6 (2010): 115–30.

Klein, M. W. "Labeling Theory and Delinquency Policy: An Experimental Test." *Criminal Justice and Behavior* 13 (1986): 47–79.

Lanctôt, N., S. A. Cernkovich, and P. C. Giordano. "Delinquent Behavior, Official Delinquency, and Gender: Consequences for Adulthood Functioning and Well-Being." *Criminology* 45 (2007): 131–57.

Lemert, E. M. *Human Deviance, Social Problems, and Social Control.* Englewood Cliffs, NJ: Prentice-Hall, 1967.

Liu, X. "The Conditional Effect of Peer Groups on the Relationship between Parental Labeling and Youth Delinquency." *Sociological Perspectives* 43 (2000): 499–514.

MacLeod, J. F., P. G. Grove, and D. P. Farrington. *Explaining Criminal Careers: Implications for Justice Policy.* Oxford: Oxford University Press, 2012.

McAra, L. and S. McVie. "Youth Justice? The Impact of System Contact on Patterns of Desistance from Offending." *European Journal of Criminology* 4 (2010): 315–45.

Moffitt, T. E. "'Life-Course Persistent' and 'Adolescence-Limited' Antisocial Behavior: A Developmental Taxonomy." *Psychological Review* 100 (1993): 674–701.

Murray, J., D. P. Farrington, and M. P. Eisner. "Drawing Conclusions about Causes from Systematic Reviews of Risk Factors: The Cambridge Quality Checklists." *Journal of Experimental Criminology* 5 (2009): 1–23.

Nagin, D. S., F. T. Cullen, and C. L. Jonson. "Imprisonment and Reoffending." In *Crime and Justice*, edited by M. Tonry, vol. 38, 115–200. Chicago: University of Chicago Press, 2009.

Palamara, F., F. T. Cullen, and J. C. Gersten. "The Effect of Police and Mental Health Intervention on Juvenile Deviance: Specifying Contingencies in the Impact of Formal Reaction." *Journal of Health and Social Behavior* 27 (1986): 90–105.

Palmer, T. B. "The Youth Authority's Community Treatment Project." *Federal Probation* 38, no. 1 (1974): 3–14.

Paternoster, R. and L. Iovanni. "The Labeling Perspective and Delinquency: An Elaboration of the Theory and Assessment of the Evidence." *Justice Quarterly* 6 (1989): 359–94.

Petrosino, A., C. Petrosino, M. Hollis-Peel, and J. Lavenberg. "Effects of Scared Straight on Subsequent Delinquency." In *Encyclopedia of Criminology and Criminal Justice*, edited by G. J. N. Bruinsma and D. Weisburd. New York: Springer-Verlag, forthcoming.

Sampson, R. J. and J. H. Laub. "A General Age-Graded Theory of Crime: Lessons Learned and the Future of Life-Course Criminology." In *Integrated Developmental and Life-Course Theories of Offending*, edited by D. P. Farrington, 165–81. New Brunswick, NJ: Transaction, 2005.

Theobald, D., D. P. Farrington, and A. R. Piquero. "Childhood Broken Homes and Adult Violence: An Analysis of Moderators and Mediators." *Journal of Criminal Justice* 41 (2013): 44–52.

Villettaz, P., M. Killias, and I. Zoder. "The Effects of Custodial vs. Noncustodial Sentences on Re-offending: A Systematic Review of the State of Knowledge." *Campbell Systematic Reviews* (2006): 13.

Wilson, D. and D. L. MacKenzie. "Boot Camps." In *Preventing Crime: What Works for Children, Offenders, Victims, and Places*, edited by B. C. Welsh and D. P. Farrington, 73–86. Dordrecht, Netherlands: Springer, 2006.

Part I

Development of Labeling Theory

2

The Natural History of Labeling Theory

Ross L. Matsueda

Labeling theory remains a major theoretical perspective in the study of crime and deviance. To gain a thorough understanding of labeling theory, it is important to trace the rich history of the perspective, including the way labeling theorists have grappled with fundamental social-scientific issues such as the definition of deviance, the use of functionalist explanations, the distinction between realist versus constructionist epistemologies, and the status of causal explanation. Despite continuing debates over key issues, labeling theory has succeeded in producing a body of important empirical research, as exemplified in this volume.

This chapter chronicles the early history of labeling theory and is divided into five parts. Part one summarizes symbolic interaction theory, the underlying set of ideas that provided the impetus for labeling perspectives. Part two presents the initial statements of labeling theory including statements by George Herbert Mead, Frank Tannenbaum, Edwin Lemert, Emile Durkheim, Kai Erikson, and Howard Becker. Part three discusses the controversy, first identified by Becker (1963), over "actual deviance," and shows how this controversy is rooted in the distinction between normative and interpretative paradigms. Part four proposes a solution to the controversy by returning to seminal ideas of Mead's pragmatism. Finally, part five discusses three promising avenues for future research, including building on recent integrated theories of primary and secondary

Acknowledgment. The author thanks Maria Grigoryeva for comments on an earlier draft.

deviance, applying the medicalization of deviance perspective to advances in pharmacology and behavioral genetics, and using labeling theory as a framework for examining the alarming trends in incarceration in the United States.

Symbolic Interactionist Theory: The Underlying Perspective for Labeling Theory

Herbert Blumer (1969) coined the term "symbolic interactionism" to refer to the ideas of George Herbert Mead, John Dewey, William James, W. I. Thomas, Charles Horton Cooley, Robert E. Park, Ernest Burgess, Robert Faris, and others. These social philosophers and social scientists drew from the philosophical school of American Pragmatism, which assumes that social reality, and by extension, society, is an ever-changing social process, rather than a static structure consisting of unchanging functional positions. Members of society both adapt to societal constraints and structures, and contribute to the creation and re-creation of such constraints and structures. Social order is not a given static property of society; rather, it is constructed through social interaction and negotiation between individuals. For Blumer (1969), the important element of social interaction is the creation of shared meanings using common language or symbols. Through symbolic interaction, individuals reciprocally interpret significant symbols and jointly construct a common definition of the situation, which in turn calls for particular purposive action. In the famous words of W. I. and Dorothy Thomas, "If men define situations as real, they are real in their consequences" (Thomas and Thomas, 1928). Thus, what is important for the consequences or outcomes of interaction is not only the objective situation, but also the situation as defined by the interactants. As we shall see later, labeling theorists applied this dictum to deviant labels, arguing that regardless of whether a person is objectively deviant or not, if that person is defined as deviant, negative consequences will result.

Mead (1934), the most important figure among symbolic interactionists, argued that a fruitful approach to studying society begins with the analysis of the social act or face-to-face interaction. Through a process of communication using language—or to use Mead's term, "significant symbols"—individuals construct shared meanings and understandings. Perhaps the most important shared meaning concerns that of the self. The self arises through role-taking, the process of taking the role of the other, that is, viewing one's self from the perspective of the other and controlling one's behavior accordingly. For example, when adults label a youth a "troublemaker," the youth may come to see himself as a troublemaker, eventually adopting an identity as a troublemaker. In this way, the self is a reflection of appraisals made by significant others (Matsueda, 1992). Cooley used the term "the looking glass self" to emphasize that one's self is a reflection of how others see one.

Among the significant others who help form stable selves or identities are members of primary groups, such as families and peers. Such groups are termed as "reference groups" because they provide an individual with a perspective, a point of reference, and a comparison group (Matsueda, 1992). By taking the roles of reference groups, one comes to see oneself from the perspective of those groups. Moreover, one can take the role of individual significant others serially, or consider the role of the organized group, as in Mead's (1934) term, the "generalized other," which includes the norms and rules by which the group is organized. In this way, symbolic interactionists link organized social groups, including their structures, to an individual's self or identity: as an individual participates in multiple groups, the self becomes multidimensional. Structural symbolic interactionists stress this link through the concepts of role-identity, identity-salience, and role-commitment (e.g., Stryker, 1980).

A key hypothesis of symbolic interactionism, derived from Mead (1934), is that an individual's line of action is influenced by the multidimensional self or identity. Most behavior is habitual, non-reflective, and automatic, following directly from past behavior and generally consistent with one's identity. But when a situation becomes problematic and habitual behavior is blocked or impeded, individuals take the role of others and consider alternative lines of action from the standpoint of those others. An alternative elicits an evaluative response and if inhibited by a negative evaluation, elicits another alternative from the standpoint of others. This continues until an alternative is tried in overt interaction and solves the problematic situation.

Mead (1934) argued that reflective behavior, which entails self-conscious thinking, is a form of role-taking that occurs in the mind and allows people to consider the consequences of their behavior before acting overtly. Dewey (1922) referred to this as engaging in an imaginative rehearsal. Thus, people are able to rehearse various lines of action in their imagination before carrying out the action, in the same way that actors rehearse scenes before going onstage. Moreover, because role-taking involves considering lines of action from the standpoint of reference groups, it follows that behavior is controlled by social groups.

In summary, symbolic interactionism implies that the labeling or appraising of individuals by social groups affects the individuals' identities or social selves. Those identities, in turn, influence subsequent behavior through taking the role of the other, which amounts to a thorough social cognitive process. It follows that, if reference groups or powerful groups, such as the adult members of a community, define a youth as "evil" or "bad," the youth may come to internalize the label as a part of his or her identity, which may increase the likelihood of future deviance. Moreover, if the legal system enters this labeling process and further stigmatizes a youth with officially legitimized designations such as "juvenile delinquent" or "person in need of supervision," the youth may not only take on the corresponding identity, but may also become isolated from conventional reference groups, thereby reinforcing his or her deviant identity and deviant behavior. It is precisely these social processes to which labeling theory turned its attention.

Initial Statements of Labeling Theory

The Psychology of Punitive Justice

The earliest statement of ideas that became central to labeling theory was made by Mead (1918) in his analysis of punitive justice. According to Mead, the usual societal response to criminal acts is hostility toward the criminal. Crime unites otherwise disparate individuals with conflicting interests, values, and attitudes against a common enemy: one who has violated the sanctity of property or individual rights. For example, the thief brings the value of private property into relief for all citizens, who put aside their differences and respond with a set of narrowly delimited impulses of hostility and anger.

Individual selves become one with the community, organizing around a hostile response to a common enemy and increasing the solidarity of the community. The community's response of hostility rather than understanding, anger rather than sympathy, and stigma rather than forgiveness reduces the criminal to a stigmatized enemy in need of retribution, deterrence, and exclusion. Moreover, the hostile response literally *constitutes or defines* the law in action as well as the sanctity of the violated rights. Without the criminal to bring property and individual rights into sharp focus, those rights could not be sustained indefinitely. The system of punishment fails to deter offenders adequately; in fact, it actually works to preserve a criminal class. For Mead (1918: 224), "the attempt to utilize these social attitudes and procedures to remove the causes of crime, to assess the kind and amount of punishment which the criminal should suffer in the interests of society, or to reinstate the criminal as a law-abiding citizen has failed utterly."

Mead (1918) contrasts the hostile response of the punitive justice system to the criminal with the response of the traditional juvenile court to the young delinquent. Here the hostile impulse is restrained, opening the perceptual field to complexities, such as a child's family situation, emotional problems, and developmental progress, and opening the range of responses for helping (not stigmatizing) the child by addressing the child's problems, integrating the child back into the community, and considering the role of the child within social institutions. The community attempts to solve a social problem using reflective intelligence rather than merely venting hostility and isolating the offender.

The Functions of Deviance for Society

Within his general functionalist theory of social integration, Emile Durkheim (1964) developed ideas, similar to Mead's, about the functions of deviance for society. For Durkheim (1964), in relatively undifferentiated and undeveloped societies, social order is achieved through mechanical solidarity, in which criminal laws reflect the collective conscience or shared morality of members of society.[1] The societal reaction to crime is punitive, which serves twin positive functions for society as a whole. First, because a criminal act shocks the collective conscience, attacks the shared morality, and therefore threatens the social order, punishment of the criminal serves to reaffirm the moral order and strengthen the collective conscience. Second, because morality is neither absolute nor inherent in objective behavior, but instead is relative to a given society and historical period, societal punishment serves the function of defining moral boundaries for members of society. On every occasion that calls for the punishment of a criminal, the line between moral and immoral behavior is explicitly drawn for members of society. Punishment is often doled out in public settings, such as floggings, hangings, and executions, which maximize its symbolic value of reaffirming the moral order and defining moral boundaries. For Durkheim (1964), in a "society of saints," in which there is no violence, theft, or robbery, crime would still exist, but would consist of trivial acts of deviance that we would consider merely "bad taste." Those acts, while trivial in seriousness, would nevertheless elicit punishment of the offender for the functions of reinforcing the moral order and defining moral boundaries. For Durkheim, a certain amount of deviant behavior is "normal"—that is, functional—for society.

Kai Erikson (1962, 1966) drew on the ideas of Durkheim, and to a lesser extent, Mead, in expanding labeling theory to include the functions of deviance for society. Erikson (1962) noted that labeling entails a very explicit process of selection. Even hardened criminals engage in conventional routine behavior most of their days, but society singles out a "moment of deviation"—a small island of deviance in a sea of conformity—as a measure of the kind of person he or she "really is." The result may be jail or hospitalization. Erikson (1966) argued that this very selective labeling occurs in a community to define moral boundaries and to develop a sense of group identity. Labeling is not a quiet act of censure; rather, as in the case of a criminal trial, it is a public ceremony used to announce the moral boundary, degrade the deviant, and thereby reaffirm the community's identity. Moreover, Erikson (1966) observed that societal reactions to deviance—including imprisonment, rehabilitation, and hospitalization—do not appear to reform the criminal, which is their manifest function. Instead they appear to stigmatize the offender, segregate the offender with other deviants, and evoke a feeling of distrust from the community. The result is a self-fulfilling prophecy, in which deviants return to their deviant ways. Thus, societal reactions serve a latent function of providing society with a pool of offenders for defining moral boundaries and reaffirming social solidarity. In *Wayward Puritans*, Erikson (1966) examined the Salem witchcraft trials in early Puritan settlements, showing that criminal laws and punishments were invoked against alleged witches in ways that defined moral boundaries and reaffirmed the moral order. The Puritans expressed their emotional hysteria by condemning the witches and labeling them sinners, criminals, and agents of the devil, which in turn helped reduce the factions and tensions between Puritans, Quakers, and other religious sects within the settlements.

Dramatization of Evil

The historian and social scientist, Frank Tannenbaum (1938), explicitly developed most of the arguments of labeling theory in *Crime and the Community*. Influenced by Chicago School sociologists, and particularly Frederic Thrasher's (1927) discussion of spontaneous play groups, sorting on the streets, and formation of delinquent gangs, Tannenbaum used the term "dramatization of evil" to characterize the labeling process, which at its core originates from conflict between youth and the adult community over definitions of situations. From the standpoint of youth, their acts of breaking windows, climbing over roofs, and stealing from street vendors are forms of play, adventure, excitement, mischief, and fun. From the standpoint of the community, these acts are forms of evil, nuisance, and delinquency, which require control, chastisement, and punishment (Tannenbaum, 1938: 17). Repeated conflict between unruly youth and the adult community creates increasing polarization and hardening of attitudes. On one side, the community gradually shifts from defining specific acts as "evil" to defining the perpetrator as "an evil person." Eventually, the youth's companions, hangouts, speech, and personality come to be regarded with suspicion, increasing the likelihood of negative labeling. On the other side, the unruly youth gradually shifts from feeling a sense of injustice at being wrongly accused and punished to recognizing that the community defines him (and his group) as different, bad, and evil. This process may produce a change in the self-identity of the youth, who comes to view himself as delinquent, which in turn causes him to integrate more fully into gangs, which provide escape, security, and mores compatible with his life situation. Of course, different youths respond to negative labeling in different ways—sometimes actively resisting with aggression, sometimes fleeing, and sometimes surrendering. In deciding between these courses of action, young members of the group are susceptible to the influence of older, more experienced youth, who may lead others into overt delinquent acts. The experiences of arrest and incarceration intensify the hardening process for youth, as they open up new social vistas, such as formal institutions of control and the worlds of hardened criminals (see Thrasher, 1927).

In summary, for Tannenbaum, relatively random acts of misbehavior in play groups come into conflict with the adult community not because the children are inherently bad, but because their behaviors are disapproved by adults. This sets in motion a process of escalating conflict, in which adults label youths as "bad" or "evil," the youths respond with resistance within their groups, which in turn elicits increased negative labeling as adults seek to control the increasingly serious behavior of the youths. Often the result is that the "person becomes the thing he is described as being" (Tannenbaum, 1938: 20). It follows that society's response to youth misbehavior, including early intervention, deterrence, and rehabilitation, at times makes matters worse. The counterfactual condition—ignoring a child's early acts of misbehavior, which may be simply due to normal childish immaturity—may have seen the youth aging out of misbehavior, rather than continuing on a career of crime.

Primary and Secondary Deviance

Labeling theory received renewed impetus with the publication of Edwin Lemert's (1951) *Social Pathology*, in which he introduced the concepts of primary and secondary deviance (see also Lemert, 1967). Primary deviance refers to initial acts of deviance that arise from original causes (some combination of social, cultural, psychological, and physiological factors) and has only minor consequences for a person's status, social relationships, or subsequent behavior. Primary deviance tends to be situational, transient, and idiosyncratic—like the minor acts of play by children in spontaneous play groups described by Thrasher (1927) and Tannenbaum (1938). Lemert (1972: 42) notes that most people "violate many laws during their lifetimes" and that the average law-abiding citizen commits many acts that technically are crimes, but are not serious enough to be viewed as crimes either by the perpetrator or the rest of society. Secondary deviance, in contrast, is explicitly a response to societal reactions to deviance and has major consequences for a person's status, relationships, and future behavior. Secondary deviance occurs when society's negative response to a person's initial deviance—such as stigmatizing, punishing, and segregating the offender—causes fundamental changes in the person's social roles, self-identity, and personality. Those changes increase the probability of future secondary deviant acts. Whereas the primary deviant's life and identity are organized around conventional activities, the "secondary deviant's life and identity are organized around the facts of deviance" (Lemert, 1967: 41).

Society's responses to crime and deviance are highly variable, ranging from expression of moral indignation to formal prosecution, stigmatization, and punishment. For Lemert, the most important societal reaction is the response of social institutions of control—such as the criminal justice system and mental health institutions—which are legitimated by the state. Criminal processing in the justice system stigmatizes the individual at every stage, from arrest, detention, court appearance to sentencing and punishment. At times the labeled deviant faces more scrutiny and is subjected to more rules—such as terms of probation and parole, rules in jails and prisons, and regulations in mental hospitals—than other members of society (Lemert, 1967). The process leading to secondary deviance is not immediate, but unfolds over time, as primary deviants are repeatedly subjected to stigmatization and degradation ceremonies by agents of social control. Such degradation ceremonies are likely to be successful when denouncers establish legitimacy with their audiences and demonstrate that the values shared by the audience are violated by the deviant (Garfinkel, 1956). The result may be that deviance achieves a "master status," organizing the deviant's life (Lofland, 1969). In addition, "normals" often structure situations to avoid encounters with deviants because they fear "guilt by association" (Goffman, 1963). Thus, labeling can segregate individuals from conventional realms even in the absence of physical separation. But stigmatization is a process of interaction between individuals and society, in which the individual plays an important role in negotiating, minimizing, and combating stigma by managing the information revealed to others about their identities (Goffman, 1963).

For Lemert, societal reactions are reactions to deviance—at least deviance in the eyes of the social audience—and therefore, one can speak of "deviance" independent of a societal reaction. He argues that societal reactions can be warranted, whereby society is responding to behaviors that are objectively deviant, or unwarranted, whereby society is falsely responding to behaviors that are not objectively deviant. If society labels as a murderer one who has actually murdered another person, the label is warranted; if society labels as mentally ill a person who is merely eccentric, the label is unwarranted. Lemert (1951: 56) uses the term putative deviation as "that portion of the societal reaction which has no foundation in objective behavior" (see Rains, 1975). But who determines whether a societal reaction is putative or not? Presumably, social scientists are best equipped to make such a determination.

Moral Entreprenuers, Moral Enforcers, and the Labeling Definition of Deviance

Perhaps the most important contribution to labeling theory, Howard Becker's (1963) *Outsiders*, helped solidify it as a dominant perspective in the study of deviance. Working within the framework laid down by Tannenbaum and Lemert, and himself a symbolic interactionist, Becker made four important contributions to labeling theory (see Matsueda, 2001): (1) he offered an explicit labeling definition of deviance; (2) he expanded the definition of societal reactions to include the creation and enforcement of social rules; (3) he applied the ideas of symbolic interactionism to describe the process of becoming a marijuana user, developing a deviant subculture, and initiating a deviant career; and (4) he contrasted the positions of labeling theory and conventional theories of deviance on the question of actual deviance.

Becker (1963: 9) provided a formal labeling definition of deviance: "deviance is not a quality of the act the person commits, but rather a consequence of the application by others of rules and sanctions to an 'offender.'" In other words, deviance is not objective norm-violating behavior, but a label conferred by society: "the deviant is one to whom that label has successfully been applied; deviant behavior is behavior that people so label." Similarly, John Kitsuse (1962: 248) defined deviance as a process by which societal members "interpret behavior as deviant, define persons who so behave as a certain kind of deviant, and accord them the treatment considered appropriate to such deviants." Erikson (1962: 11) argued that "Deviance is not a property *inherent in* certain forms of behavior; it is a property *conferred upon* these forms by the audiences which directly or indirectly witness them."

Becker's second major contribution to labeling theory was his conceptualization of societal reactions to include rule creation and enforcement. He argued that the process of creating deviance begins not at the point when a person is labeled deviant—for allegedly violating some rule—but earlier, when social groups and moral crusaders first create those rules. According to Becker (1963: 9), "Social groups create deviance by making the rules whose infraction constitutes deviance, and by applying those rules to particular people and labeling them as outsiders." Rule creation is often instigated by moral crusaders, who are typically from upper classes, motivated by humanitarian concerns, and preoccupied with the substantive ends (rather than the logistical means) of their crusades. They bring attention to their cause using the mass media, organize support from disparate interest groups who share an interest in the cause, and lobby legislators to write laws favorable to their cause. Moral crusades tend to have a natural history, beginning with a broad set of values—like self-determination or the protestant work ethic—passing a specific rule or law based on those values, and then creating a bureaucratic system to enforce those rules.

The task of enforcing rules falls to "rule enforcers"—police, prison guards, security guards—who tend to be more concerned with the bureaucratic imperatives of enforcement than with the actual substantive content of the rules. The law is almost never enforced uniformly to all who fall under its purview; rather, it is selectively enforced. For Becker, law is more likely to be enforced against members of lower classes or racial minorities, and the reasons for selective enforcement are highly variable, often having to do with organizational and political imperatives. Police may perceive that delinquency is largely a problem of lower class minorities and view upper class white rule violators as good kids having adolescent fun. Or they may respond to a public outcry against drunk driving or prostitution and step up their enforcement. In general, the powerless may be more susceptible to labeling than the powerful, even when committing the same infractions. These observations led to a key proposition of labeling theory: social control institutions disproportionately label the disadvantaged and powerless as deviant, regardless of their actual behavior (e.g., Paternoster and Iovanni, 1989). In this way, labeling theory became linked to group conflict theories, which depicted society as segmented into groups with conflicting values and interests (e.g., Turk, 1969; Quinney, 1970). Here, laws are viewed as an expression of one group's political power over others, as powerful groups mobilize the law and law enforcers to sanction behaviors that violate their interests or values.

Becker's third contribution to labeling theory was his analysis of becoming a marijuana user. Here he showed how "deviant motives actually develop in the course of experience with the deviant activity" (Becker, 1963: 42). Thus, novice smokers take the role of experienced users to learn to smoke marijuana, including how to inhale and hold the smoke in the lungs, how to recognize the effects of being high, and how to define the effects as pleasurable. In this way, an inherently ambiguous physiological experience—potentially experienced as dizziness, nauseous, euphoric, or comical—is transformed and redefined into a social object defined as being "high," and more importantly, being *pleasurable*. Such definitions are built up through symbolic interaction in groups, as other experienced peers demonstrate how to smoke properly, how to recognize the feeling of being high (including having the "munchies"), and how to interpret the high feeling as pleasurable and even euphoric. Thus, "marijuana acquires meaning for the user as an object which can be used for pleasure," and with repeated experiences of this sort, "there grows a stable set of categories for experiencing the drug's effects" (Becker, 1963: 56). Moreover, because marijuana is illegal, whether one progresses from a beginning user to occasional user and then to a regular user depends on how one adapts to rule enforcers' attempts to limit supply of the drug, detect drug users, and define the behavior as immoral. Regular users must have developed contacts with drug dealers, must have learned verbalizations that neutralize definitions of the behavior as immoral, and must have dealt with the possibility of being caught by segregating acquaintances into users versus non-users, by withdrawing into groups who condone marijuana, or by realizing that detection would not be so bad. Through these processes, regular users adopt a stable conception of self as a marijuana smoker. In summary, the process of becoming a marijuana user is built up through social interactions, in which social definitions of marijuana smoking derived from peers, is a crucial component.

Becker's fourth contribution to labeling theory was to explicate, using his well-known four-fold table of "types of deviant behavior," a fundamental distinction between conventional etiological theories of deviant behavior and a societal reactions perspective. This is presented in Table 2.1, which cross-classifies types of deviant behavior by whether the behavior violates social rules or norms and whether society perceives the behavior as deviant or not.

The off-diagonal cells refer to the unproblematic cases: obedient behavior that is correctly perceived as conforming, and rule-breaking behavior correctly perceived as deviant. If deviance consisted only of these two categories—that is the other cells were zero—labeling would not be problematic, statistics on criminals would be accurate, and etiological and labeling theories would study the identical phenomenon (Matsueda, 2001). Of more interest are the diagonal cells. The falsely accused is the conforming person who is labeled a deviant anyway. This is the criminal who receives a "bum rap," the normal person whose eccentricity is viewed as mental illness, the effeminate heterosexual male who is labeled gay. The secret deviant is one who violates social norms but avoids being labeled a deviant. Labeling theorists tended to focus on this category. Self-report surveys of delinquency suggest that nearly everyone has committed at least one act of deviance or delinquency. Only a very small segment of society, however, is labeled deviant and that segment appears to be not representative of the population at large, but instead disproportionately drawn from the ranks of the disadvantaged, powerless, poor, and racial and ethnic minorities. Therefore, labeling theorists concluded that deviance is largely a societal reaction rather an objective act. They called for more research on the process of labeling, thereby shifting the focus away from primary deviance and toward institutions, such as the

Table 2.1
Types of deviant behavior

	Obedient behavior	Rule-breaking behavior
Perceived as deviant	Falsely accused	Pure deviant
Not perceived as deviant	Conforming	Secret deviant

Source: Becker (1963: 20).

legal system and mental health system, which dole out labels with the legitimacy of conventional society.

The Controversy over Actual Deviance: Normative and Interpretative Paradigms

Internal Contradiction in the Four-Fold Table

Becker's four-fold table contains an internal contradiction noted by Jack Gibbs (1966) from a positivist position and later analyzed by Melvin Pollner (1974) from an ethnomethodological perspective and by Prudence Rains (1975) from a societal reactions position (see Matsueda, 2001). If deviance is defined not as a "quality of the act," but as a reaction or label by a social group, then how can we speak of *"obedient" or "rule-breaking" behavior independent of the societal reaction*? Those are presumably "qualities of the act." In his retrospective on labeling theory, Becker (1973: 186–87) stated the dilemma concisely: "If we begin by saying that an act is deviant when it is so defined, what can it mean to call an act an instance of secret deviance? Since no one has defined it as deviance, it cannot, by definition, be deviant; but secret indicates that *we* know it is deviant, even if no one else does."

This contradiction created substantial controversy, including attacks on labeling theory by traditionally oriented positivist social scientists. Gibbs (1966) recognized that statements by Kitsuse (1962), Erikson (1962), and Becker (1963) shared a common perspective, which he called "the societal reactions perspective," and argued that at times the perspective appeared to propose a theory of deviance. If so, it needed to explain why actual deviant *acts* (not *reactions*) are greater in some populations but not others, are committed by some individuals but not others, and are labeled in some societies but not others. Subsequently, Walter Gove (1970) criticized Thomas Scheff's (1966) labeling theory of mental illness, arguing that people enter a role of mental illness primarily because of a serious disturbance and not because their random behavior is singled out as instances of mental illness, which is then exacerbated by the labeling process (see also Scheff, 1974; Gove, 1975). Hirschi (1975) criticized Tannenbaum's (1938) initial thesis of deviance amplification on similar grounds.

A different form of criticism, by Woolgar and Pawluch (1985), attacked societal reactions researchers for selectively treating some definitions or labels as problematic, and others—often the researchers' own definitions—as unproblematic. Woolgar and Pawluch argue, for example, that labeling theorists and proponents of the social constructionist view of social problems (e.g., Spector and Kitsuse, 1977) typically assert that a social problem (such as marijuana smoking) has changed little, whereas the societal definition of the problem has changed dramatically (such as being defined as a highly addictive drug). The researchers' assumption that marijuana smoking has changed little is treated as an unproblematic and unanalyzed statement of fact—remaining in the background—whereas the social definition of marijuana as an addictive drug is treated as a problematic statement in need of research. Thus, one category of claims is "laid open to ontological uncertainty" and "made the target for explanation" whereas another category of claims—that of the author—is accepted on faith (Woolgar and Pawluch, 1985: 218). Woolgar and Pawluch (1985) refer to this practice as "ontological gerrymandering," whereby labeling researchers question the realist assumptions of the labelers, while keeping their own realist assumptions hidden. In their conclusions, they ask whether it is possible to move beyond this espousal of relativism within a presentation that is conventional and objectivist. Or in other words, "what would an argument free from ontological gerrymandering look like?" (Woolgar and Pawluch, 1985: 224).

This controversy led to a trifurcation of labeling theory and research into camps differentiated by their stance on "actual deviance." First, most labeling theorists followed Lemert's (1951, 1972) writings, which emphasized the societal reaction component of deviance, but allowed for variation in whether the reaction is warranted or not. Indeed, he defined putative deviance as "that portion of societal reaction" that is unwarranted—for example, blind persons are often treated as if they were hard of hearing even though their hearing is fine, and runaway girls are often treated as sexually delinquent even though they are sexually inactive. Becker (1973) himself adopted such a position, suggesting the term "potentially deviant" to apply to behaviors that have yet to be labeled deviant. For Becker, then, the entire process beginning with rule creation, infraction or potential deviance, and societal reaction are included within an overall interaction perspective. With respect to mental illness, Scheff (1966) introduced the term "residual rule breaking," and argued that such initial deviance has diverse causes, tends to be denied by the actor, is typically transient, and is less important than negative labeling in producing deviant careers.

Second, others, including Kitsuse (1962), maintained a labeling definition of deviance as a label and not objective behavior, and refused to take a stance on "actual" deviance (Rains, 1975). This is consistent with phenomenologists' method of "bracketing" (Husserl's "epoché") the objective world when studying the subjective experience of the actor. This led to studies of how the social reality of deviance is constructed in social interaction, how a sense of deviance is accomplished, and how invariant methods of members are used, including ethnomethodological studies of members' methods (Garfinkel, 1967), studies of the medicalization of deviance (Conrad and Schneider, 1980), and studies of the social construction of social problems (Spector and Kitsuse, 1977).

Third, still others have recently taken the ideas of labeling and symbolic interactionism and incorporated them into causal theories of not only secondary deviance, but primary deviance as well. These theories include Link's modified labeling theory of mental illness (Link et al., 1989), Braithwaite's (1989) theory of reintegrative shaming, Sherman's (1993) theory of defiance, and Matsueda and Heimer's symbolic interactionist theory of differential social control (Matsueda, 1992; Heimer and Matsueda, 1994).

These three lines of research, defined by their stance on "actual deviance," developed largely independently. Societal reaction researchers used ethnographic and qualitative methods to examine societal reactions to putative deviance, ethnomethodologists used conversation and phenomenological analysis to examine the methods that members use to accomplish a sense of deviance, and deductive theorists used quantitative methods to test propositions derived from labeling and interactionist theories.

An important question for labeling theory is whether these three seemingly disparate research camps can be viewed as contributing to a single enterprise, such as an "interactionist framework of deviance," to use Becker's (1973) term. The early answer to this question was a resounding "no," based on fundamental differences in assumptions about whether interaction consists of interpretive processes beyond literal description, and whether descriptions can be adequate for the deductive explanations favored by the natural sciences. These issues were clearly illuminated in Wilson's (1970) well-known distinction between normative and interpretive paradigms, which became influential in debates over the proper way of studying society from a labeling perspective (see especially Pollner, 1974; Hawkins and Tiedeman, 1975).

Normative and Interpretative Paradigms

In an influential article published in the *American Sociological Review*, Thomas Wilson (1970) contrasted the positions of two perspectives in sociology: the interpretive paradigm, which assumes social interaction is an interpretive process among interactants; and the normative paradigm, which assumes social interaction is rule governed.[2] Building on Blumer's (1969) description of how meanings are jointly produced in symbolic interaction through the interpretive process of role-taking, Wilson (1970) argued that Garfinkel's (1967) concept of the documentary method of interpretation shows how multiple indexical particulars (observables) serve as indexes of an underlying pattern in a reflexive relationship in which index and pattern are mutually determining. Applied to labeling, a member of society—either a citizen or social control agent—observes a series of indexical particulars of an individual (strange clothing, abnormal comportment, peculiar behavior) and infers an underlying pattern of "deviant." For Wilson, the interpretive paradigm implies that because all sociological phenomena—including groups, organizations, and social structures—are all rooted in role-taking, all sociological research must assume the subjective role of the actor, using the documentary method of interpretation to arrive at "interpretive" rather than "literal" description.

The normative paradigm, by contrast, assumes that social interaction is governed by rules, norms, or dispositions that are not reflexively tied to the occasions of their use. Based on the assumption of a shared system of symbols and meanings, such rules allow for context-free literal descriptions of situated action. Moreover, literal description, without explicit reference to the perspective of the actors, provides the foundation for deductive explanations that generalize across situations, rather than being inextricably tied to context. A literal description of deviance could eschew interpretive procedures by which each deviant act is initially constituted in interaction, and merely assume that deviance is behavior that violates shared rules that span the situations of their use. In turn, such descriptions would allow researchers to use deductive generalizable explanations. In other words, the normative paradigm justifies social scientists' attempts to conduct research using the model and tools of the natural sciences.

Wilson concludes by arguing that social interaction is indeed an interpretive process. Literal description, possible in the natural sciences, is incomplete in the social sciences because interaction is inherently interpretive rather than deductive. This means that sociological explanation is not deductive but must conform to Blumer's (1969) notion of sensitizing concepts induced through an interpretive process. Therefore, one cannot rely on literal descriptions of deviance but must engage in interpretive descriptions, which must be true to the subjective perceptions of actors. Observation and coding of social interaction cannot be conceptualized as "problems of measurement error" in literal description used in the natural sciences, but must be treated as interpretive processes requiring the researcher to make explicit the "context and grounds for his interpretations" (Wilson, 1970: 706). In the end, Wilson argues for an interpretive sociology that focuses on how members of society produce a social world that is objectified and of which they are themselves a part. Rather than assuming a shared system of symbols that can be taken for granted by the researcher, the accomplishment of those symbols can be investigated as a topic in its own right.

Although rarely articulated so powerfully, this view of interpretive sociology was implicitly adopted by most labeling theorists, who ignored the question of actual deviance and used qualitative methods to study the process by which social control officials labeled some individuals deviant. Researchers using quantitative methods to examine hypotheses derivable from labeling theory tended not to be proponents, but rather critics, who embraced a version of the normative paradigm and rejected the interpretive paradigm. The unfortunate result was the development of lines of research that appeared contradictory and researchers who seemed to talk past one another (e.g., Gove, 1970; Scheff, 1974).

Beyond Normative and Interpretative Paradigms

I argue here for a move beyond the polemics of normative and interpretative paradigms by returning to the pragmatist position of Mead. Such a move will allow us to embrace the disparate research projects conducted by interactionists, constructionists, and positivists under a single interactionist perspective based on pragmatism. We can establish this by distinguishing between patterns of meanings versus situated meanings in Mead's work, and then examining Mead's and Dewey's views on scientific inquiry.

Stable Meanings and Selves versus Situated Meanings and Selves

Mead (1934) began with a methodological holism, in which the society or group is logically prior to the individual. Recall that he begins with the organization of the society or group, and then identifies social interaction, role-taking, and joint action with reference to that organization. Methodologically, this implies that one cannot hope to understand social action without first understanding the structure of the larger groups within which that action takes place. It is this broader social and institutional organization that structures interaction, allows for patterned action, and gives structure to selves.

At the same time, Mead (1934) analyzed symbolic interaction, showing how interactants adjust to each other's conduct, negotiate common meanings, and thereby coordinate their conduct into joint action. A crucial feature of this analysis is a duality of the self, which arises in problematic situations, consisting of an image of a larger organized group (the generalized other or "me") and an acting agent (the "I"). This internal conversation between phases of the self, the "I" and the "me," constitutes cognition, which occurs in the mind to solve a problem. The impulsive response of the "I," which cannot be entirely predicted in advance, gives rise to emergence, creativity, and novelty; the structuring of the "me," which derives from organized groups embedded in social institutions, gives rise to patterned action. Agency, then, arises from the dialectic between the "I" and the "me" (Matsueda, 2006).

The study of symbolic interaction—the way in which meanings are interpreted, actors adjust to each other, and conduct is coordinated—requires direct observation or reconstruction of the interaction process. This is the methodological emphasis of Blumer's (1969) symbolic interactionism, which argues for using naturalistic inquiry, sensitizing concepts, and exploring social phenomena to refine concepts and construct explanations, rather than being imprisoned by rigid theoretical concepts and mindless testing of hypotheses derived from such concepts. Naturalistic inquiry focuses on the social act, stressing the emergent properties of social interaction, which is irreducible to the biographical histories of the individual participants. Such direct observation and inductive reasoning are particularly powerful when examining a phenomenon about which we lack strong theories (Matsueda, 2006).

But many of Blumer's followers have taken literally the polemical arguments of his essay (1956), "Sociological Analysis and the Variable," and rejected the use of statistical analysis of variables to study social phenomena. This is misguided. Statistical analyses are crucial for identifying the structures of organized groups and patterns of meanings that transcend situations. Because individuals are embedded in organized groups and social institutions, they develop consistent reference groups or generalized others. Although complex, overlapping, and ever changing, such embeddedness accounts for stability of reference groups and therefore, stability of the self, which in turn explains continuity in behavior. Individuals, then, are distributed in social groups in ways structured in part by social networks, which cannot be revealed in case studies or studies of interaction sequences. Therefore, researchers must use variables measuring the features of certain organized groups—such as commitments to lawful activities or roles as "bad asses" in school—relevant to the social action investigated.

This is consistent with Blumer's (1969: 139) largely ignored conclusion that "in the area of interpretative life, variable analysis can be an effective means of unearthing stabilized patterns of interpretation, which are not likely to be detected through the direct study of the experience of people." It is also consistent with Mead's (1930) methodological recommendations revealed in his appraisal of Cooley's contributions to social psychology. There, he advocated for the use of statistical methods and community surveys as part of the application of the scientific method to study society, following W. I. Thomas, Park, Burgess, and Faris (see Matsueda, 2006). But what does it mean to apply the scientific method to the study of society?

Scientific Inquiry, Scientific Knowledge, and Taken-for-Granted Knowledge

Mead's (1938) characterization of scientific inquiry follows pragmatist philosophy as well as his specific theory of minds, selves, and societies. Like Dewey, Mead argues that scientific inquiry is the use of reflective intelligence to identify objects and their meanings to solve a problem arising within human experience. That is, scientific inquiry, and the resulting product, scientific knowledge, is concerned with problems arising within human experience, not with an absolute reality arising outside of experience. Within a world largely taken for granted—a "world that is there"—the scientist uses the experimental method of formulating hypotheses, making observations and collecting data, and then testing those hypotheses against observable data. In scientific inquiry, the "world that is there" consists of an unproblematic common world made possible by role-taking, a common language, and a common social organization of perspectives (Mead, 1938). Within this world, problems requiring scientific inquiry arise and "appear as anomalies or exceptions that do not fit the structures of the common world" (Cook, 1993: 179). As in Thomas Kuhn's (1962) analysis of scientific revolutions, anomalies provide transitional guides to scientific knowledge; for Kuhn, anomalies stimulate paradigmatic shifts out of one period of normal science to another. For Mead (1938), to solve an anomaly, scientists must use their creative intelligence to reconstruct the problematic situation, to bring various hypotheses to bear, and to test those hypotheses against data made observable to the scientific community, until a hypothesis is found that resolves the problem. In contrast to unsuccessful hypotheses, which remain largely in the biographies of their producers, successful hypotheses become a part of the reconstructed, common, organized, social world of science (Cook, 1993).

Implications for Research on Crime and Deviance

This discussion has important implications for the contrast between normative and interpretive paradigms and for the conduct of scientific inquiry from a labeling perspective. First, scientific inquiry applied to the physical world does not differ fundamentally from scientific inquiry into the social world. Second, scientific knowledge is not an attempt to grasp absolute reality or absolute truth lying outside of human experience, but instead arises in a thorough social process, in which anomalies or exceptions create problematic situations requiring the construction of hypotheses and the testing of hypotheses against socially observable data. Third, scientific inquiry, addressing an immediate problem, always takes place within a larger taken-for-granted world, in which meanings are assumed unproblematic. Fourth, once a hypothesis solves a problematic situation, it becomes a part of the structure of scientific knowledge, a part of the taken-for-granted world, but its status is always tentative because a future problem may cause it to be disconfirmed or reformulated.

We can apply this approach to the controversy over the status of actual deviance in labeling theory. An objective reality independent of human experience does exist, but it is an indefinite reality that can be characterized in the present in multiple ways, depending on the problematic situation at hand. Thus, social scientists can conceive of actual deviance independent of labeling, which, for the purpose of explaining actual deviance, would constitute a part of the "world that is there." But even as "actual deviance" is treated as unproblematic, it is no less socially constituted. Here it is constituted by the social scientist's measurement instruments, which, for example, could be self-report surveys or official arrest reports. Moreover, "actual deviance," like any other object of inquiry, is always *provisionally* unproblematic. Conceivably, an anomalous finding could be hypothesized to be a result of a measurement problem, which would focus attention on how deviance is measured, in the same way that for many scientists, Heisenberg's uncertainty principle made sense of the effect of shining a light on an electron. At times, then, research on the labeling process, which highlights how deviance is socially constituted, can be crucial for etiological researchers. Such research is of interest to etiological researchers insofar as it determines whether labeling yields measures congruent with the researchers' conception of actual deviance. In contrast, ethnomethodological studies of labeling examine how deviance is socially constituted as a topic in its own right, contributing to a different area of scientific knowledge (e.g., Kitsuse and Cicourel, 1963).

Even though meaningful interaction relies on interpretive processes by interactants to study social phenomena, it is not always necessary to have the subjective perspective of every concrete interactant. There are two reasons for this. First, meaningful interactions are structured and patterned across situations. Those patterns of meaningful action, which are highly stable in institutionalized settings, reveal the subjective perspective of multiple interactants. In such settings, meanings are shared and relatively unproblematic and can often be safely—but always contingently—taken for granted. Second, scientific inquiry seeks to solve problems within a "world that is there," including the common taken-for-granted organization of meanings and scientific knowledge. Applied to etiological research, the taken-for-granted meanings may include the meaning of deviant behavior, such as homicide, which remains contingently unproblematic.[3] Of course, such meanings make up the taken-for-granted world only provisionally, and in the future, they could become objects of inquiry when existing explanations become problematic. At that point, the investigation of interpretive procedures could become essential to etiological research. For example, etiological research using data from the Uniform Crime Reports came under scrutiny with the creation of self-report and victimization surveys. Later, self-reports came under severe criticism until researchers conducted careful studies of the self-report method, finding that within the domain of content—relatively non-serious to moderately serious offenses—self-reports had good measurement properties, and, for the purpose of testing etiological theories of crime, self-reports may be the best measure (Elliott and Ageton, 1980; Hindelang et al., 1981; Huizinga and Elliott, 1986). Such research entails hypotheses tested against observable data, showing what is now taken to "have been there all along." Note that for etiological research, such interpretive research is important precisely because it addresses measurement error.

Finally, this discussion suggests that the implicitly pejorative term "ontological gerrymandering" is misguided. Social scientific research necessarily addresses problematic meanings within a context of a taken-for-granted background. At times, to solve the problem at hand, elements of the taken-for-granted background might be treated as problematic in the form of a hypothesis, and insofar as the hypothesis solves the problem, the background is reconstructed for the scientific community. The distinction between unproblematic background and problematic foreground is constituted in practice by scientists, who create consensus over what can be taken for granted in the present. Rather than being a product of gerrymandering, this distinction is necessarily made in the practice of scientific inquiry.

Directions for Research

Labeling theory has enjoyed a renaissance over the last two decades. Much of this resurgence of interest is the result of new theoretical developments that seek to integrate labeling ideas into a general interactionist theory of both primary and secondary deviance. These advances have the potential for positioning labeling theory to provide a general theoretical framework for interpreting two important recent trends: the advances in pharmacology and behavioral genetics that has expanded the legitimacy of the medicalization of deviance, and the precipitous increase in incarceration in the United States, particularly among young black men, and the dire consequences that have resulted.

Interactionist Theories of Crime, Deviance, and Labeling

Over the last two decades, major advances on labeling theory have been made by integrating labeling ideas with interactionist theories of criminal and deviant behavior. This approach has the potential to treat primary and secondary deviance within a single unified framework. We discuss three of these developments: Link's modified labeling theory, Braithwaite's theory of reintegrative shaming, and Matsueda and Heimer's differential social control.

Link's Modified Labeling Theory

Bruce Link and his colleagues have made substantial advances on Scheff's (1966) classic labeling approach to mental illness. For Scheff, stereotypical notions of how the mentally ill behave are learned through socialization beginning in childhood. A person's residual rule violation may be singled out by others who view it as an instance of their stereotype of mental illness, resulting in a negative label. That label, in turn, constrains the person to adopt the role of a mentally ill person—as social control agents reward such conformity to the role—organize an identity around that role, and ultimately "become" mentally ill.

Link et al. (1989) expanded this theory to a five-stage process of labeling. The first stage concerns the extent to which people believe that mental patients will be devalued and discriminated against by the community. Both patients and other community members will learn these beliefs through socialization. The greater this belief, the more likely mental patients will expect to be rejected by the larger community, and the more likely other community members will in fact reject mental patients. In the second stage, the person is officially labeled by treatment agencies, which makes societal conceptions of mental illness relevant to the self. In the third stage, the patient responds to the labeling with three possible responses: *secrecy*, whereby the treatment history is concealed from employers, relatives, or potential lovers; *withdrawal*, in which the patient limits interactions to those who accept their illness and stigma; and *education*, in which the patient seeks to minimize stigma by enlightening others. Each of these responses suggests that patients view stigmatization as a threat to self. The fourth stage entails negative consequences of labeling for the patients' lives, including self-esteem, social networks, and earning power. This can arise directly from the patient's beliefs about the community's devaluation and discrimination toward mental illness (stage one) or from the patient's responses to labeling, secrecy, withdrawal, and education (stage three). In the fifth stage, the patient becomes more vulnerable to repeat episodes of mental illness because of the labeling and stigma outlined in the first four stages.

Link and his colleagues found empirical support for the perspective, particularly for the first four stages (Link et al., 1987, 1989). Patients and non-patients alike believe that mental patients will be rejected by most people. Patients believe that coping mechanisms, like secrecy and withdrawal are advisable for mental patients. Finally, the stigma of labeling undermines social support derived from relations within households and the community.

Braithwaite's Reintegrative Shaming

John Braithwaite (1989) has expanded a labeling theory of crime with his work on shame and reintegration. Braithwaite (1989) begins with the observation that labeling and stigmatization sometimes increase crime but sometimes do not. His theory of reintegrative shaming seeks to identify the conditions under which secondary deviance occurs.

Specifically, secondary deviance occurs when society's response to crime stigmatizes the offender as an outcast. Isolated from conventional society, the offender is likely to affiliate with deviant subcultural groups—assuming the individual has a taste for subcultures and has the structural opportunity to affiliate—which further ensnarls the offender into a web of criminality. In contrast, when community disapproval—particularly *public shaming*—is followed by *reacceptance* into the community of law-abiding citizens, the offender is likely to refrain from crime. This is reintegrative shaming and it effectively reduces crime because (1) social disapproval is embedded in the wider context of social acceptance; (2) the effect of stigmatization and being pushed into subcultures is minimized; and (3) shaming and repentance build a person's conscience, which will reduce future crimes in the absence of external controls.

Sherman (1993) contributes to these propositions with his defiance theory, arguing that shame is more likely to be acknowledged when punishment is experienced as fair or legitimate, leading to reduction in future crime. In contrast, when punishment is experienced as illegitimate, due to procedural injustice, shame is less likely to be acknowledged, resulting in a defiant pride that increases future crime. Defiance can be specific to individuals, or general among a collectivity, but in either case its effects may counterbalance the corresponding specific and general deterrent effects of sanctions. Thus, procedural justice—by which police, judges, and courts treat all citizens fairly and respectfully—may reduce crime more than deterrence.

Braithwaite (1989) argues that reintegrative shaming is more effective in communitarian societies characterized by interdependencies based on mutual obligations, trust, and group loyalties. In communitarian societies like traditional Japanese society, members are intertwined in each others' lives and, therefore, more likely to engage in the shaming of others and more likely to be affected by shaming when it is applied to themselves. In contrast, within individualistic societies like America, members are less collectively oriented and more individualistic. Consequently, disintegrative shaming, which stigmatizes offenders and pushes them toward subcultures, is more likely to occur. Within both communitarian and individualistic societies, those individuals who are most committed to community—such as women, the employed, and the elderly—are more likely to engage in shaming behavior, more likely to respond to shaming themselves, and less likely to deviate. Finally, effective shaming begins in early child socialization within the family, as parents punish children while expressing love for the child, rather than expressing rejection. As the child develops, socialization relies less on shaming, and more on internal controls, appealing to the child's own standards of right and wrong and respect for others. Shaming is needed primarily as a refresher, reinforcing what is already known. Braithwaite's theory of reintegrative shaming has been supported by research using survey data (e.g., Ahmed et al., 2001) and field experiments of restorative justice (e.g., Strang, 2002).

Matsueda and Heimer's Differential Social Control

Matsueda (1992) and his colleagues (Heimer and Matsueda, 1994; Bartusch and Matsueda, 1996; Heimer, 1996) have returned to the symbolic interaction principles of George Herbert Mead in developing a theory of differential social control. Matsueda (1992) and Heimer and Matsueda (1994) argue that a symbolic interactionist theory of delinquency provides a theory of self-control and social control, and thus is able to explain not only labeling and secondary deviance, but primary deviance as well. They begin with the concept of role-taking. Most of our everyday activities are routine and do not require extensive thought. Behaviors are a stream of habitual responses to routine situations. However, when a situation becomes problematic—that is, the habitual responses somehow do not work properly—the person stops and engages in reflection, thinking, or cognition. As noted earlier, cognition consists of role-taking: the person takes the role of the other, views the problematic situation from the standpoint of significant others, and evaluates alternative lines of action from the perspective of others. This serial process of cognition—which is an imaginative rehearsal of alternatives—continues until the problem is resolved.

This implies that the self is a reflection of appraisals made by significant others, including organized groups, such as generalized others and reference groups. Matsueda (1992) incorporated labeling hypotheses into this perspective, arguing that negative labeling by parents, teachers, and peers would influence future delinquency through the role-taking process. Furthermore, the differential labeling process predicts that socially disadvantaged youth are more likely to be labeled: partly because of their greater delinquency and partly because of discrimination. He found support for a causal chain in which parental appraisals affected reflected appraisals, which in turn affected delinquency, but failed to find strong support for the status characteristics hypothesis.

Heimer and Matsueda (1994) expanded the role-taking process to include learned definitions of delinquency, anticipated reactions to delinquency, and delinquent peers. They used the term "differential social control" to emphasize that social control through role-taking can take a conventional direction (e.g., when taking the role of conventional groups) or a criminal direction (e.g., when taking the role of criminal groups). They also showed how classical theories of crime could be viewed as special cases of differential social control. Their analyses supported the hypothesis that reflected appraisals, delinquent peers, and delinquent attitudes affect delinquent behavior. Heimer (1996) and Bartusch and Matsueda (1996) used differential social control to explain gender differences in delinquent behavior, finding that the role-taking process varied somewhat by gender and explained substantial variance in the gender gap. Finally, Matsueda and Heimer (1997) applied differential social control to explain delinquency through the life course, arguing that symbolic interaction provided a bio-social theory of development and selection into life-course roles, a theory of the meaning of those roles, and a theory of how those roles affect crime (see also Matsueda, 2006).

Mental Health and the Medicalization of Deviance

A specific application of labeling theory to the medical profession, that is, the "medicalization of deviance perspective," developed in the 1970s to address the way in which deviance becomes defined as a medical problem and treated by the medical model. According to Conrad (1975: 12), medicalization refers to the process of "defining behavior as a medical problem or illness and mandating or licensing the medical profession to provide some form of treatment for it." Once the deviant act—such as mental illness, alcoholism, drug addiction, violence, and hyperactivity—is medicalized, other approaches to explaining, treating, and policy making are ignored, downplayed, or dismissed. But proponents of the medicalization perspective emphasize the negative consequences of medicalizing deviance (Conrad, 1975; Conrad and Schneider, 1980). Once defined as a medical problem, the deviant behavior is removed from public discourse and placed in the domain of the medical profession, which now has a monopoly over illness by virtue of its power and prestige. The deviance is individualized, divorced from its social context, separated from its political implications, and encapsulated in hospitals and clinics. Here, deviance becomes defined as an individual malady, never a problem of the social system. Hyperactivity is a neurological problem, not a problem of the organization of school classrooms; violence is a brain disorder or genetic defect, not an outcome of social inequality; depression is a chemical disorder, not a problem of social relations. As a medical problem, the deviant behavior is subject to social controls that are legitimate in the world of medicine, such as control using psychoactive drugs or psychosurgery. Some recent research has combined medicalization with ethnomethodology and examined the ways doctors and patients accomplish diagnoses of illnesses in conversation (e.g., Heritage and Maynard, 2006).

Given the recent advances in pharmacology and DNA research, studies of the social organization of medicine may be more important than ever. The increased legitimacy of medicine to diagnose and treat mental disorders, such as depression, obsessive compulsive disorder, bipolar disease, and schizophrenia, could foster a general belief in the legitimacy of the medical model to treat virtually all behaviors that depart from normative expectations. The medicalization of deviance perspective has the potential not only to examine how medical delivery, diagnoses, and treatments are socially organized, but also the political processes by which the medical approach to deviance is legitimized, and the degree to which that legitimacy is warranted.

The latter question requires addressing the question of whether the medical conception of actual deviance is warranted rather than merely bracketing the question of actual deviance. Although typically unstated, the medicalization of deviance perspective tacitly implies that the problems of deviance that come under the purview of medical practice might be better addressed using a non-medical approach. To see this, consider the counterfactual: if such deviant actions were each perfectly addressed by medicine, studies of the medicalization of deviance would lose much of its luster.

From a pragmatist perspective, whether the conception of deviance is warranted or not depends on assessing the practical implications of medicalization—including treatment, transformation into an individual malady, and ignoring alternatives—for different actors involved, including the patient, the patient's family, the medical personnel (doctors and nurses), as well as the society as a whole. For example, at times, defining deviant behavior as an illness can reduce stigma by transforming deviance from a bad or evil act in need of punishment to a medical problem in need of treatment. For example, alcoholism is viewed as disease rather than a character defect; hyperactivity is viewed as an illness, rather than an evil, disobedient child.

Mass Incarceration in the United States

A disturbing trend in the United States concerns the precipitous increase in incarceration rates beginning in the mid-1970s through the first decade of the twenty-first century. After five decades of relatively constant rates of incarceration (about one-tenth of one percent of the population), the rate jumped nearly five-fold between 1970 and 2005 (to about seven-tenths of one percent). Over two million Americans are now behind bars. The rising incarceration rates have persisted even as crime rates have been dropping since the mid-1990s. The increase in imprisonment shows strong racial disparities: blacks are now eight times more likely to be incarcerated than whites. Moreover, incarceration rates are also disparate by age, sex, and educational attainment, resulting in extraordinary incarceration rates for young black males who have dropped out of school. Nearly one third of young black male dropouts were in prison or jail during the 2000s (Western, 2006). Pettit and Western (2004) estimate that the lifetime risk of incarceration for black male high school dropouts reached 60 percent by 1999, making imprisonment a "normal" life-course transition in midlife.

Recent research, conducted largely outside of labeling theory, has documented the negative consequences of mass incarceration, particularly for African American men. Audit studies, which randomly assign felony status to job applicants find that, compared to felons, non-felons are twice as likely to be called back among whites and three times as likely among blacks (Pager, 2003). Analysis of statistical data suggests that, compared with those without a prison record, ex-felons earned nearly 40 percent fewer dollars a year (Western, 2006). Research has also examined the consequences of felon disenfranchisement laws, in which ex-felons are deprived of the right to vote. Because ex-felons are more likely to vote Democrat, several key Republican electoral victories may have been reversed under the counterfactual condition in which felons were allowed to vote (Manza and Uggen, 2006).

The sharp rise in incarceration rates is unique to the United States: compared to western European nations, the U.S. incarceration rate was four times higher in the 1980s and more than five times higher at the turn of the century. The events behind the increase in punishment in the United States likely are the product of political processes endemic to U.S. capitalism, particularly in late modernity. For example, Beckett (1997: 11–12) argues that rising punishment rates in the United States are rooted in conservative politics, in which crimes of poor blacks were "used as evocative symbols of their undeserving nature" to undermine support for civil rights in the 1960s, in which the war on crime became intertwined with the war on drugs during the 1980s, and in which the neoclassical depiction of crime as an individual choice, a retrenchment from welfare policies, and the success of get tough on crime policies led to the creation of the "penal-industrial complex" with support from Republicans and Democrats.

At a more abstract level, Garland (2001) compares the United States to England, and despairs that in late modernity a culture of risk management (backed by economic rationality), centralized state power (which has shifted decision making away from criminal justice practitioners to politicians), and a shift from welfare (rehabilitation and prevention) to penal orientations has led to policies of severe punishment, increasing surveillance, and determinant sentencing. Garland's analysis rests on commonalities between the United States and England during late modernity. By contrast, Whitman (2003) holds late modernity constant by distinguishing contemporary United States from France and Germany. He concludes that the confluence of a strong state—in which bureaucrats are free to interpret (soften) the law to fit individual circumstances—and memories of the brutal punishments doled out to the lower classes during the "reign of terror" led to mild punishments (mercy) for all offenders in France and Germany. This "leveling up" of treatment to approximate that of aristocrats is absent in the United States because of its weak state and because Americans lack a shared history of brutality. The result is a shift from the judicial to the legislative, whereby mechanical punishments are subject to political processes in which parties clamor to appear tough on crime.

Labeling theory potentially provides a broader theoretical framework within which to interpret these contemporary findings. Thus, a return to labeling theory would help to identify the specific causal mechanisms by which stigma, the result of negative labeling by social control agents, unfolds in a social process of symbolic interaction. Here stigma would be conceptualized within a context of power differentials between institutionalized social control agents and the disadvantaged who are likely to come under their purview. Integrating research on labeling with the macro-historical development of law and punishment would build on the classic work of Becker (1963), who traced the historical treatment of marijuana smokers to the politics behind laws such as the marijuana tax act. Macro-level theorizing would link labeling and stigmatizing processes to larger political-economic structures within which they are embedded.

Notes

1. For Durkheim, under mechanical solidarity, social order is based on common moral values, and punishment is mechanically administered to offenders. By contrast, as societies grow and differentiate into specialized occupational positions, the collective conscience breaks down and in its place arises organic solidarity—reflected in civil law—in which social order is based on the functional interrelationships of specialized positions. Here, violators of civil laws are sanctioned with reparation between individuals, rather than punishment by the state. Of course, when the division of labor outstrips the development of organic solidarity, a state of anomie ensues.
2. Here I am arguing not that all labeling theorists agree with the arguments of Wilson (1970), but rather that his discussion is the best and clearest explication of the internal problems raised by various proponents of labeling perspectives.
3. This holds for interpretive research as well: here the taken-for-granted meanings may include the definition of the social audience, the identification of labelers, and designation of cues that signify a common symbol of deviance.

References

Ahmed, E., N. Harris, J. Braithwaite, and V. Braithwaite. *Shame Management through Reintegration.* Cambridge: Cambridge University Press, 2001.

Bartusch, D. J. and R. L. Matsueda. "Gender, Reflected Appraisals, and Labeling: A Cross-Group Test of an Interactionist Theory of Delinquency." *Social Forces* 75, no. 1 (1996): 145–76.

Becker, H. S. *Outsiders: Studies in the Sociology of Deviance.* New York: Macmillan, 1963.

———. "Labeling Theory Reconsidered." In *Outsiders: Studies in the Sociology of Deviance*, edited by H. S. Becker, 177–212. New York: Free Press, 1973.

Beckett, K. *Making Crime Pay: Law and Order in Contemporary American Politics.* New York: Oxford University Press, 1997.

Blumer, H. "Sociological Analysis and 'the Variable.'" *American Sociological Review* 32 (1956): 683–90.

———. *Symbolic Interactionism: Perspective and Method.* Englewood Cliffs, NJ: Prentice-Hall, 1969.

Braithwaite, J. *Crime, Shame, and Reintegration.* Cambridge: Cambridge University Press, 1989.

Conrad, P. "The Discovery of Hyperkinesis: Notes on the Medicalization of Deviant Behavior." *Social Problems* 23 (1975): 12–21.

Conrad, P. and J. W. Schneider. *Deviance and Medicalization: From Badness to Sickness.* St. Louis, MO: Mosby, 1980.

Cook, G. A. *George Herbert Mead: The Making of a Social Pragmatist.* Urbana: University of Illinois Press, 1993.

Dewey, J. *Human Nature and Conduct.* New York: Modern Library, 1922.

Durkheim, E. *The Division of Labor in Society.* New York: Free Press, 1964.

Elliott, D. S. and S. S. Ageton. "Reconciling Race and Class Differences in Self-Reported and Official Estimates of Delinquency." *American Sociological Review* 45 (1980): 95–110.

Erikson, K. T. "Notes on the Sociology of Deviance." *Social Problems* 9 (1962): 307–14.

———. *Wayward Puritans.* New York: Wiley, 1966.

Garfinkel, H. "Conditions of Successful Degradation Ceremonies." *American Journal of Sociology* 61 (1956): 420–24.

———. *Studies in Ethnomethodology*. Englewood Cliffs, NJ: Prentice-Hall, 1967.

Garland, D. *The Culture of Control*. Chicago: University of Chicago, 2001.

Gibbs, J. P. "Conceptions of Deviant Behavior: The New and the Old." *Pacific Sociological Review* 9 (1966): 9–14.

Goffman, E. *Stigma: Notes on the Management of Spoiled Identity*. New York: Simon and Schuster, 1963.

Gove, W. R. "Societal Reaction as an Explanation of Mental Illness: An Evaluation." *American Sociological Review* 35 (1970): 873–84.

———. "The Labelling Theory of Mental Illness: A Reply to Scheff." *American Sociological Review* 40 (1975): 242–48.

Hawkins, R. and G. Tiedeman. *The Creation of Deviance: Interpersonal and Organizational Determinants*. Columbus, OH: Charles E. Merrill, 1975.

Heimer, K. "Gender, Interaction, and Delinquency: Testing a Theory of Differential Social Control." *Social Psychology Quarterly* 59 (1996): 39–61.

Heimer, K. and R. L. Matsueda. "Role-Taking, Role-Commitment, and Delinquency: A Theory of Differential Social Control." *American Sociological Review* 59 (1994): 365–90.

Heritage, J. and D. W. Maynard. *Communication in Medical Care: Interaction between Primary Care Physicians and Patients*. Cambridge: Cambridge University Press, 2006.

Hindelang, M. J., T. Hirschi, and J. G. Weis. *Measuring Delinquency*. Beverly Hills, CA: Sage, 1981.

Hirschi, T. "Labeling Theory and Juvenile Delinquency: An Assessment of the Evidence." In *The Labelling of Deviance: Evaluating a Perspective*, edited by W. R. Gove, 181–203. New York: Wiley, 1975.

Huizinga, D. and D. S. Elliott. "Reassessing the Reliability and Validity of Self-Report Delinquency Measures." *Journal of Quantitative Criminology* 2 (1986): 293–328.

Kitsuse, J. I. "Societal Reaction to Deviant Behavior: Problems of Theory and Method." *Social Problems* 9 (1962): 247–56.

Kitsuse, J. I. and A. V. Cicourel. "A Note on the Use of Official Statistics." *Social Problems* 11 (1963): 131–39.

Kuhn, T. S. *The Structure of Scientific Revolutions*. Chicago: University of Chicago Press, 1962.

Lemert, E. M. *Social Pathology: A Systematic Approach to the Theory of Sociopathic Behavior*. New York: McGraw-Hill, 1951.

———. *Human Deviance, Social Problems, and Social Control*. Englewood Cliffs, NJ: Prentice-Hall, 1967.

———. *Human Deviance, Social Problems, and Social Control*. 2nd ed. Englewood Cliffs, NJ: Prentice-Hall, 1972.

Link, B. G., F. T. Cullen, J. Frank, and J. Wozniak. "The Social Rejection of Ex-Mental Patients: Understanding Why Labels Matter." *American Journal of Sociology* 92 (1987): 1461–500.

Link, B. G., F. T. Cullen, E. Struening, P. E. Shrout, and B. P. Dohrenwend. "A Modified Labeling Theory Approach to Mental Disorders: An Empirical Assessment." *American Sociological Review* 54 (1989): 400–23.

Lofland, J. *Deviance and Identity*. Englewood Cliffs, NJ: Prentice-Hall, 1969.

Manza, J. and C. Uggen. *Locked Out: Felon Disenfranchisement and American Democracy*. New York: Oxford University Press, 2006.

Matsueda, R. L. "Reflected Appraisals, Parental Labeling, and Delinquency: Specifying a Symbolic Interactionist Theory." *American Journal of Sociology* 97 (1992): 1577–611.

————. "Labeling Theory: Historical Roots, Implications, and Recent Developments." In *Explaining Criminals and Crime*, edited by R. Paternoster and R. Bachman, 223–41. Los Angeles: Roxbury, 2001.

————. "Criminological Implications of the Thought of George Herbert Mead." In *Sociological Theory and Criminological Research: Views from Europe and the United States*, edited by M. Deflem, 77–108. Oxford: Elsevier Science, 2006.

Matsueda, R. L. and K. Heimer. "A Symbolic Interactionist Theory of Role Transitions, Role Commitments, and Delinquency." In *Advances in Criminological Theory, Volume 7, Developmental Theories of Crime and Delinquency*, edited by T. Thornberry, 163–214. New Brunswick, NJ: Transaction, 1997.

Mead, G. H. "The Psychology of Punitive Justice." *American Journal of Sociology* 23 (1918): 577–602.

————. "Cooley's Contribution to American Social Thought." *American Journal of Sociology* 35 (1930): 693–706.

————. *Mind, Self, and Society*. Chicago: University of Chicago Press, 1934.

————. *The Philosophy of the Act*. Chicago: University of Chicago Press, 1938.

Pager, D. "The Mark of a Criminal Record." *American Journal of Sociology* 108 (2003): 937–75.

Paternoster, R. and L. Iovanni. "The Labeling Perspective and Delinquency: An Elaboration of the Theory and Assessment of the Evidence." *Justice Quarterly* 6 (1989): 359–94.

Pettit, B. and B. Western. "Mass Imprisonment and the Life Course: Race and Class Inequality in U.S. Incarceration." *American Sociological Review* 69 (2004): 151–69.

Pollner, M. "Sociological and Common-Sense Models of the Labelling Process." In *Ethnomethodology*, edited by R. Turner, 27–40. Harmondsworth: Penguin, 1974.

Quinney, R. *The Social Reality of Crime*. Boston: Little, Brown and Company, 1970.

Rains, P. "Imputations of Deviance: A Retrospective Essay on the Labeling Perspective." *Social Problems* 23 (1975): 1–11.

Scheff, T. J. *Being Mentally Ill: A Sociological Theory*. Chicago: Aldine, 1966.

————. "The Labelling Theory of Mental Illness." *American Sociological Review* 39 (1974): 444–52.

Sherman, L. W. "Defiance, Deterrence, and Irrelevance: A Theory of the Criminal Sanction." *Journal of Research in Crime and Delinquency* 30 (1993): 445–73.

Spector, M. and J. I. Kitsuse. *Constructing Social Problems*. Menlo Park, CA: Cummings, 1977.

Strang, H. *Repair or Revenge: Victims and Restorative Justice*. Oxford: Oxford University Press, 2002.

Stryker, S. *Symbolic Interactionism*. Menlo Park, CA: Benjamin/Cummings, 1980.

Tannenbaum, F. *Crime and the Community*. Boston: Ginn, 1938.

Thomas, W. I. and D. S. Thomas. *The Child in America*. New York: Knopf, 1928.

Thrasher, F. M. *The Gang*. Chicago: University of Chicago Press, 1927.

Turk, A. *Criminality and Legal Order*. Chicago: Rand McNally, 1969.

Western, B. *Punishment and Inequality in America*. New York: Russell Sage, 2006.

Whitman, J. Q. *Harsh Justice*. Oxford: Oxford University Press, 2003.

Wilson, T. P. "Conceptions of Interaction and Forms of Sociological Explanation." *American Sociological Review* 35 (1970): 697–710.

Woolgar, S. and D. Pawluch. "Ontological Gerrymandering: The Anatomy of Social Problems Explanations." *Social Problems* 32 (1985): 214–27.

3

Labeling Theory and Mental Illness

Fred E. Markowitz

Much has changed since the introduction of the labeling theory of mental illness. Scientific and public understanding of the causes of serious mental illness has shifted to acknowledge the role of genetic and social causes, yet mental illness still carries a powerful stigma and is often associated with dangerousness (Corrigan and Penn, 1999; Phelan et al., 2000; Corrigan, 2005). Effective medications help to control the symptoms of the most debilitating illnesses, yet many patients lack the insight and support required to comply with treatment regimens. Most mental health treatments are no longer conducted on a long-term basis in the "total institution" of large psychiatric hospitals, but instead are conducted on a voluntary, outpatient basis. At the same time, the loss of public psychiatric hospital capacity to treat and monitor severely ill and economically disadvantaged patients has not been offset by adequate community treatment and has led to an alarming number of persons with mental illness in the criminal justice system (Torrey, 1997; Markowitz, 2006). In this chapter, I review developments in labeling theory as applied to mental illness. First, I review T.J. Scheff's (1974, 1984) initial version with emphasis on how the theory holds up given the shifts in understanding and treatment of mental illness. Next, I discuss the influential, modified labeling theory (MLT) and the series of studies that have followed, highlighting causal processes revealed and those that remain untested. Finally, I discuss extensions of the theory focused on identity formation and conclude with directions for further study emphasizing data requirements.

Labeling and Stigma

A central aspect of labeling theory is the focus on the *stigma* associated with mental illness. According to the classic definition provided by Erving Goffman, stigma is ". . . an attribute that is deeply discrediting . . ." that reduces the bearer ". . . from a whole and usual person to a tainted, discounted one" (1963: 3). Mental illness is perhaps one of the most discrediting attributes. It is linked to an array of negative stereotypical traits (e.g., dangerousness, weakness, and incompetence). It is widely misunderstood by the general public, and is often inaccurately and negatively portrayed in the media (Wahl, 1995; Corrigan and Lundin, 2001). Stigma can be understood in two related ways: (1) public stigma—the attitudes and behavior of persons in the general public with regard to mental illness and (2) self-stigma—the internalization of stigma among persons with mental illness (Corrigan, 2005). The consequences of both forms of stigma include discrimination, loss of socioeconomic status, lowered self-esteem, and increased symptoms (Link and Phelan, 2001).

Labeling theory is an important framework for understanding the effects of stigma associated with the devalued status of "person with mental illness" (Lemert, 1951, 1967; Becker, 1963; Scheff, 1974, 1984). The theory is rooted in the *symbolic interactionist* perspective within sociology (Mead, 1934; Blumer, 1969; Stryker, 1980). The basic premise of symbolic interactionism is that the meanings of social objects (persons and actions) are socially constructed. Responses in social interaction are based on assigned meanings ("definitions of the situation") that are drawn from shared cultural knowledge and the internalized attitudes of the "generalized other." Within this framework, self-conceptions result from perceptions of how *significant others* (e.g., family, friends, and teachers) view the self. This is known as the *reflected appraisals process* (Kinch, 1963). Based on others' responses to the self as a social object, we come to see ourselves as we think others see us (Cooley, 1902). Self-conceptions that are linked to occupied social positions are *role-identities* (Stryker, 1980). Persons normally occupy many roles (e.g., employee, spouse, and parent) with accompanying behavioral expectations. According to labeling theory, persons may be cast in the role of "mentally ill."

The early version of labeling theory must be understood within the climate of the 1960s, when prevailing norms were being questioned and power imbalances among social groups, including so-called "deviants" were the focus of much public and academic discourse. The theory specified the process by which deviant labels are applied and persons' self-conceptions and social opportunities are altered. Scheff (1974, 1984) argued that many behaviors violating social norms constitute "residual" forms of deviance, such as social withdrawal, talking to oneself, or displaying inappropriate affect—the kinds of behaviors that treatment professionals (and many lay persons) might consider indicative of mental illness. The theory questioned the legitimacy of psychiatric diagnosis, and following Goffman (1961, 1963), emphasized the role of formal labeling in setting into motion stigmatizing processes that lead to sustained symptomatic behavior.

It is worth reviewing the formal propositions in Scheff's theory to see how they have withstood the test of time and empirical research. They include (1) *residual rule-breaking arises from fundamentally diverse sources*. According to Scheff, these sources include genetics, peculiar upbringing, and external stress. While emphasis on faulty parenting by the psychoanalytic perspective has receded, the prevailing view among both medical and sociological researchers is that severe mental illness (e.g., schizophrenia, depression, and bi-polar disorder) is the product of inherited, bio-genetic predispositions towards mental illness that are facilitated by social factors. Among those predisposed, mental illness may be triggered by the stress of economic disadvantage, role strains, and alienation, but may also arise without any particular stressors (Horwitz, 2001; Mirowsky and Ross, 2003). There is, however, less professional consensus regarding causes of substance–dependence/abuse and personality disorders. Thus, while mental illness is not considered merely "residual rule-breaking," but a legitimate, treatable medical condition, the sources of mental illness remain somewhat consistent with Scheff's original theory.

Scheff also argued that (2) *relative to the rate of treated "mental illness," the rate of unrecorded residual rule-breaking is extremely high*. Most of Scheff's proposition of "residual rule-breaking" was recognized as legitimate psychiatric illness. Based on this, studies indicating prevalence of mental illness used survey-administered Diagnostic and Statistic Manual (DSM) criteria in general population samples and estimated that only about a third of the almost 30 percent of persons meeting diagnostic criteria receive treatment (Kessler et al., 2005). This is partially consistent with Scheff's next proposition, that (3) *most residual rule-breaking is "denied" and is of transitory significance*. However, it may not only be that symptoms are explained away, but also that they are often not severe enough to interfere with functioning to such an extent to warrant treatment. Symptoms may also be viewed as normal, expected responses to life events, such as divorce, death, or unemployment (Horwitz, 2001). However, when disturbing behavior becomes severe enough and seems to be out of the ordinary, treatment-seeking is more likely (Karp, 1996; Pescosolido and Boyer, 1999). Critically, this requires that persons must engage in a degree of "self-labeling," recognizing that their emotions and behavior fall outside of the normal range (Thoits, 1985). Treatment that may follow is most likely to be voluntary, administered by primary-care physicians, rather than psychiatrists, and likely to be on an outpatient basis (Wang et al., 2002, 2005). Nevertheless, persons with the most severe and persistent mental illnesses such as schizophrenia are, at some time, likely to seek specialty care and be hospitalized (Wang et al., 2002, 2005).

Scheff's propositions regarding the development of public stigma remain highly relevant. His proposition that (4) *stereotyped imagery of "mental disorder" is learned in early childhood* is confirmed by media studies that find children's TV shows contain a fair amount of references to "crazy" characters and that children indeed acquire negative conceptions of mental illness from such programming (Wahl, 2002). His proposition that (5) *stereotypes of insanity are continually reaffirmed, inadvertently, in ordinary social interaction* has not been systematically tested. Yet it is consistent with studies that show that, although public understanding of mental illness has become somewhat more sophisticated over the last several decades in terms of recognizing various disorders and their causes, the public often associates mental illness (especially psychosis and substance abuse) with dangerousness (Phelan et al., 2000). The association of mental illness with dangerousness, while perhaps overstated, is not entirely unreasonable. The best studies, using general population samples, find that persons with mental illness are indeed at a slightly higher risk of violent behavior. In one major study, about 16 percent of those with depression, schizophrenia, or bi-polar disorder, reported violent behavior as compared to about 7 percent of those without a disorder (Swanson, 1994). However, the risk of violence among persons with mental disorder is on par with demographic factors, such as gender, age, and race (Link et al., 1992, 1999). The risk is also more pronounced among those experiencing certain psychotic symptoms (e.g., hearing voices and experiencing thoughts that seem to be not one's own) and among those with substance abuse problems (Link et al., 1992, 1999; Swanson, 1994; Eblogen and Johnson, 2009; Teasdale, 2009). The public is comparatively less afraid and thus less likely to reject persons with depression or anxiety disorders (Link et al., 1999).

Scheff attempted to specify how public attitudes translate into discriminatory behavior in proposition (6): *Labeled deviants may be rewarded for playing the stereotyped role of "mentally ill"* and (7): *Labeled deviants are punished when they attempt to return to conventional roles.* While perhaps not being "rewarded," patients demonstrating "insight" into their disorders and complying with treatment regimens (medication) are likely to be seen as more cooperative and have better relationships with treatment providers. Efforts at gaining insight and compliance are not so much an attempt to keep persons in the role of patient, but to reduce symptoms, foster independence, and facilitate recovery from the illness (Angell et al., 2006; Angell and Mahoney, 2007). Moreover, while there is much evidence to suggest that persons labeled as mentally ill are at risk of being discriminated against, particularly in the areas of employment and housing (Corrigan and Watson, 2002), it is sometimes difficult to determine whether negative outcomes are due to discrimination since mental illness is often "concealable." Others may not know a person has it unless it is revealed. This presents an important dilemma for those with mental illness—whether, when, and to whom it should be revealed (Corrigan and Matthews, 2003). MLT (discussed below) addresses this issue to some extent.

Scheff also proposed that (8) *in a "crisis," when a residual rule-breaker is publically labeled, the deviant is highly suggestible, and may accept the proffered role of "insane" as the only alternative.* This proposition is likely an overstatement and has many contingencies. In earlier decades, psychiatric hospitalization was more common and it was relatively easier to involuntarily hospitalize patients (Mechanic, 2008). Currently, psychiatric hospitalization is much less likely (although arguably still essential at times) and the criteria for involuntary hospitalization—dangerousness to self or others—stricter. As a result, many persons in psychiatric crisis, displaying disturbing behavior, may not get appropriate treatment until after a law has been violated (Torrey, 2008). Others are fortunate if their family members can convince them to go to the hospital on their own accord. Depending on the behavior involved, availability of treatment options, and police discretion, some may be brought to the hospital by police or may end up in jail, where they may not receive treatment. In any event, persons in crisis are often not aware of the diagnostic labels that are employed by treatment professionals, labels that can be rather quickly applied, followed by administration of medication, in the context of very short stays in hospital (Luhrmann, 2000). They are frequently discharged without adequate follow-up care or monitoring.

Thus, whether patients "accept" the label of mental illness is likely to depend on their treatment history, including the number of prior "crisis" situations, the degree of insight into their disorder, medication effectiveness and compliance, as well as availability and engagement of follow-up care.

An auxiliary proposition in Scheff's theory is that *the likelihood of being labeled depends on the rule-breaker's power and social distance from agents of social control.* This proposition assumes involuntary, inpatient treatment of those less advantaged and, therefore, must be revaluated, given the predominance of voluntary treatment. Both classic and contemporary studies of treatment for mental illness find that, in general, persons with greater, not fewer, resources are likely to seek treatment (Pescosolido and Boyer, 1999). The evidence that indicates disadvantaged minorities are more likely to find themselves in treatment involuntarily is somewhat mixed, with some studies finding support for a "social control" hypothesis (Rosenfield, 1984) and others not (Thoits, 2005; Lincoln, 2006). The findings in more recent studies may reflect the change in how psychiatric hospitalization is accessed, with many disadvantaged patients *not* admitted because of an inability to pay for their care. In terms of voluntary treatment, disadvantaged persons' limited access to quality mental health services and lack of understanding of the need for medical intervention may also contribute to a lower likelihood of receiving treatment (Schnittker, 2003). Consequently, untreated mental illness is a significant factor that leads to homelessness and involvement in the criminal justice system. Recent studies find high rates of mental illness among persons in jails and prisons (Ditton, 1999; James and Glaze, 2006). As several critics have pointed out, for many disadvantaged persons, jails and prisons have replaced psychiatric hospitals as the largest sites for the management of persons with untreated disturbing symptoms of mental illness (Torrey, 2007, 2008).

Perhaps Scheff's most influential proposition is that, (9) *among residual rule-breakers, labeling is the single most important cause of careers of residual deviance.* It is this proposition of labeling theory that has been most strongly contested in the literature. The principal empirical rejoinders include the evidence of both a biological and social basis for many mental disorders and the fact that treatment of all forms (inpatient, outpatient, medication, and therapy), involving the assignment of diagnostic labels generally reduces symptoms and improves functioning (Gove and Fain, 1973; Gove and Howell, 1974; Gove, 1979, 1982; Weinstein, 1979, 1983; Warner et al., 1989; Frank and Glied, 2006). Thus, a central issue surrounding the theory became whether social rejection and negative outcomes are due to the stigmatizing consequences of the label of "mentally ill" or whether they are due to disturbing, symptomatic behavior resulting from a medical condition. Early and more recent studies using experimental vignettes show that although labeling through treatment increases rejection, the effect of symptomatic behavior is greater (Phillips, 1963; Link et al., 1987; Martin et al., 2000). In addition, studies integrating insights from attribution theory show that when persons perceive others as responsible for causing their mental illness, there is less sympathy, less willingness to help, and a greater likelihood of social rejection (Corrigan et al., 2003a). Lack of social support and opportunities may then worsen symptoms (Markowitz, 2001).

Scheff's original version of labeling theory predated the "genetic revolution" and is tempered substantially by a wide body of evidence supporting the effectiveness of labeling and treatment in improving symptoms of mental illness. This evidence, thus, limits the theory's ability to fully explain the development and trajectory of illness. Genetic explanations have led to an emphasis on mental illness as a "no fault" illness and as "an illness like any other" (Albee and Joffe, 2004; Read et al., 2006). However, this does not provide a straightforward way to reduce the stigma associated with diagnostic labeling. Some evidence suggests that genetic explanations for mental illness may result in persons being viewed as "fundamentally flawed," thus leading to social rejection (Phelan, 2005). Moreover, unlike other medical conditions, mental illness can include disturbing thoughts and behaviors. Taking into account the realities of mental illness and the enduring presence of stigma, labeling theory has been modified to further our understanding of how stigma impedes recovery.

Modified Labeling Theory

In a landmark study using a community sample, Bruce Link (1982) examined the effects of both the symptoms of mental illness and being labeled mentally ill (through treatment) on employment and income. He found that, controlling for other variables (marital status, education, age, and occupation), patient status had as much of an effect on income and employment as did the symptoms. This study led to persuasive arguments for the continued importance of understanding how the stigma associated with labeling affects the functional outcomes of people with mental disorders, encapsulated in a framework known as MLT (Link et al., 1987, 1989).

In MLT, the strong claim made by Scheff that labeling causes "careers in residual deviance" is replaced by a more subtle approach to how stigma affects the course of illness *among those in treatment* (labeled). According to the modified theory, widely held stereotypical attitudes about persons with mental illness (e.g., of being incompetent and dangerous) become *personally relevant* to individuals diagnosed with a mental illness. Because of these attitudes, many of those diagnosed expect to be devalued and discriminated against. This anticipated rejection is experienced as demoralizing (i.e., self-esteem is lowered and depression increases). Also, to avoid rejection, persons who are labeled engage in various coping strategies, such as secrecy, disclosure, or social withdrawal, enhancing the effects of expected rejection by constricting social networks, leading to unemployment and lowered income. Thus, stigmatizing beliefs act as *self-fulfilling prophecies* (Darley and Fazio, 1980). Drawing on the *stress-process model* (Pearlin et al., 1981; Turner et al., 1995), the theory further predicts that lowered self-esteem, constricted interpersonal networks, unemployment, and low income increase stress. Stress, in turn, places persons at risk for increased symptoms. In this way, while labeling and stigma are not the sole causes of sustained mental illness, they *indirectly* affect the course of illness through changes in the self-concept and key social outcomes, such as social networks and employment.

In a series of studies, Link and colleagues tested MLT using combined community and treatment samples (Link, 1987; Link et al., 1989, 1991). In these studies, stigma is operationalized using the devaluation–discrimination (DD) scale, a twelve-item index that measures the extent of *expected rejection*—beliefs that persons treated for mental illness will be rejected as friends, teachers, employees, dating partners, etc. First, these studies show that, on an average, persons with a mental disorder who are either treated (i.e., labeled) or are not, and persons without a mental disorder believe that those who are labeled will experience a degree of devaluation and discrimination, supporting the notion of generalized expectations of rejection. Second, they show that, among persons in treatment, expectations of rejection have adverse effects on demoralization, income, employment, and social support networks. Third, endorsement of strategies for coping with stigma, such as secrecy, education (trying to explain mental illness/treatment to others), and social withdrawal, may produce more harm than good—they interact with DD beliefs, enhancing its adverse effects on social networks and economic outcomes.

In an influential study, Sarah Rosenfield (1997) directly addressed the issue of how labeling via treatment can have both beneficial and detrimental effects on subjective quality of life. Using a sample from a model treatment program, she showed that receipt of certain services (e.g., vocational rehabilitation, financial support, mental illness chemical abuse group, and leisure activities) had positive effects on quality of life, whereas, controlling for staff-reported symptoms and stigma (operationalized using the DD scale) it had negative effects on quality of life. She also found that self-esteem and self-efficacy mediated much of the effects of stigma and services on quality of life.

Follow-up studies provide stronger evidence for MLT by using longitudinal data. In one study, Link et al. (1997) surveyed eighty-four men with mental illness and substance abuse at two points in time (upon entering a treatment program and one year later). They found that even though symptoms declined and functioning improved at follow-up, expected and experienced stigma and endorsement of socially isolating coping orientations remained at the same levels. The study also showed how stigma increased depressive symptoms. In a related study, Markowitz (1998), using two-wave data (eighteen months) from persons with mental illness in outpatient treatment and self-help groups, found adverse effects of both expected and experienced rejection on evaluative dimensions of self-concept (esteem, efficacy) and life satisfaction. He also found that much of the effects of anticipated rejection diminished when a limited (dichotomous) measure of discriminatory experiences was controlled. This suggests that part of the effects of anticipated rejection may be due to rejection experiences. However, this still leaves the causal relationship between anticipated and experienced rejection undetermined—to what extent do people experience rejection because they expect it and expect it because they experience it? Although the findings showed that the negative effect of stigma on life satisfaction is partly mediated by self-concept, reciprocal effects models indicated that the relationship between self-concept and life satisfaction is bi-directional—self-concept not only affects interpersonal and economic outcomes, but is affected by them as well. Another longitudinal study using data from formerly institutionalized persons showed how stigmatizing experiences negatively impacted self-esteem and self-efficacy (Wright and Gronfein, 2000). However, that study had a very small sample size ($n = 88$), and did not include measures of anticipated rejection (DD), degree of symptoms, or interpersonal and social outcomes. These studies point out the necessity of considering the bi-directionality of stigma processes, so that the impact of stigma is not overestimated. They also indicate the need to develop and estimate models that integrate stigma within a

Figure 3.1
Integrated stigma-recovery model

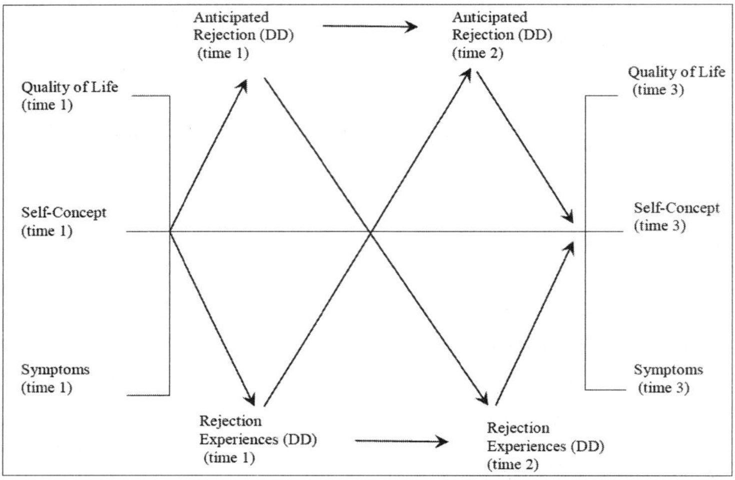

framework of dynamic recovery processes (Markowitz, 2004a, 2004b) (see Figure 3.1).

Labeling, Reflected Appraisals, and Identity

The role of the self-concept in stigma processes is a central concern, yet MLT-based research has been limited to an examination of how stigma negatively affects global self-evaluation (esteem) and self-efficacy (i.e., sense of personal control) among persons with mental illness (Rosenfield, 1997; Markowitz, 1998; Wright and Gronfein, 2000). It has not examined how labeling and stigma affect other dimensions of self, including *personal attributes* (e.g., smart, attractive, and intelligent) or the salience of mental illness as a *role-identity*. Stigma may adversely impact these dimensions of self, having important consequences for recovery. Persons who, for example, consider themselves as less competent, capable, or successful may act in ways that reduce their quality of life by not making friends, furthering their education, or seeking jobs. Diminished quality of life may then increase stress, triggering symptoms of psychiatric disorder (Markowitz, 2001). The integration of MLT with the reflected appraisals process of self-concept formation offers a framework to provide a more detailed understanding of how stigma affects self-conceptions. Central questions include how stigmatizing beliefs and perceived discrimination associated with a diagnosis of mental illness affect self-conceptions as "deviant," "abnormal," or, in Goffman's terms, as having a "spoiled identity." For example, to what extent do family members' (and service providers' and employers') stigma-related beliefs affect how they view the person with mental illness and their prospects for recovery? In turn, how do the beliefs of these "significant others" affect self-conceptions? Finally, how do stigmatized self-conceptions—consistent with the stereotypes associated with mental illness—impact well-being outcomes?

Recent studies examined the relationships among informal labeling, identity, and mental illness. Following the model developed by Matsueda (1992), Stacy DeCoster and Karen Heimer (2001) used a representative sample of adolescents and showed that prior levels of depression affected perceived (reflected) appraisals of oneself by parents, teachers, and friends as "distressed." Reflected appraisals, in turn, led to increased depression (and delinquency). The study did not, however, show whether the effect of reflected appraisals on outcomes was due to self-appraisals. Other studies, integrating insights from MLT with Affect Control Theory, show how "stigma sentiments"—the evaluation (e.g., good versus bad), potency (e.g., strong versus weak), and activity (sharp versus dull) of "a person with mental illness" is related to the corresponding (evaluation, potency, and activity) dimensions of reflected appraisals ("how others see me") and self-evaluations ("myself as I really am") (Kroska and Harkness, 2006, 2008). The study did not, however, examine the effects of appraisals on outcomes. In order to provide a more detailed understanding of how stigma affects recovery from mental illness, a similar approach needs to be applied to a sample of persons with serious mental illness. Studies must include all elements of the reflected appraisals process—others' actual appraisals, reflected appraisals, and self-appraisals—in terms of stigmatized self-conceptions consistent with the stereotypes associated with mental illness and examine their impact on important outcomes including symptoms, functioning, and quality of life (see Figure 3.2).

According to the reflected appraisals process, the self-concept is shaped, in large part, by the perceived responses of significant others, such as family, friends, or teachers (McCall and Simmons, 1966; Stryker, 1980; Matsueda, 1992; Gecas and Burke, 1995). Therefore, what is needed is a focus on the most significant groups in the lives of persons with mental illness, including family members. While there has been research on "family burden," care giving, and "expressed emotion" among family members (see Avison, 1999a, 1999b), the study of stigma and families remains limited to describing how stigma impacts the family members

Figure 3.2
Stigma and reflected appraisals process

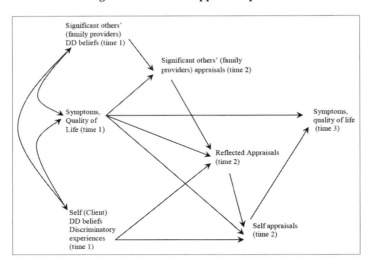

of persons with mental illness (Lefley, 1989; Wahl and Harmon, 1989; Struening et al., 2001; Angell et al., 2003). Even though families are often the targets of "courtesy" stigma, they may also inadvertently act as sources of stigma to their mentally ill family member. For example, studies of persons with mental illness report that, after employers and the general population, family members and mental health providers are a frequent source of stigmatizing responses, such as viewing respondents as less than competent, lacking understanding, making offensive comments, and expressing concern about potential dangerousness (Wahl, 1999; Dickerson et al., 2002a, 2002b). These expressions are likely to impact the way that persons with mental illness think about themselves.

It is important to acknowledge that many of these messages towards ill relatives grow out of positive intentions and reflect the frustrations and attempts to cope with the difficulties of having a relative with serious mental illness, yet they are of concern because of their potential adverse effects (Karp, 2001). Prior research, for example, has shown that significant others' expectations may affect the role performance of persons with mental illness and the quality of their family relationships (Greenley, 1979; Barrowclough et al., 2001; Struening et al., 2001). These findings suggest that the stigma-related attitudes of family about the devaluation and discrimination associated with mental illness are likely to be key sources of how persons with mental illness come to think of themselves, in turn affecting prospects for recovery. One recent study, using a sample of adults with schizophrenia and their mothers provides some tentative support for how the reflected appraisals process affects stigmatized self-conceptions that in turn affect recovery outcomes (Markowitz et al., 2011).

Conclusions

While MLT has helped frame the countervailing forces at play when persons are treated for mental illness as well as other stigmatized conditions (e.g., smoking, homosexuality, and obesity), there is room to expand the theory to specify more elaborate causal processes and to employ new measures of experienced rejection (Ritscher and Phelan, 2004) and stigmatized identity, administered to those with mental illness as well as key persons in their lives. Most notably, studies are needed that examine mediating variables (especially identity formation) that provide the link between public attitudes, internalized attitudes among persons with mental illness, and outcomes. Also, further examination of contingencies in stigma processes is needed. For example, to what extent do persons with mental illness reject stereotypes or employ strategies that moderate the effects of anticipated and experienced rejection (Corrigan et al., 2003b)? The centrality of persons' illness relative to other features of identity also remains unexamined. Importantly, it must also be acknowledged that the effects of stigma are not unidirectional, but likely reciprocal—persons experience and anticipate stigmatization with adverse effects on symptoms and functioning. Yet those with severe symptoms or low levels of functioning are likely at risk for greater social rejection.

The data requirements for furthering our understanding of labeling and stigma processes are challenging. Larger, longitudinal samples of persons with mental illness at all stages of treatment (entry, ongoing, and formerly treated) with a variety of diagnoses (e.g., depression, schizophrenia, and bi-polar disorder) are needed to estimate complex causal models with sub-group comparisons. Moreover, it would be useful to include the extent to which the appraisals of other family members such as spouses, parents, siblings, as well as treatment providers play a role in the recovery process. Finally, it is important to include measures such as the DD (devaluation–discrimination beliefs) items to examine how more widely held stigmatizing attitudes towards mental illness (perceived expectations held by "most people in the community") influence recovery through their effects on others', reflected, and self-appraisals. In this way, following symbolic interactionist theory, we can link the attitudes of the "generalized other" with those of "significant others" to better understand self-concept formation and outcomes among persons with mental illness. Integrating MLT with the reflected appraisals process may help further our understanding of how the stigma that accompanies labeling impedes recovery.

References

Albee, G. W. and J. M. Joffe. "Mental Illness is NOT 'An Illness Like Any Other.'" *Journal of Primary Prevention* 24, no. 4 (2004): 419–36.

Angell, B., A. Cooke, and K. Kovac. "First Person Accounts of Stigma." In *A Comprehensive Review of the Stigma of Mental Illness: Implications for Research and Social Change*, edited by P. W. Corrigan, 69–98. Washington, DC: American Psychological Association, 2003.

Angell, B. and C. Mahoney. "Re-Conceptualizing the Case Management Relationship in Intensive Treatment: A Study of Staff Perceptions and Experiences." *Administration and Policy in Mental Health and Mental Health Services Research* 34, no. 2 (2007): 172–88.

Angell, B., C. Mahoney, and N. Martinez. "Promoting Treatment Adherence in Assertive Community Treatment." *Social Service Review* 80, no. 3 (2006): 485–526.

Avison, W. A. "Family Structure and Processes." In *A Handbook for the Study of Mental Health: Social Contexts, Theories, and Systems*, edited by A. Horwitz and T. L. Scheid, 228–40. Cambridge: Cambridge University Press, 1999a.

———. "Impact of Mental Illness on the Family." In *Handbook for the Sociology of Mental Health*, edited by C. Anheshensel and J. Phelan, 495–518. New York: Academic/Plenum, 1999b.

Barrowclough, C., G. Haddock, I. Lowens, A. Connor, J. Pidliswyi, and N. Tracey. "Staff Expressed Emotion and Causal Attributions for Client Problems on a Low Security Unit: An Exploratory Study." *Schizophrenia Bulletin* 27, no. 3 (2001): 517–26.

Becker, H. S. *Outsiders: Studies in the Sociology of Deviance*. New York: Free Press, 1963.

Blumer, H. *Symbolic Interactionism: Perspective and Method*. Englewood Cliffs, NJ: Prentice-Hall, 1969.

Cooley, C. H. *Human Nature and the Social Order*. New York: Scribner's, 1902.

Corrigan, P. W. *On the Stigma of Mental Illness*. Washington, DC: American Psychological Association, 2005.

Corrigan, P. W. and D. Penn. "Lessons from Social Psychology on Discrediting Psychiatric Stigma." *American Psychologist* 54, no. 9 (1999): 765–76.

Corrigan, P. W. and R. Lundin. *Don't Call Me Nuts: Coping with the Stigma of Mental Illness*. Chicago: Recovery Press, 2001.

Corrigan, P. W. and A. Watson. "The Paradox of Self-Stigma and Mental Illness." *Clinical Psychology: Science and Practice* 9, no. 1 (2002): 35–53.

Corrigan, P. W., F. E. Markowitz, A. Watson, D. Rowan, and M. Kubiak. "Attribution and Dangerousness Models of Public Discrimination against Persons with Mental Illness." *Journal of Health and Social Behavior* 44, no. 2 (2003a): 162–79.

Corrigan, P. W. and A. Matthews. "Stigma and Disclosure: Implications for Coming Out of the Closet." *Journal of Mental Health* 12, no. 3 (2003): 235–48.

Corrigan, P. W., V. Thompson, D. Lambert, Y. Sangster, J. G. Noel, and J. Campbell. "Perceptions of Discrimination among Persons with Serious Mental Illness." *Psychiatric Services* 54, no. 8 (2003b): 1105–10.

Darley, J. M. and R. H. Fazio. "Expectancy Confirmation Processes Arising in the Social Interaction Sequence." *American Psychologist* 35 (1980): 867–81.

DeCoster, S. and K. Heimer. "The Relationship between Law Violation and Depression: An Interactionist Analysis." *Criminology* 39, no. 4 (2001): 799–836.

Dickerson, F. B., J. L. Sommerville, and A. Origoni. "Mental Illness Stigma: An Impediment to Psychiatric Rehabilitation." *Psychiatric Rehabilitation Skills* 6, no. 2 (2002a): 186–200.

Dickerson, F. B., J. Sommerville, A. E. Origoni, N. B. Ringel, and F. Parente. "Experiences of Stigma among Outpatients with Schizophrenia." *Schizophrenia Bulletin* 28, no. 1 (2002b): 143–55.

Ditton, P. M. *Mental Health and Treatment of Inmates and Probationers.* Washington, DC: Bureau of Justice Statistics, 1999.

Eblogen, E. B. and S. Johnson. "The Intricate Link between Violence and Mental Disorder: Results from the National Epidemiologic Survey on Alcohol and Related Conditions." *Archives of General Psychiatry* 66, no. 2 (2009): 152–61.

Frank, R. G. and S. Glied. *Better but Not Well: Mental Health Policy in the United States since 1950.* Baltimore, MD: Johns Hopkins Press, 2006.

Gecas, V. and P. Burke. "Self and Identity." In *Social Psychology: Sociological Perspectives*, edited by K. S. Cook, G. A. Fine, and J. S. House, 41–67. Boston: Allyn and Bacon, 1995.

Goffman, E. *Asylums.* Garden City, NY: Anchor/Doubleday, 1961.

———. *Stigma: Notes on the Management of Spoiled Identity.* Englewood Cliffs, NJ: Prentice-Hall, 1963.

Gove, W. R. "The Labeling versus Psychiatric Explanation for Mental Illness: A Debate that has Become Substantively Irrelevant." *Journal of Health and Social Behavior* 20, no. 3 (1979): 301–4.

———. "The Current Status of the Labeling Theory of Mental Illness." In *Deviance and Mental Illness*, edited by W. R. Gove, 273–300. Beverly Hills, CA: Sage, 1982.

Gove, W. R. and T. Fain. "The Stigma of Mental Hospitalization: An Attempt to Evaluate its Consequences." *Archives of General Psychiatry* 29, no. 4 (1973): 494–500.

Gove, W. R. and P. Howell. "Individual Resources and Mental Hospitalization: A Comparison and Evaluation of the Societal Reaction and Psychiatric Perspectives." *American Sociological Review* 39, no. 1 (1974): 86–100.

Greenley, J. R. "Familial Expectations, Posthospital Adjustment, and the Societal Reaction Perspective on Mental Illness." *Journal of Health and Social Behavior* 20, no. 3 (1979): 217–27.

Horwitz, A. V. *Creating Mental Illness.* Chicago: University of Chicago Press, 2001.

James, D. J. and L. Glaze. *Mental Health Problems of Prison and Jail Inmates.* Washington, DC: U.S. Department of Justice, Bureau of Justice Statistics, 2006.

Karp, D. A. *Speaking of Sadness: Depression, Disconnection, and the Meanings of Illness.* New York: Oxford University Press, 1996.

———. *The Burden of Sympathy: How Families Cope with Mental Illness.* New York: Oxford University Press, 2001.

Kessler, R. C., O. Demler, R. G. Frank, M. Olfson, H. A. Pincus, and E. Walters. "Prevalence and Treatment of Mental Disorders 1990 to 2003." *New England Journal of Medicine* 352 (2005): 2515–23.

Kinch, J. W. "A Formalized Theory of the Self-Concept." *American Journal of Sociology* 68, no. 4 (1963): 481–86.

Kroska, A. and S. Harkness. "Stigma Sentiments and Self-Meanings: Exploring the Modified Labeling Theory of Mental Illness." *Social Psychology Quarterly* 69, no. 4 (2006): 325–48.

————. "Exploring the Role of Diagnosis in the Modified Labeling Theory of Mental Illness." *Social Psychology Quarterly* 71, no. 2 (2008): 193–208.

Lefley, H. P. "Family Burden and Family Stigma in Major Mental Illness." *American Psychologist* 44, no. 3 (1989): 556–60.

Lemert, E. *Social Pathology*. New York: McGraw-Hill, 1951.

————. *Human Deviance: Social Problems and Social Control*. Englewood Cliffs, NJ: Prentice-Hall, 1967.

Lincoln, A. "Psychiatric Emergency Room Decision-Making, Social Control, and the 'Undeserving Sick.'" *Sociology of Health and Illness* 28, no. 1 (2006): 54–75.

Link, B. G. "Mental Patient Status, Work, and Income: An Examination of the Effects of a Psychiatric Label." *American Sociological Review* 47, no. 2 (1982): 202–15.

————. "Understanding Labeling Effects in the Area of Mental Disorders: An Empirical Assessment of the Effects of Expectations of Rejection." *American Sociological Review* 52, no. 1 (1987): 96–112.

Link, B. G., H. Andrews, and F. Cullen. "The Violent and Illegal Behavior of Mental Patients Reconsidered." *American Sociological Review* 57, no. 3 (1992): 275–92.

Link, B. G., F. T. Cullen, J. Frank, and J. Wozniak. "The Social Rejection of Former Mental Patients: Understanding Why Labels Matter." *American Journal of Sociology* 92, no. 6 (1987): 1461–500.

Link, B. G., F. T. Cullen, E. Struening, P. E. Shrout, and B. Dohrenwend. "A Modified Labeling Theory Approach to Mental Disorders: An Empirical Assessment." *American Sociological Review* 54, no. 3 (1989): 400–23.

Link, B. G., J. Mirotznik, and F. Cullen. "The Effectiveness of Stigma Coping Orientations: Can Negative Consequences of Mental Illness Labeling be Avoided?" *Journal of Health and Social Behavior* 32, no. 3 (1991): 302–20.

Link, B. G., J. Monahan, A. Steuve, and F. Cullen. "Real in their Consequences: A Sociological Approach to Understanding the Association between Psychotic Symptoms and Violence." *American Sociological Review* 64, no. 2 (1999): 316–32.

Link, B. G. and J. Phelan. "Conceptualizing Stigma." *Annual Review of Sociology* 27 (2001): 363–85.

Link, B. G., E. Struening, M. Rahav, J. C. Phelan, and L. Nuttbrock. "On Stigma and its Consequences: Evidence from a Longitudinal Study of Men with Dual Diagnoses of Mental Illness and Substance Abuse." *Journal of Health and Social Behavior* 38, no. 2 (1997): 177–90.

Luhrmann, T. M. *Of Two Minds: The Growing Disorder in American Psychiatry*. New York: Alfred A. Knopf, Inc., 2000.

Markowitz, F. E. "The Effects of Stigma on the Psychological Well-Being and Life Satisfaction of Persons with Mental Illness." *Journal of Health and Social Behavior* 39, no. 4 (1998): 335–48.

————. "Modeling Processes in Recovery from Mental Illness: Relationships between Symptoms, Life Satisfaction, and Self-Concept." *Journal of Health and Social Behavior* 42, no. 1 (2001): 64–79.

————. "Sociological Models of Mental Illness Stigma: Progress and Prospects." In *On the Stigma of Mental Illness: Implications for Research and Social Change*, edited by P. W. Corrigan, 129–44. Washington, DC: American Psychological Association, 2004a.

————. "Sociological Approaches to Recovery." In *Recovery in Mental Illness: Broadening Our Understanding of Wellness*, edited by R. O. Ralph and P. W. Corrigan, 85–100. Washington, DC: American Psychological Association, 2004b.

————. "Psychiatric Hospital Capacity, Homelessness, and Crime and Arrest Rates." *Criminology* 44 (2006): 45–72.

Markowitz, F. E., B. Angell, and J. S. Greenberg. "Stigma, Reflected Appraisals, and Recovery Outcomes in Mental Illness." *Social Psychology Quarterly* 74 (2011): 144–65.

Martin, J. K., B. A. Pescosolido, and S. Tuch. "Of Fear and Loathing: The Role of 'Disturbing Behavior,' Labels, and Causal Attributions in Shaping Public Attitudes toward Persons with Mental Illness." *Journal of Health and Social Behavior* 41 (2000): 208–23.

Matsueda, R. L. "Reflected Appraisals, Parental Labeling, and Delinquency: Specifying a Symbolic Interactionist Theory." *American Journal of Sociology* 97, no. 6 (1992): 1577–611.

McCall, G. L. and J. Simmons. *Identities and Interaction.* New York: Free Press, 1966.

Mead, G. H. *Mind, Self, and Society.* Chicago: University of Chicago Press, 1934.

Mechanic, D. *Mental Health and Social Policy: Beyond Managed Care.* Boston: Pearson/Allyn and Bacon, 2008.

Mirowsky, J. and C. Ross. *Social Sauses of Psychological Distress.* Hawthorne, NY: Aldine de Gruyter, 2003.

Pearlin, L. I., E. G. Menaghan, M. A. Lieberman, and J. Mullan. "The Stress Process." *Journal of Health and Social Behavior* 22 (1981): 337–56.

Pescosolido, B. A. and C. Boyer. "How Do People Come to Use Mental Health Services? Current Knowledge and Changing Perspectives." In *A Handbook for the Study of Mental Health: Social Contexts, Theories, and Systems*, edited by A. V. Horwitz and T. L. Scheid, 392–411. New York: Cambridge University Press, 1999.

Phelan, J. C. "Geneticization of Deviant Behavior and Consequences for Stigma: The Case of Mental Illness." *Journal of Health and Social Behavior* 46 (2005): 307–22.

Phelan, J. C., B. G. Link, A. Steuve, and B. Pescosolido. "Public Conceptions of Mental Illness in 1950 and 1996: What is Mental Illness and Is It to Be Feared?" *Journal of Health and Social Behavior* 41, no. 2 (2000): 188–207.

Phillips, D. "Rejection: A Possible Consequence of Seeking Help for Mental Disorders." *American Sociological Review* 28, no. 6 (1963): 963–72.

Read, J., N. Haslam, L. Sayce, and E. Davies. "Prejudice and Schizophrenia: A Review of the 'Mental Illness is an Illness Like Any Other' Approach." *Acta Psychiatrica Scandinavica* 114, no. 16 (2006): 303–18.

Ritscher, J. and J. Phelan. "Internalized Stigma Predicts Erosion of Morale among Psychiatric Outpatients." *Psychiatry Research* 129, no. 3 (2004): 257–65.

Rosenfield, S. "Race Differences in Involuntary Hospitalization: Psychiatric vs. Labelling Perspectives." *Journal of Health and Social Behavior* 25, no. 1 (1984): 14–23.

———. "Labeling Mental Illness: The Effects of Services vs. Stigma." *American Sociological Review* 62, no. 4 (1997): 660–72.

Scheff, T. J. "The Labelling Theory of Mental Illness." *American Sociological Review* 39 (1974): 444–52.

———. *Being Mentally Ill: A Sociological Theory.* 2nd ed. Chicago: Aldine, 1984.

Schnittker, J. "Misgivings of Medicine? African Americans' Skepticism of Psychiatric Medication." *Journal of Health and Social Behavior* 44, no. 4 (2003): 506–24.

Struening, E., D. Perlick, B. G. Link, F. Hellman, and J. Sirey. "The Extent to Which Caregivers Believe Most People Devalue Consumers and Their Families." *Psychiatric Services* 52, no. 12 (2001): 1633–38.

Stryker, S. *Symbolic Interactionism: A Social Structural Version.* Menlo Park, CA: Benjamin Cummings, 1980.

Swanson, J. W. "Mental Disorder, Substance Abuse, and Community Violence: An Epidemiological Approach." In *Violence and Mental Disorder: Developments in Risk*

Assessment, edited by J. Monahan and H. J. Steadman, 101–36. Chicago: University of Chicago Press, 1994.

Teasdale, B. "Mental Disorder and Violent Victimization." *Criminal Justice and Behavior* 36, no. 5 (2009): 513–35.

Thoits, P. A. "Self-Labeling Processes in Mental Illness: The Role of Emotional Deviance." *American Journal of Sociology* 91, no. 2 (1985): 221–49.

———. "Differential Labeling of Mental Illness by Social Status: A New Look at an Old Problem." *Journal of Health and Social Behavior* 46, no. 1 (2005): 102–19.

Torrey, E. F. *Out of the Shadows: Confronting America's Mental Illness Crisis*. New York: John Wiley and Sons, 1997.

———. *The Insanity Offense: How America's Failure to Treat the Seriously Mentally Ill Endangers Its Citizens*. New York: W. W. Norton, 2008.

Turner, R. J., B. Wheaton, and D. Lloyd. "The Epidemiology of Social Stress." *American Sociological Review* 60, no. 1 (1995): 104–25.

Wahl, O. F. *Media Madness: Public Images of Mental Illness*. New Brunswick, NJ: Rutgers University Press, 1995.

———. "Mental Health Consumers' Experience of Stigma." *Schizophrenia Bulletin* 25, no. 3 (1999): 467–78.

———. "Children's Views of Mental Illness: A Review of the Literature." *Psychiatric Rehabilitation Skills* 6 (2002): 134–58.

Wahl, O. F. and C. Harmon. "Family Views of Stigma." *Schizophrenia Bulletin* 15, no. 1 (1989): 131–39.

Wang, P. S., O. Demler, and R. Kessler. "Adequacy of Treatment for Serious Mental Illness in the United States." *American Journal of Public Health* 92, no. 1 (2002): 92–8.

Wang, P. S., M. Lane, M. Olfson, H. A. Pincus, K. B. Wells, and R. Kessler. "Twelve-Month Use of Mental Health Services in the United States: Results from the National Comorbidity Survey Replication." *Archives of General Psychiatry* 62, no. 6 (2005): 629–40.

Warner, R., D. Taylor, M. Powers, and J. Hyman. "Acceptance of the Mental Illness Label by Psychotic Patients: Effects on Functioning." *American Journal of Orthopsychiatry* 50, no. 3 (1989): 398–409.

Weinstein, R. M. "Patient Attitudes toward Mental Hospitalization: A Review of Quantitative Research." *Journal of Health and Social Behavior* 20, no. 3 (1979): 237–58.

———. "Labeling Theory and the Attitudes of Mental Patients: A Review." *Journal of Health and Social Behavior* 24, no. 1 (1983): 70–84.

Wright, E. R. and W. Gronfein. "Deinstitutionalization, Social Rejection, and the Self-Esteem of Former Mental Patients." *Journal of Health and Social Behavior* 41, no. 1 (2000): 68–90.

4

Labeling Theory and Correctional Rehabilitation: Beyond Unanticipated Consequences

Francis T. Cullen and Cheryl Lero Jonson

As Louis Schneider (1975: 331) notes, "the sociologist always has an understandable desire . . . to get away from the obvious, to penetrate deeper, to be analytically resourceful, to bring enlightenment." This is often achieved by pointing out what is latent in social life and has unanticipated consequences (Merton, 1936). Particularly valued are those revelations that illuminate the ironic—how efforts to reach one social goal actually have the opposite results. Unmasking "fatal remedies," as Sam Sieber (1981) calls them, brings special status, for here the scholar shows sufficient wisdom to depict how the road to social hell is paved with good intentions.

Much of labeling theory's initial appeal as a sociological perspective was its embrace of the ironic, of showing how the very efforts made to stop crime and deviance exacerbated the conduct (Schneider, 1975). Frank Tannenbaum (1938) called this the "dramatization of evil," whereas for Edwin Lemert (1951) it was a case of transforming otherwise transitory experimentation with "primary deviance" into more organized, life-encapsulating "secondary deviance." Scholars were quick to borrow Robert Merton's (1968) construct of the "self-fulfilling prophecy" to explain how labeling—and the subsequent societal reaction it evoked—created the very thing it was meant to eliminate: career criminality. This was scholarly fun, showing how common-sense thinking blinded the sociological unwise from seeing reality. The latent was made manifest; rich irony was disclosed—and it was possible to be smarter than the average person. Advocating labeling theory was, as John Hagan (1973) wonderfully described it, a case of engaging in the "sociology of the interesting."

Labeling theory, however, was attractive for another reason: it offered a withering criticism of state power. Stephen Cole's (1975) citational analysis shows that labeling theory emerged as a popular perspective in the late 1960s and then became the dominant criminological paradigm in the early 1970s (see also Cullen and Cullen, 1978). This was a time, of course, in which the United States was gripped by revelation after revelation of the abuse of state power. Government lies about the Vietnam War, unnecessary shootings at Kent State University and during the Attica prison insurgency, racism tolerated but urban riots repressed, the Watergate scandal denied but in the end disclosed, the use of undercover FBI agents to disrupt countercultural movements and radical political organizations—these and other events robbed the state of its legitimacy. There was now a "confidence gap" as trust in the government plummeted (Lipset and Schneider, 1983). In this context—described by Tom Brokaw (2007) with the word *Boom!*—the taken for granted was no longer taken for granted, as the assumptions underlying society were shattered. This was true of criminological assumptions as well. Scholars were prepared to endorse a theory that did not rely on the state to solve lawlessness but, rather, blamed the exercise of state power—through the criminal justice system—for the crime problem burdening society.

Thus, labeling theory—and its embrace of irony and the unanticipated—was both interesting and politically correct. It would be a mechanism to illuminate why arresting and, in particular, locking people up would merely serve to create hardened criminals. In so doing, the perspective was useful in challenging social control practices that were, upon closer inspection, indefensible. But labeling theorists failed to consider the ironic, unanticipated consequences of the paradigm's own ideas. In the end, it was a criminological theory that legitimated a prescription for crime control—do nothing since nothing works—that was vacuous and unable to repel conservative answers to crime. In particular, labeling theory was particularly critical of correctional rehabilitation, again without any sense of what the alternative to offender treatment might be: unprecedented punitiveness and mass incarceration.

To have a future, contemporary labeling theory must be more sophisticated. It must be part of an effort to build a theory of the criminal sanction in which the conditions under which labeling and societal action have crime-inducing or crime-preventative effects are spelled out (Cullen and Cullen, 1978; Palmara et al., 1986; Sherman, 1993). In the area of corrections, labeling theory must learn from the extant research what does and does not "work" to reduce reoffending (Cullen and Gendreau, 2000; MacKenzie, 2006). We contend that a key to this effort is for labeling theorists to focus on the known risk factors for recidivism and to specify which interventions increase or decrease these factors. By rooting the perspective more fully in what is known about offending, labeling theory can be commensurately enriched.

Notably, labeling theory and correctional rehabilitation theory are seemingly at opposite ends of the criminological enterprise—one explaining why intervention increases crime through unanticipated consequences, the other explaining why intervention decreases crime through planned treatment. We argue that these perspectives should be reconciled. In the sections that follow, we first note how labeling theory was part of a general movement in criminology to reject rehabilitation—that is, to "turn on the therapeutic." This position led labeling theorists to embrace radical non-intervention—a policy position that proved untenable in the face of what Todd Clear (1994) calls the "penal harm movement." Subsequent research on rehabilitation is instructive in showing that labeling theory had a point—some sanctions make offenders more criminogenic. But the effects of interventions are characterized not by homogeneity but by heterogeneity: some interventions also make offenders less criminal. Scholarship probing what differentiates criminogenic from crime-preventative sanctions reveals that there are principles of effective correctional treatment. This literature also provides the basis for us to derive five principles of labeling effects, with the larger goal of moving toward a theory of the criminal sanction.

Turning on the Therapeutic

Post-World War II American criminology was thoroughly liberal and reformist. Although often covered with the veneer of value-free science, there was a clear belief that science could serve the goal of incremental societal betterment. In the area of corrections, rehabilitation was hegemonic. Punishment was seen as ineffective and thus as lacking scientific credibility. Karl Menninger (1968) would be widely acclaimed for writing a book entitled *The Crime of Punishment*. Indeed, the movement toward treatment was seen as part of a broader civilizing process in which the brutalities inflicted on offenders were being replaced with efforts to correct through treatment. Scholars were not naïve about prisons; many major theorists had conducted prison studies themselves and were helping us to understand life in the "society of captives" (see, e.g., Sykes, 1958). Nonetheless, despite programmatic failures in the past, there was a cautious optimism that progress rested not in returning to hangings, whippings, and mean-spirited prison regimes but to trumpeting the humane intervention with offenders within therapeutic correctional communities. There was, as Philip Rieff (1966) put it, the "triumph of the therapeutic."

Unfortunately, correctional rehabilitation became intertwined with labeling theory's critique of state power. As the dominant ideology justifying the exercise of state power over offenders, rehabilitation was portrayed as the government's accomplice in doing harm and thus was ripe for attack. The key concern was that the rehabilitative ideal—and its notion of providing offenders with individualized treatment—gave the state unfettered discretion over the lives of the wayward. A treatment or medical model depended on officials using their discretionary expertise to design interventions capable of addressing—or curing—the unique criminogenic difficulties driving each person to break the law. But what if this discretion were not used for therapeutic purposes? What if this discretion were abused to the point where decisions over offenders' lives were shaped by ignorance, by race and class bias, or by bureaucratic interests? If so, then rehabilitation would serve as a benevolent mask for malevolent practices. This is precisely what labeling theorists believed to be happening.

These themes were elaborated in convincing ways by the revisionist histories of the day. Traditionally, historians tended to see corrections as an arena in which successive reformers ("great men") and waves of change incrementally contributed to the humanization of prisons and punishment practices (see, e.g., Eriksson, 1976). Blake McKelvey (1977), for example, could write about the "history of good intentions." This benign view, which embraced a vision of American society as in a steady march toward progress and a higher plane of humanity, was rejected by the social historians of the late 1960s and beyond (Ignatieff, 1981). Correctional rehabilitation was seen as an ideology to be unmasked as a tricky servant of increasing state power.

Anthony Platt's (1969) *The Child Savers* was a brilliant investigation of the origins of the juvenile court in Cook County (Chicago), Illinois in the late 1800s. On the surface, the middle-class women who led this reform were filled with good intentions in their efforts to rescue delinquent youths from the squalor of the slums and the meanness of adult courts by creating a treatment-oriented juvenile court. Platt revealed, however, that their "good intentions" were corrupted by the realities of what they produced (inhumane and ineffective juvenile reformatories) and by their class interests. Thus, rather than probe the ethnic and class inequalities at the root of delinquency, they engaged in reform efforts that gave their lives meaning and status but did nothing to challenge the prevailing power structure.

David Rothman's two social histories, *Discovery of the Asylum* (1971) and *Conscience and Convenience* (1980), similarly illuminated the inevitable corruption of great ideas to save the wayward from a life in crime. Both the invention of the penitentiary in Jacksonian America (1830s) and the renovation of the justice system in the Progressive era (1900–1920) ran aground in the face of the stubborn realities of institutional life. Prisons were no place to cure people, both because the very nature of institutional life is inhumane and because of the primacy that custodians place on control over the betterment of their charges. In the end, "convenience" would always trump—indeed, would always corrupt—"conscience."

And to provide but one other example, we can consider Michel Foucault's (1977) *Discipline and Punish*, a volume impenetrable to read but from which a chilling message nonetheless can be distilled. Punishment of the body is easily seen and its brutality is easily appreciated. But the movement in the modern state toward more therapeutic, science-driven interventions, warned Foucault, is neither an advance nor is benign. Therapeutic knowledge is a latent technology of power—another way of controlling individuals. It is especially insidious precisely because it is mistakenly depicted as a civilized departure from a barbaric past. In reality, it is a less visible means by which the state and those wielding power exert control not simply over the body but over the mind.

Two further considerations prompted scholars to turn on the therapeutic state. First, the treatment given to offenders and to other deviant populations was "enforced" (Kittrie, 1971). This was not a therapeutic relationship in which the therapist and patient were present through mutual acquiescence. Rather, control infused the relationship of the state to the offender. The exchange hinged on a massive inequality in power in which offenders had the obligation to be "cured" lest they spend years under correctional supervision. Second and related, the therapy was to take place oftentimes behind prison walls. By the early 1970s, the critique of "total institutions" was virtually complete (Goffman, 1961). Zimbardo and his colleagues' Stanford prison experiment, in which a sample of psychologically normal college students created a coercive prison in a few short days, seemed to cement the view that nothing good could occur in the so-called correctional facilities (Zimbardo et al., 1973; see also Zimbardo, 2007).

This intellectual context reflected and invigorated labeling theory. Labeling theorists were part of a broader coalition of scholars seeking to unmask the role of therapeutic ideology in justifying, in benevolent language, the expansion and abuse of state power. Arrest, conviction, and supposed treatment did not save children or adults from a life in crime. Rather, this legal reaction prompted labeled individuals to embrace criminal identities, to be stigmatized and cut off from pro-social relationships, and to be thrown into institutions where dehumanization and schooling in crime was inevitable. Correctional rehabilitation thus was not simply fraudulent but a willing facilitator in the creation of career criminals. It was time to deconstruct the therapeutic so that its coercive effects would be fully understood.

The Unanticipated Consequences of Non-Intervention

If state power as expressed through correctional interventions is the cause of crime—as labeling theory hypothesizes—then the solution to crime is manifest: limit state power. In the words of Edwin Schur (1973), this means a call for "radical non-intervention"—of leaving people alone "whenever possible." Two strategies formed the core of such non-intervention.

First, there was the embrace of efforts to constrain state discretionary powers. Taken together, these efforts comprised the "justice model" for corrections (American Friends Service Committee Working Party, 1971; Conrad, 1973; Morris, 1974; von Hirsch, 1976; Fogel, 1979). Hopes of reforming offenders or, for that fact, of stopping crime were discarded. Instead, the goal was to ensure justice for all. This was to be accomplished through the extension of due process rights so as to protect offenders against inequitable and abusive legal intrusions. The other key policy criterion was determinate sentencing, which would eradicate individualized treatment. Instead, punishments would be linked to the seriousness of the crime and release from prison would be known at the time of sentencing.

Second, labeling theorists and their allies favored diversion and deinstitutionalization. Their intent was to get offenders out of the system and, in particular, out of prison. This anti-institutional view became part of the general professional ideology of criminologists, thus, representing an enduring legacy of labeling theory (Cullen and Gendreau, 2001). Indeed, scholars who endorse the use of prisons, such as James Q. Wilson (1975) or John DiIulio (1994), are labeled as conservatives and are the object of much critique if not outright scorn.

The non-interventionist position, while morally pleasing and popular among scholars, proved to be naïve both criminologically and politically. Let us first comment on why this do-nothing position was criminologically naïve. Early on, critics of labeling theory, such as Walter Gove (1975), realized that societal reaction was neither a necessary nor a sufficient condition for stable crime and deviance to occur (Cullen and Cullen, 1978). Subsequent insights from life-course criminology reveal that criminal careers have their roots early in life and are well under way before formal mechanisms of social control, especially the criminal justice system, are typically invoked (Farrington, 2005; Piquero et al., 2007). Non-intervention thus may not result in the disappearance of primary deviance, but rather, in the continual abatement of chronic criminality (Stouthamer-Loeber et al., 1995). The chief issue is not non-intervention but how to intervene in a way that does not have iatrogenic effects.

Non-interventionism also proved politically naïve. To be sure, at the time, limiting state intervention appeared to be a reasonable policy strategy. Prison populations were under 200,000 in the early 1970s, and rates of incarceration had remained relatively stable for a half century (Blumstein and Cohen, 1973). In Massachusetts, Jerome Miller (1991) had successfully deinstitutionalized the state's juvenile facilities, with no apparent increase in crime. And on the legal front, the Warren Court had ushered in an era of unprecedented concern with and extension of due process rights. Still, from a policy standpoint, non-invention suffered three fatal flaws that rendered this optimism sadly misplaced (Travis and Cullen, 1984).

First, labeling theorists misread the times and the feebleness of their response to crime. They failed to appreciate the rising "law and order" rhetoric infusing the crime agenda espoused by conservatives. Faced with escalating crime and a sense of breakdown, Americans did not wish to hear that criminals should receive a slap on the wrist and be allowed to roam free in the community. Non-intervention might play well in the halls of academia but it seemed silly, if not irresponsible, in the city streets where lawlessness was creating havoc.

Second, in its efforts to constrain state power, non-interventionists endorsed determinate sentences. They advocated that these sentences be kept short, a wish that now seems absurdly utopian. More than this, by taking decision making power away from corrections officials, they inadvertently placed it into the hands of politicians (who set the determinate sentences) and prosecutors (who decided what to charge an offender). This redistribution of discretionary power could not have come at a worse time. As American politics shifted to the right on crime, legislators engaged in a punitive orgy, passing one draconian law after another.

Third, labeling theorists confused the extension of rights with social caring. But this is not the case. Legal rights delimit what the state can do *to you*, but they do not mandate the state to do anything *for you*. The genius of the rehabilitative ideal was that it served a higher social purpose (Allen, 1981). Its mission was not simply to protect the public but also to improve the offender. Phrased differently, the therapeutic state intended to make corrections an instrument of social welfare. In rejecting rehabilitation, scholars willingly embraced a system that was to provide justice—rights—but little else to offenders. They made a disastrous trade: social welfare for procedural justice. The poverty of this approach is most apparent in the deinstitutionalization of mental patients, who were given the right to fend for themselves in the streets with few services provided. In corrections, the consequence was to absolve the state of any obligation to care for the wayward (Cullen and Gilbert, 1982; Rotman, 1990).

Foolishly, non-interventionism assumed that the culprit for the ills in the correctional system was therapeutic ideology and practices. But thirty years after labeling theory informed the attack on rehabilitation, we have seen what the correctional system is like when the reigning ideology is stripped of its social welfare sentiments and made explicitly punitive. To be sure, many factors contributed to the lengthy mean season in corrections and to the rise of mass incarceration (see, e.g., Garland, 2001; Gottschalk, 2006; Simon, 2007; Useem and Piehl, 2008). Still, it is instructive that non-intervention and its partner, the justice model, offered no credible ideological alternative to the calls to get tough on crime. Advocates failed to realize that rehabilitation remains a powerful public ideology in the United States and one of the few means for debating and defeating ineffective punitive policies (Cullen et al., 2000; Cullen, 2007). Ironically, non-intervention thus must be seen as having the unanticipated consequence of creating the very thing it hoped to prevent: unprecedented intervention through the mass imprisonment of offenders.

Lessons from Rehabilitation: Heterogeneity of Effects

Labeling theory coincided with and drew added legitimacy from the "nothing works" movement in corrections. In 1974, Robert Martinson published his classic essay in *The Public Interest* in which he concluded that treatment programs had "no appreciable effect" on recidivism.

Technically, Martinson did not say that "nothing works," but he did ask the question, "does nothing work?" Further, in later interviews and writings, he made it clear that "nothing works" was the take away message from his synthesis of evaluation studies (Cullen and Gendreau, 2000).

The remarkable feature of Martinson's work was not his conclusion—others had supplied similar findings previously—but how readily the criminological community accepted his assessment. Scientific norms of organized skepticism (Merton, 1973) were cast aside, as scholars took Martinson's nothing works message as the final word—as empirical confirmation of what by now was criminological common sense, that is, of what "everyone already knew." Challenges to this professional ideology were met with dismissal or with the use of what Michael Gottfredson (1979) called "treatment destruction techniques" to render positive program findings methodologically suspect. Labeling theory provided a clear rationale for why rehabilitation programs were ineffective or, at worse, iatrogenic. It was bad medicine that did not work or made the patient more ill.

As Ted Palmer (1975) pointed out, nearly half (48 percent) of the studies reviewed by Martinson had positive results (see also Gendreau and Ross, 1979). Martinson, however, never claimed that programs did not reduce recidivism. Rather, he argued that within any category of treatment—for example, group counseling or education programs—the interventions did not work reliably. Sometimes they might reduce recidivism, sometimes they did not. Accordingly, it was impossible to advise policy makers on what should be done to rehabilitate offenders. He also made the assumption of *homogeneity of effects*. He assumed that regardless of the category of treatment, this glass half-full and half-empty effect would be found. Thus, it was not so much that nothing works, but that nothing works reliably and nothing works better than anything else (Lipton et al., 1975; see also Cullen and Gendreau, 2000).

Subsequent meta-analytic assessments of the treatment evaluation literature, however, proved Martinson incorrect in two ways (Cullen, 2005). First, across all studies, there was a positive effect size of around .10 to .12, suggesting roughly a five percentage point difference in recidivism rates (i.e., 50 percent for the control group versus 45 percent for the treatment group). Second, and more consequential, across types of treatment modalities *heterogeneity in effects*, not homogeneity, was found (Lipsey, 1992, 2009; Lösel, 1995; Lipsey and Wilson, 1998; McGuire, 2002; Lipsey and Cullen, 2007). In short, some interventions are ineffective, but others have large and consistent effects in reducing reoffending (see, e.g., Andrews et al., 1990; see also Andrews and Bonta, 2006).

Contemporary labeling theorists, however, generally ignore this evaluation literature, much to the impoverishment of the perspective. The correctional rehabilitation area is home to perhaps the most extensive and rigorous set of evaluations of the impact of criminal sanctions on offenders. This research has important implications for a more sophisticated, nuanced labeling theory. To wit: not all criminal sanctions are the same. As early labeling theorists suspected, interventions that are punitive and pregnant with a dislike of offenders tend to make matters worse (see also Braithwaite, 1989). But this research also reveals that turning on the therapeutic was a mistake—a case of throwing the baby out with the bathwater. Offender rehabilitation can work.

The Quality of the Criminal Sanction: What Does and Does Not Work

What should be done with offenders who break the law? With over seven million offenders under state supervision in the United States—including over 2.4 million incarcerated on any given day—it is silly to talk about "radical non-intervention." Massive numbers of people are being criminally labeled and sanctioned and thus the choice of doing nothing is not viable in most instances. The critical issue is thus the *quality of the sanction* being imposed (see also Braithwaite, 1989; Sherman, 1993). Again, the treatment evaluation literature provides clear guidance on what does, and does not work, to reduce recidivism—that is, on what does and does not have "labeling effects."

What Does Not Work

In the assessment of labeling theory, the key issue is whether applying a criminal sanction to an offender makes the person more or less likely to break the law. This leaves aside issues of general deterrence or crime savings that might accrue from incapacitation. Instead, the focus is on whether labeling is criminogenic and causes individuals to recidivate. The opposite point of view, embraced by economists and common-sense get-tough politicians, is that raising costs and thus lowering the expected utility of crime makes people less likely to offend. This is the *specific deterrence thesis* (see Thorsell and Klemke, 1972; Tittle, 1975; Cullen and Cullen, 1978).

As it turns out, the empirical literature—with a few exceptions here and there—is an economist's nightmare. The "rational human" does not seem to be very responsive to criminal justice efforts at specific deterrence.

Existing meta-analyses and related research reveal that punishment-oriented correctional programs have few positive effects, typically have no impact on recidivism, and at times are criminogenic (Cullen et al., 1996; Lipsey and Wilson, 1998; Cullen et al., 2002; McGuire, 2002; MacKenzie, 2006; Lipsey and Cullen, 2007; Lipsey, 2009).

The results of control-oriented or punishment-oriented intensive supervision programs (ISPs) are especially instructive. This is an ideal test of specific deterrence. Offenders are placed in a program in which they are subjected to close surveillance and are threatened with punishment for any misconduct. There are no bleeding-heart liberals seeking to save the wayward or social workers hoping to hold offenders' hands. Rather, the members of the surveillance staff are instructed to have a harder edge—to know that they are watching offenders who need watching and who should be cut little, if any, slack.

Of course, the extant research shows that ISPs are largely ineffective (Byrne and Pattavina, 1992; Cullen et al., 1996; MacKenzie, 2006). Joan Petersilia and Susan Turner's (1993) classic experimental study of ISPs across fourteen sites provided the most damning evidence. In no site did the experimental group have lower recidivism rates than the control group. In fact, across all offenders, the experimental groups had a slightly higher recidivism rate (37 percent to 33 percent). The only glimmer of hope was that the minority of offenders exposed to treatment were less likely to recidivate than those receiving only control (see also Bonta et al., 2000; Paparozzi and Gendreau, 2005).

A more recent study by Christopher Lowenkamp et al. (2009) of fifty-eight ISPs in Ohio furnishes more discouraging evidence for the specific deterrence thesis. They examined whether or not a program was characterized by treatment integrity and whether the program's philosophy was oriented toward deterrence or human services (treatment). Lowenkamp et al. discovered that programs that lacked integrity and were deterrence-oriented increased recidivism by 9 percent and 11 percent, respectively. This was also true of deterrence-oriented programs that were high on treatment integrity, though the jump in reoffending was not statistically significant. By contrast, human services-oriented programs, especially those with high-treatment integrity, lowered reduced recidivism (by 17 percent).

Advocates of deterrence might protest that anything done in the community is a slap on the wrist and thus is not a fair test of the power of punishment to teach offenders that crime does not pay. Here, the argument is that the key to deterrence is imposing a custodial sanction. In fact, the idea that the sting of imprisonment is special is at the heart of mandatory sentencing policies and to the very logic of deterrence. Steven Levitt (2002: 443) captures this sentiment, noting that "it is critical to the deterrence hypothesis that longer prison sentences be associated with reductions in crime."

Alas, beyond any incapacitation effects, there is scant evidence that custodial sanctions reduce criminal participation more than non-custodial sanctions. Four reviews of existing studies lend credence to these conclusions. First, Paul Gendreau et al. (2000) examined 103 comparisons, encompassing over 265,000 offenders, of custodial versus non-custodial sanctions. There was no evidence that a prison sentence reduced recidivism. In fact, the opposite was discovered, with custodial sentences being associated with a 7 percent increase in recidivism.

Second, extending the work of Gendreau et al. (2000), Paula Smith et al. (2002) also reported no deterrent effect associated with a custodial sentence. When comparing incarceration to community-based sanctions, Smith et al. found that incarceration was associated with a 7 percent increase in recidivism. Notably, when they examined studies with a strong quality of design, they uncovered an even stronger iatrogenic effect of prison, with incarceration associated with an 11 percent increase in recidivism.

In a third review of the research, Patrice Villettaz et al. (2006) systematically analyzed twenty-three studies, which included twenty-seven comparisons examining the effect of custodial versus non-custodial sanctions on recidivism. Of the twenty-seven comparisons, only two were associated with a reduction in recidivism. By contrast, in fourteen comparisons there was no difference between those subjected to custodial versus non-custodial sanctions, and in eleven comparisons custodial sanctions were associated with increases in reoffending.

Finally, in a more recent study, Daniel Nagin et al. (2009) reported results consistent with those in the previous three reviews. Examining six experimental/quasi-experimental, eleven matching, and thirty-one regression-based studies, Nagin et al. found that overall incarceration had either a null or slight criminogenic effect on recidivism.

Thus, across four major reviews of the extant literature, little evidence has been found in support of the specific deterrence argument. Those still clinging to a belief in punitiveness, however, might claim that the issue really is the length of the prison sentence. Admittedly, research in this area is limited. Still, the studies that do exist are not favorable to the specific deterrence thesis. Indeed, three reviews of the literature have found that longer prison terms are associated with an increase in recidivism. For example, in a meta-analysis of twenty-three studies, Gendreau et al. (1999) determined that offenders who spent more time in prison were 2 to 3 percent more likely to recidivate than those who served less time. Similarly, extending the Gendreau et al. (1999) meta-analysis by examining twenty-six studies, Smith et al. (2002) found that longer sentences were associated with a 3 percent increase in recidivism; this figure rose to 4 percent when studies with the strongest quality of design were analyzed separately. Finally, when reviewing two experimental and seventeen non-experimental studies, Nagin et al. (2009) concluded that longer custodial sentences had either a null effect or a slightly increased likelihood of recidivism.

Well, might a deterrent effect be unmasked if we probed the pains of imprisonment? At present, there is little research on whether the harshness of prison conditions impact reoffending. Still, a study by Keith Chen and Shapiro (2003) is instructive and, again, contrary to the prediction of the specific deterrence thesis. Based on offenders within the Federal Bureau of Prisons, they examined the relationship between recidivism and confinement in higher or lower security, with the presumption that life in a higher security placement was harsher. Their results indicated that being housed in a higher security level had no deterrent effect and that, "if anything, harsher prison conditions lead to more post-release crime" (2003: 1). Similar results have been found with Italian inmates, with no evidence that harsher living conditions decrease recidivism (Drago et al., 2008).

Deterrence scholars might try one final line of argument: punishing low-risk offenders would be effective because the shock of incarceration would nip their criminal careers in the bud. Of course, this prediction is directly contrary to the *primary deviance thesis* of labeling theory. As articulated by Lemert (1951), this idea of punishing low-risk offenders solidifies their criminality. Once again, although limited, the available data are inconsistent with the logic of specific deterrence. It appears that over-sanctioning low-risk offenders helps turn their primary deviance into secondary deviance. Thus, in a study of 5,469 male offenders in the Canadian federal penitentiary system, Smith (2006) discovered that imprisonment increased recidivism among low-risk but not among high-risk offenders.

What Does Work

Thus, there is growing evidence that punitively oriented criminal sanctions have little, no, or iatrogenic effects. Accordingly, this research is consistent with labeling theory and argues for the perspective's continued elaboration. Other research, however, contravenes a rigid labeling theory prediction that all criminal sanctions are criminogenic. There is persuasive evidence that well-designed interventions can reduce recidivism (MacKenzie, 2006). Most notably, a group of Canadian scholars—Don Andrews, Jim Bonta, and Gendreau among the most known—have developed a systematic paradigm for undertaking rehabilitation programs (Cullen, 2002). Their perspective is called the "principles of effective correctional treatment" and has accumulated substantial empirical support (Andrews et al., 1990; Andrews, 1995; Gendreau, 1996; Andrews and Bonta, 2006; Gendreau et al., 2006; Smith et al., 2009b). The paradigm is organized around three principles—risk, need, and responsivity—that have implications for when "labeling" has positive or, as we shall see below, negative effects on behavior.

The Canadians, as we will term them here, start their paradigm with a simple but powerful observation: correctional interventions must be based on a clear knowledge of the risk factors associated with recidivism (Gendreau et al., 1996). They distinguish between "static risk factors" (e.g., age and race), which cannot change, and "dynamic risk factors" (e.g., antisocial attitudes), which can change. They call dynamic risk factors "criminogenic needs," and they argue that interventions must target these empirically established factors for change. This is called the "need principle."

Their logic next proceeds to the observation that correctional programs will only work if they are "responsive to"—that is, are capable of changing—dynamic risk factors or "criminogenic needs." Virtually all punitively oriented programs are incapable of altering empirically established risk factors. They are not "responsive" to these needs. By contrast, treatment programs, especially those that are behavioral or cognitive behavioral, are responsive. This is called the "responsivity principle."

The Canadians also offer a "risk principle." Research indicates that correctional interventions should be delivered to high-risk offenders. Risk level should be determined by actuarial methods, which is why the Canadians developed the Level of Service Inventory—an assessment instrument shown to have predictive validity (Vose et al., 2008; Smith et al., 2009a). High-risk offenders are prime candidates for treatment because they are marked by criminogenic needs and thus have "room" to change quite a bit. Low-risk offenders are unlikely to recidivate if "left alone" and thus have "room" to become more criminogenic if subject to criminal justice interventions.

As noted, there is increasing evidence supporting the principles of effective correctional treatment (Andrews et al., 1990; Andrews and Bonta, 2006; Gendreau et al., 2006; Smith et al., 2009a, 2009b). However, the validity of these principles gains added support from the experimental evaluation literature in the area of early intervention programs. Successful programs are "risk focused" (Farrington and Welsh, 2007; see also Farrington, 1994; Farrington and Coid, 2003). According to David Farrington and Brandon Welsh (2007: 94), "the basic idea of this approach is very simple: identify the key risk factors for offending and implement prevention methods designed to counteract them." In other words, these programs conform to the principles of criminogenic needs and of responsivity. Not all early interventions focus only on high-risk youths; for example, some are schoolwide. Even so, a number of prominent initiatives—such as the nurse-visitation program (Olds, 2007), the High/Scope Perry Preschool project (Schweinhart, 2007), functional family therapy (Alexander et al., 1998), and multisystemic therapy (Henggeler, 1998)—do target high-risk children and/or families for treatment. In short, they adhere to the risk principle.

Principles of Labeling Effects: Toward a Theory of the Criminal Sanction

As Sherman (1993) understood when proposing his defiance theory, there is a need for a theory of the criminal sanction that specifies the conditions under which labeling and subsequent societal reaction produce "defiance, deterrence, or irrelevance" (see also Cullen and Cullen, 1978; Palmara et al., 1986). This challenge means embarking on a process whereby *principles of labeling effects* can be theoretically and empirically derived from the extant literature. It is premature to develop a complete theory of the criminal sanction, but it is possible to take steps toward this goal. In this context, the insights from the research on correctional treatment programs—on what works and what does not—provide a basis of adding to an understanding of labeling effects. Specifically, we are able to propose five principles of labeling effects based on the discussion in the previous section.

Before proceeding, a caveat is necessary. Beyond the principles we derive from the correctional rehabilitation literature, a complete theory of the criminal sanction would incorporate insights from a range of extant works. For example, an accumulating body of empirical studies exists, which documents that labeling effects do exist and vary by socio-demographic characteristics (for a summary, see Chiricos et al., 2007). Longitudinal research shows how official intervention can deepen juvenile delinquency and later criminal participation as well by increasing involvement in deviant groups and diminishing educational attainment and employment (Bernburg and Krohn, 2003; Bernburg et al., 2006). It also appears that criminal justice sanctions are likely to exacerbate offending when they are perceived as unfair and violate norms of procedural justice (Sherman, 1993; Tyler, 2003). And consistent with John Braithwaite's (1989) reintegrative shaming theory, official reactions that are restorative tend to reduce recidivism and avoid the potential criminogenic consequences of punitive penalties (Braithwaite, 2002; Latimer et al., 2005; McGarrell and Hipple, 2007). Again, our limited goal here is to extend the discussion of the impact of labeling on reoffending by developing hypotheses based on our knowledge about correctional treatment.

First, we offer the *principle of primary deviance*. This principle proposes that interventions focused on low-risk offenders will escalate the probability of increasing recidivism. This insight builds on the work of Lemert (1951) and traditional labeling theorists. It differs in the sense that it does not assume that all offenders are "primary deviants." Even so, it confirms the central idea that interventions with those who are not at risk for further criminal conduct are likely to be criminogenic. Whenever possible, interventions should select high-risk offenders for treatment (see also Chiricos et al., 2007).

Second, we offer the *principle of criminogenic risks*. In general, labeling theory has tended to be anti-positivist and has ignored the criminological literature on risk factors. Most often, labeling is seen as fostering increased criminal conduct by prompting individuals to embrace a criminal identity. Other times, there is a general discussion of how labeling might cut off ties from conventional society and deepen ties with criminal society. More specificity, however, is needed. Thus, if labeling is criminogenic, it must operate through specific risk factors—increasing those shown to be related to offending at different developmental periods (Farrington, 1994; Gendreau et al., 1996; Loeber and Farrington, 1998; Farrington and Welsh, 2007).

Third, we offer the related *principle of targeting non-criminogenic risks*. Many correctional interventions are not evidence based (Latessa et al., 2002; MacKenzie, 2006; Cullen et al., 2009). They often target factors for change that have little to do with recidivism (e.g., self-esteem). Thus, when non-criminogenic risks are the focus of intervention, the result is likely to be what Sherman (1993) calls "irrelevance"—that is, a null effect. We make this prediction because little about the offender will have changed. However, a criminogenic effect cannot be ruled out (Wormith, 1984).

Fourth, we offer the *principle of non-responsivity*. This is another consequence of interventions that are not evidence based. Here, the focus is not on what is targeted but on the use of inappropriate interventions. Again, interventions that are not responsive to criminogenic risk factors—that is, that are not capable of changing them—are likely to produce irrelevance or, if they exacerbate risk factors, to increase recidivism (e.g., foster anger or defiance). This is comparable to iatrogenic effects in medicine when patients are given incorrect medication, which may have a placebo effect or make the person more ill. In corrections, the use of non-responsive programs often amounts to quackery because professional norms do not mandate the use of interventions shown to be effective (Latessa et al., 2002; Cullen et al., 2009).

Fifth, we offer the *principle of punitive interventions*. This principle proposes that interventions that are punitively oriented—that is, that seek exclusively to impose surveillance, pain, discipline, or fear on offenders— will be criminogenic. This thesis might be seen as a special case of the principle of non-responsivity, given that get-tough sanctions are not designed to alter the known risk factors for reoffending. They are always non-responsive. However, because of the centrality of punitive rhetoric to the correctional enterprise, it warrants a separate analysis.

Conclusion: Beyond Unanticipated Consequences

Labeling theory was the academic child of a particular historical period in which scholars used ideas to challenge the prevailing taken-for-granted social constructions of reality and to challenge the hypocritical and ruthless exercise of state power. Irony was thus a means for deconstructing cultural and hierarchical regimens that served repressive functions. Revealing the unanticipated consequences of criminal justice was particularly satisfying because it showed the ignorance of using state power, disproportionately focused on disadvantaged populations, to end the crime problem. There was a sense of glee in pointing out that state authorities were creating the very conduct they smugly claimed to be stopping.

Times change, however, and so too should labeling theory. In its earliest stages, an extreme, socially conscious version of the perspective was understandable. Now, a more mature labeling theory needs to play a central role in specifying the conditions under which interventions have criminogenic effects. As noted, these insights will contribute to a general theory of the criminal sanction. This theory needs to draw on diverse literatures so as to distill principles of labeling effects.

Finally, it was unfortunate that a special target of labeling theory in its formative stages was correctional rehabilitation. This was, in a sense, a historical accident. As the hegemonic ideology justified the exercise of state power, the therapeutic was castigated for enabling state repression in the name of benevolent motives. This anti-rehabilitation bent in labeling theory merits reconsideration. As argued, the alternative to correctional rehabilitation is much worse, and a body of research has been developed that shows the conditions under which treatment interventions not only have labeling effects but also preventative effects. Labeling theory and correctional intervention thus are two paradigms that should be reconciled; they have much to learn from one another.

References

Alexander, J., C. Pugh, and B. Parsons. *Functional Family Therapy: Book Three in the Blueprints in Violence Prevention Series*. Boulder, CO: Center for the Study and Prevention of Violence, University of Colorado, 1998.

Allen, F. A. *The Decline of the Rehabilitative Ideal: Penal Policy and Social Purpose*. New Haven, CT: Yale University Press, 1981.

American Friends Service Committee Working Party. *Struggle for Justice: A Report on Crime and Punishment in America*. New York: Hill and Wang, 1971.

Andrews, D. A. "The Psychology of Criminal Conduct and Effective Treatment." In *What Works: Reducing Reoffending—Guidelines from Research and Practice*, edited by J. McGuire, 35–62. New York: John Wiley, 1995.

Andrews, D. A. and J. Bonta. *The Psychology of Criminal Conduct*. 4th ed. Cincinnati, OH: LexisNexis/Anderson, 2006.

Andrews, D. A., I. Zinger, R. D. Hoge, J. Bonta, P. Gendreau, and F. T. Cullen. "Does Correctional Treatment Work? A Clinically Relevant and Psychologically Informed Meta-Analysis." *Criminology* 28 (1990): 369–404.

Bernburg, J. G. and M. D. Krohn. "Labeling, Life Chances, and Adult Crime: The Direct and Indirect Effects of Official Intervention in Adolescence on Crime in Early Adulthood." *Criminology* 41 (2003): 1287–318.

Bernburg, J. G., M. D. Krohn, and C. J. Rivera. "Official Labeling, Criminal Embeddedness, and Subsequent Delinquency: A Longitudinal Test of Labeling Theory." *Journal of Research in Crime and Delinquency* 43 (2006): 67–88.

Blumstein, A. and J. Cohen. "A Theory of the Stability of Punishment." *Journal of Criminal Law and Criminology* 64 (1973): 198–206.

Bonta, J., S. Wallace-Capretta, and J. Rooney. "A Quasi-Experimental Evaluation of an Intensive Rehabilitation Supervision Program." *Criminal Justice and Behavior* 27 (2000): 312–29.

Braithwaite, J. *Crime, Shame and Reintegration*. Cambridge: Cambridge University Press, 1989.

————. *Restorative Justice and Responsive Regulation*. New York: Oxford University Press, 2002.

Brokaw, T. *Boom! Voices of the Sixties*. New York: Random House, 2007.

Byrne, J. M. and A. Pattavina. "The Effectiveness Issue: Assessing What Works in the Adult Community Corrections System." In *Smart Sentencing: The Emergence of Intermediate Sanctions*, edited by J. M. Byrne, A. J. Lurigio, and J. Petersilia, 281–303. Newbury Park, CA: Sage, 1992.

Chen, M. K. and J. M. Shapiro. "Do Harsher Prison Conditions Reduce Recidivism? A Discontinuity-Based Approach." *American Law and Economic Review* 9 (2003): 1–29.

Chiricos, T., K. Barrick, W. Bales, and S. Bontrager. "The Labeling of Convicted Felons and Its Consequences for Recidivism." *Criminology* 45 (2007): 547–81.

Clear, T. R. *Harm in American Penology: Offenders, Victims, and Their Communities*. Albany: State University of New York Press, 1994.

Cole, S. "The Growth of Scientific Knowledge: Theories of Deviance as a Case Study." In *The Idea of Social Structure: Papers in Honor of Robert K. Merton*, edited by L. A. Coser, 175–220. New York: Harcourt Brace Jovanovich, 1975.

Conrad, J. P. "Corrections and Simple Justice." *Journal of Criminal Law and Criminology* 64 (1973): 208–17.

Cullen, F. T. "Rehabilitation and Treatment Programs." In *Crime: Public Policies for Crime Control*, edited by J. Q. Wilson and J. Petersilia, 253–89. Oakland, CA: ICS Press, 2002.

————. "The Twelve People Who Saved Rehabilitation: How the Science of Criminology Made a Difference—The American Society of Criminology 2004 Presidential Address." *Criminology* 43 (2005): 1–42.

————. "Make Rehabilitation Corrections' Guiding Paradigm." *Criminology and Public Policy* 6 (2007): 717–28.

Cullen, F. T. and J. B. Cullen. *Toward a Paradigm of Labeling Theory* (Monograph Number 58, University of Nebraska Studies). Lincoln: University of Nebraska, 1978.

Cullen, F. T., B. S. Fisher, and B. K. Applegate. "Public Opinion about Punishment and Corrections." In *Crime and Justice: A Review of Research*, edited by M. Tonry, vol. 27, 1–79. Chicago: University of Chicago Press, 2000.

Cullen, F. T. and P. Gendreau. "Assessing Correctional Rehabilitation: Policy, Practice, and Prospects." In *Criminal Justice 2000: Vol. 3, Policies, Processes, and Decisions of the Criminal Justice System*, edited by J. Horney, 109–75. Washington, DC: U.S. Department of Justice, National Institute of Justice, 2000.

————. "From Nothing Works to What Works: Changing Professional Ideology in the 21st Century." *Prison Journal* 81 (2001): 313–38.

Cullen, F. T. and K. E. Gilbert. *Reaffirming Rehabilitation*. Cincinnati, OH: Anderson, 1982.

Cullen, F. T., A. J. Myer, and E. J. Latessa. "Eight Lessons from *Moneyball*: The High Cost of Ignoring Evidence-Based Corrections." *Victims and Offenders* 4 (2009): 197–213.

Cullen, F. T., T. C. Pratt, S. L. Micelli, and M. M. Moon. "Dangerous Liaison? Rational Choice Theory as the Basis for Correctional Intervention." In *Rational Choice and Criminal Behavior: Recent Research and Future Challenges*, edited by A. R. Piquero and S. G. Tibbetts, 279–96. New York: Routledge, 2002.

Cullen, F. T., J. P. Wright, and B. K. Applegate. "Control in the Community: The Limits of Reform?" In *Choosing Correctional Interventions That Work: Defining the Demand and Evaluating the Supply*, edited by A. T. Harland, 69–116. Newbury Park, CA: Sage, 1996.

DiIulio, J. J., Jr. "The Question of Black Crime." *The Public Interest* 117 (1994): 3–32.

Drago, F., R. Galbiati, and P. Vertova. *Prison Conditions and Recidivism.* IZA Discussion Paper No. 3395, 2008.

Eriksson, T. *The Reformers: An Historical Survey of Pioneer Experiments in the Treatment of Criminals.* New York: Elsevier, 1976.

Farrington, D. P. "Early Developmental Prevention of Juvenile Delinquency." *Criminal Behaviour and Mental Health* 4 (1994): 209–27.

———, ed. *Integrated Developmental and Life-Course Theories of Offending: Advances in Criminological Theory.* Vol. 14. New Brunswick, NJ: Transaction, 2005.

Farrington, D. P. and J. W. Coid, eds. *Early Prevention of Adult Antisocial Behavior.* Cambridge: Cambridge University Press, 2003.

Farrington, D. P. and B. C. Welsh. *Saving Children from a Life of Crime: Early Risk Factors and Effective Interventions.* New York: Oxford University Press, 2007.

Fogel, D. ". . . *We are the Living Proof . . .": The Justice Model for Corrections.* 2nd ed. Cincinnati, OH: Anderson, 1979.

Foucault, M. *Discipline and Punish: The Birth of the Prison.* New York: Pantheon, 1977.

Garland, D. *The Culture of Control: Crime and Social Order in Contemporary Society.* Chicago: University of Chicago Press, 2001.

Gendreau, P. "The Principles of Effective Intervention with Offenders." In *Choosing Correctional Interventions That Work: Defining the Demand and Evaluating the Supply,* edited by A. T. Harland, 117–30. Newbury Park, CA: Sage, 1996.

Gendreau, P., C. Goggin, and F. T. Cullen. *The Effect of Prison Sentences on Recidivism.* Ottawa, Canada: Solicitor General Canada, 1999.

Gendreau, P., C. Goggin, F. T. Cullen, and D. A. Andrews. "The Effects of Community Sanctions and Incarceration on Recidivism." *Forum on Corrections Research* 12 (2000): 10–13.

Gendreau, P., T. Little, and C. Goggin. "A Meta-Analysis of the Predictors of Adult Offender Recidivism: What Works!" *Criminology* 34 (1996): 575–607.

Gendreau, P. and R. R. Ross. "Effective Correctional Treatment: Bibliotherapy for Cynics." *Crime and Delinquency* 25 (1979): 463–89.

Gendreau, P., P. Smith, and S. French. "The Theory of Effective Correctional Intervention: Empirical Status and Future Directions." In *Taking Stock: The Status of Criminological Theory—Advances in Criminological Theory,* edited by F. T. Cullen, J. P. Wright, and K. R. Blevins, vol. 15, 419–46. New Brunswick, NJ: Transaction, 2006.

Goffman, E. *Asylums.* Garden City, NY: Doubleday, 1961.

Gottfredson, M. R. "Treatment Destruction Techniques." *Journal of Research in Crime and Delinquency* 16 (1979): 39–54.

Gottschalk, M. *The Prison and the Gallows: The Politics of Mass Incarceration in America.* New York: Cambridge University Press, 2006.

Gove, W. R., ed. *The Labeling of Deviance: Evaluating a Perspective.* New York: Halsted Press, 1975.

Hagan, J. "Labeling and Deviance: A Case Study in the 'Sociology of the Interesting.'" *Social Problems* 20 (1973): 447–58.

Henggeler, S. W. *Multisystemic Therapy: Book Six in the Blueprints in Violence Prevention Series.* Boulder, CO: Center for the Study and Prevention of Violence, University of Colorado, 1998.

Ignatieff, M. "State, Civil Society, and Total Institutions: A Critique of Recent Social Histories of Punishment." In *Crime and Justice: An Annual Review of Research,* edited by M. Tonry and N. Morris, vol. 3, 153–92. Chicago: University of Chicago Press, 1981.

Kittrie, N. *The Right to be Different: Deviance and Enforced Therapy*. Baltimore, MD: Penguin Books, 1971.

Latessa, E. J., F. T. Cullen, and P. Gendreau. "Beyond Correctional Quackery: Professionalism and the Possibility of Effective Treatment." *Federal Probation* 66, no. 2 (2002): 43–9.

Latimer, J., C. Dowden, and D. Muise. "The Effectiveness of Restorative Justice Practices: A Meta-Analysis." *Prison Journal* 85 (2005): 127–44.

Lemert, E. M. *Social Pathology*. New York: McGraw-Hill, 1951.

Levitt, S. D. "Deterrence." In *Crime: Public Policies for Crime Control*, edited by J. Q. Wilson and J. Petersilia, 435–50. Oakland, CA: ICS Press, 2002.

Lipset, S. M. and W. Schneider. *The Confidence Gap: Business, Labor, and Government in the Public Mind*. New York: The Free Press, 1983.

Lipsey, M. W. "Juvenile Delinquency Treatment: A Meta-Analytic Inquiry into the Variability of Effects." In *Meta-Analysis for Explanation: A Casebook*, edited by T. D. Cook, H. Cooper, D. S. Cordray, H. Hartmann, L. V. Hedges, R. J. Light, T. A. Lewis, and F. Mosteller, 83–127. New York: Russell Sage, 1992.

———. "The Primary Factors That Characterize Effective Interventions with Juvenile Offenders: A Meta-Analytic Overview." *Victims and Offenders* 4 (2009): 124–47.

Lipsey, M. W. and F. T. Cullen. "The Effectiveness of Correctional Rehabilitation: A Review of Systematic Reviews." *Annual Review of Law and Social Science* 3 (2007): 297–320.

Lipsey, M. W. and D. B. Wilson. "Effective Interventions for Serious Juvenile Offenders: A Synthesis of Research." In *Serious and Violent Juvenile Offenders: Risk Factors and Successful Interventions*, edited by R. Loeber and D. P. Farrington, 313–66. Thousand Oaks, CA: Sage, 1998.

Lipton, D., R. Martinson, and J. Wilks. *The Effectiveness of Correctional Treatment: A Survey of Treatment Evaluation Studies*. New York: Praeger, 1975.

Loeber, R. and D. P. Farrington, eds. *Serious and Violent Juvenile Offenders: Risk Factors and Successful Interventions*. Thousand Oaks, CA: Sage, 1998.

Lösel, F. "The Efficacy of Correctional Treatment: A Review and Synthesis of Meta-Evaluations." In *What Works: Reducing Reoffending—Guidelines from Research and Practice*, edited by J. McGuire. New York: John Wiley, 1995.

Lowenkamp, C. T., A. W. Flores, A. M. Holsinger, M. D. Makarios, and E. J. Latessa. "Intensive Supervision Probation? Does Program Philosophy and the Principles of Effective Intervention Matter?" Unpublished manuscript, University of Cincinnati, 2009.

MacKenzie, D. L. *What Works in Corrections? Reducing the Criminal Activities of Offenders and Delinquents*. New York: Cambridge University Press, 2006.

Martinson, R. "What Works? Questions and Answers about Prison Reform." *The Public Interest* 35 (1974): 22–54.

McGarrell, E. F. and N. K. Hipple. "Family Group Conferencing and Re-Offending among First-Time Juvenile Offenders: The Indianapolis Experiment." *Justice Quarterly* 24 (2007): 221–46.

McGuire, J. "Integrating Findings from Research Reviews." In *Offender Rehabilitation and Treatment: Effective Programmes and Policies to Re-Offending*, edited by J. McGuire, 3–38. West Sussex: John Wiley, 2002.

McKelvey, B. *American Prisons: A History of Good Intentions*. Montclair, NJ: Patterson Smith, 1977.

Menninger, K. *The Crime of Punishment*. New York: Penguine Books, 1968.

Merton, R. K. "The Unanticipated Consequences of Purposive Social Action." *American Sociological Review* 22 (1936): 635–59.

————. *Social Theory and Social Structure*. New York: Free Press, 1968.

————. *The Sociology of Science: Theoretical and Empirical Investigations* (N. W. Storer, ed.). Chicago: University of Chicago Press, 1973.

Miller, J. G. *Last One over the Wall. The Massachusetts Experiment in Closing Reform Schools*. Columbus: Ohio State University Press, 1991.

Morris, N. *The Future of Imprisonment*. Chicago: University of Chicago Press, 1974.

Nagin, D. S., F. T. Cullen, and C. L. Jonson. "Imprisonment and Reoffending." In *Crime and Justice: An Annual Review*, edited by M. Tonry, vol. 38, 115–200. Chicago: University of Chicago Press, 2009.

Olds, D. L. "Preventing Crime with Prenatal and Infancy Support of Parents." *Victims and Offenders* 2 (2007): 205–25.

Palmara, F., F. T. Cullen, and J. Gersten. "The Effect of Police and Mental Health Intervention on Juvenile Deviance: Specifying the Impact of Formal Reaction." *Journal of Health and Social Behavior* 27 (1986): 90–105.

Palmer, T. "Martinson Revisited." *Journal of Research in Crime and Delinquency* 12 (1975): 133–52.

Paparozzi, M. A. and P. Gendreau. "An Intensive Supervision Program That Worked: Service Delivery, Professional Orientation, and Organizational Supportiveness." *Prison Journal* 85 (2005): 445–66.

Petersilia, J. and S. Turner. "Intensive Probation and Parole." In *Crime and Justice: A Review of Research*, edited by M. Tonry, vol. 17, 281–335. Chicago: University of Chicago Press, 1993.

Piquero, A. R., D. P. Farrington, and A. Blumstein. *Key Issues in Criminal Career Research: New Analyses from the Cambridge Study in Delinquent Development*. New York: Cambridge University Press, 2007.

Platt, A. M. *The Child Savers: The Invention of Delinquency*. Chicago: University of Chicago Press, 1969.

Rieff, P. *The Triumph of the Therapeutic: Use of Faith after Freud*. New York: Harper and Row, 1966.

Rothman, D. J. *Discovery of the Asylum: Social Order and Disorder in the New Republic*. Boston: Little, Brown and Co., 1971.

————. *Conscience and Convenience: The Asylum and Its Alternatives in Progressive America*. Boston: Little, Brown and Co., 1980.

Rotman, E. *Beyond Punishment: A New View of the Rehabilitation of Criminal Offenders*. Westport, CT: Greenwood Press, 1990.

Schneider, L. "Ironic Perspective and Sociological Thought." In *The Idea of Social Structure: Papers in Honor of Robert K. Merton*, edited by L. A. Coser, 323–37. New York: Harcourt Brace Jovanovich, 1975.

Schur, E. M. *Radical Non-Intervention: Rethinking the Delinquency Problem*. Englewood Cliffs, NJ: Prentice-Hall, 1973.

Schweinhart, L. J. "Crime Prevention by the High/Scope Perry Preschool Program." *Victims and Offenders* 2 (2007): 141–60.

Sherman, L. W. "Defiance, Deterrence, and Irrelevance: A Theory of the Criminal Sanction." *Journal of Research in Crime and Delinquency* 30 (1993): 445–73.

Sieber, S. *Fatal Remedies: The Irony of Social Intervention*. New York: Plenum, 1981.

Simon, J. *Governing through Crime: How the War on Crime Transformed American Democracy and Created a Culture of Fear*. New York: Oxford University Press, 2007.

Smith, P. "The Effects of Incarceration on Recidivism: A Longitudinal Examination of Program Participation and Institutional Adjustment in Federally Sentenced Adult Male Offenders." Unpublished Ph.D. dissertation, University of New Brunswick, Canada, 2006.

Smith, P., F. T. Cullen, and E. J. Latessa. "Can 14,737 Women be Wrong? A Meta-Analysis of the LSI-R and Recidivism." *Criminology and Public Policy* 8 (2009a): 183–208.

Smith, P., P. Gendreau, and K. Swartz. "Validating the Principles of Effective Intervention: A Systematic Review of the Contributions of Meta-Analysis in the Field of Corrections." *Victims and Offenders* 4 (2009b): 148–69.

Smith, P., C. Goggin, and P. Gendreau. *The Effects of Prison Sentences and Intermediate Sanctions on Recidivism: General Effects and Individual Differences.* Ottawa, Canada: Solicitor General of Canada, 2002.

Stouthamer-Loeber, M., R. Loeber, W. van Kammen, and Q. Zhang. "Uninterrupted Delinquent Careers: The Timing of Parental Help-Seeking and Juvenile Court Contact." *Studies on Crime and Crime Prevention* 4 (1995): 236–51.

Sykes, G. M. *The Society of Captives: A Study of a Maximum Security Prison.* Princeton, NJ: Princeton University Press, 1958.

Tannenbaum, F. *Crime and Community.* New York: Columbia University Press, 1938.

Thorsell, B. A. and L. W. Klemke. "The Labeling Process: Reinforcement and Deterrent?" *Law and Society Review* 6 (1972): 393–403.

Tittle, C. R. "Deterrents or Labeling?" *Social Forces* 53 (1975): 399–410.

Travis, L. F., III and F. T. Cullen. "Radical Non-Intervention: The Myth of Doing No Harm." *Federal Probation* 48, no. 1 (1984): 29–32.

Tyler, T. R. "Procedural Justice, Legitimacy, and the Effective Rule of Law." In *Crime and Justice: A Review of Research*, edited by M. Tonry, vol. 30, 283–357. Chicago: University of Chicago Press, 2003.

Useem, B. and A. M. Piehl. *Prison State: The Challenges of Mass Incarceration.* New York: Cambridge University Press, 2008.

Villettaz, P., M. Killias, and I. Zoder. *The Effects of Custodial vs. Noncustodial Sentences on Re-Offending: A Systematic Review of the State of Knowledge.* Philadelphia, PA: Campbell Collaboration Crime and Justice Group, 2006.

Von Hirsch, A. *Doing Justice: The Choice of Punishment.* New York: Hill and Wang, 1976.

Vose, B., F. T. Cullen, and P. Smith. "The Empirical Status of the Level of Service Inventory." *Federal Probation* 72, no. 3 (2008): 22–9.

Wilson, J. Q. *Thinking about Crime.* New York: Vintage Books, 1975.

Wormith, J. S. "Attitude and Behavior Change of Correctional Clientele: A Three Year Follow-Up." *Criminology* 22 (1984): 595–618.

Zimbardo, P. *The Lucifer Effect: Understanding How Good People Turn Evil.* New York: Random House, 2007.

Zimbardo, P. G., W. C. Banks, C. Haney, and D. Jaffe. "A Pirandellian Prison: The Mind is a Formidable Jailer." *New York Times Magazine*, April 8, 1973, 38–40.

Part II
Reviews of Empirical Tests

5

A Review of Prior Tests of Labeling Theory

Kelle Barrick

Introduction

Ascending to popularity in the 1960s, labeling theory shifted the focus of criminological theory away from the offender. Labeling theorists argued that initial delinquency is normal and occurs for a variety of reasons, but official reactions to it may lead to future offending. For the first time in almost 200 years, the legal system itself became an object of inquiry and researchers began examining the societal reaction to deviance. This represented a marked shift from mainstream sociological thought at the time. Generally, labeling theorists proposed that publicly defining and treating an individual as a deviant may result in exclusions from conventional society, a possible identity change, and an increase in the likelihood of subsequent deviance. Labelists also argued that extralegal characteristics, such as race and class, influence whether official intervention will be imposed.

While popular for over twenty years, some proclaimed the perspective dead by 1985 (Paternoster and Iovanni, 1989). Critics claimed it lacked both theoretical specificity and empirical support, and classical labeling theory seemed for some time to have fallen out of favor as a viable criminological theory (Paternoster and Iovanni, 1989). The empirical literature had been criticized on many grounds, including the failure to properly model the theoretical propositions. Raymond Paternoster and LeeAnn Iovanni (1989: 360) went so far as to state that, "For the most part, empirical tests of labeling propositions have been conducted with grossly misrepresented hypotheses that are more caricature than characteristic of the theory." More specifically, much of the research, which was instrumental in the demise of labeling theory by the mid-1980s, failed to consider either the proposition that labeling effects may be contingent on individual characteristics or the process by which labels actually produce secondary deviance (Paternoster and Iovanni, 1989).

Although the field seemed to accept that labeling theory had been empirically disproven, the research itself was not so conclusive. Even Charles Tittle (1980), who was critical of the theory, thought it premature to reject the idea that labels have some effect on criminal behavior. He reviewed three studies which he thought most closely met methodological demands and found one study with results supportive of the perspective. One criticism of these studies was that they relied on offender populations and did not include any individuals who had never been convicted. Tittle (1980) argued that this may obscure the effect of labeling if there is little difference in reoffending between those already labeled but a large difference between those who have never been labeled and those who have. This raises the issue of relative and absolute labeling effects. While absolute labeling effects refer to comparisons between those who are and are not labeled, relative effects refer to comparisons between those with different types of labels, such as arrest versus conviction (Paternoster and Iovanni, 1989).

Tittle (1980) also felt that adequate controls had not been used and argued that there was likely a selection bias among those sentenced to prison and those sentenced to probation. Specifically, the courts may sentence individuals to prison rather than probation because they are seen, for a variety of reasons, as more likely to recidivate. If these factors are not controlled in tests of labeling, then it is possible that pre-selection alone accounted for differences in recidivism.

Even in a review of what were thought to be the most methodologically rigorous studies, Tittle felt that there had not been an adequate test of the perspective and that labeling theory's poor formulation almost invited falsification because specific hypotheses are required before tests can be conducted. He suggested the importance of specifying the circumstances under which labeling may increase crime. Tittle's disappointment with both the labeling theory and the research presuming to test it can best be summarized by his concluding comments:

> Labelists must get down to serious theoretical business. Evasiveness, lauding of ambiguity, and hiding behind a façade of sensitizing concepts will no longer suffice.

Researchers, on the other hand, must apply themselves with more facility and care. The meagerness and sloppiness of research on a question of this importance is embarrassing. (Tittle, 1980)

Subsequent reviews of the research reached similar conclusions. Paternoster and Iovanni's (1989) review of labeling discussed nine secondary deviance studies and argued that they (and similar studies) have contributed to the downfall of labeling theory by relying on inadequate methodologies and thus did not constitute valid tests of the theory. Most of these studies used sanctions experienced by only a small proportion of deviants (e.g., juvenile court appearance, probation, and incarceration) as the independent variable, examined relative rather than absolute labeling effects, and were formulated simplistically, without considering intervening mechanisms.

Paternoster and Iovanni (1989) concluded by saying that while many empirical tests are inconsistent with labeling propositions, more theoretically relevant work is needed in the future. Similar to Tittle (1980), Paternoster and Iovanni (1989) felt that most tests of labeling were not adequate and thought it was necessary to examine the contingencies and intervening mechanisms that may be at work.

In a more recent review, Jón Bernburg (2002) examined three studies using samples containing only offenders and five studies using a general population including both those who have and have not been labeled. The three offender sample studies (Horwitz and Wasserman, 1979; Smith and Gartin, 1989; Smith and Paternoster, 1990) produced inconclusive results, and Bernburg (2002) suggested that studies based on non-random samples of offenders may not be valid tests of labeling theory. He claimed that the best tests of secondary deviance would be longitudinal, would sample from a population with some labeled and some unlabeled individuals, and would control for prior criminal behavior. Other important controls, including race and socioeconomic status, were also suggested.

Bernburg (2002) proceeded to examine five studies (Farrington, 1977; Thomas and Bishop, 1984; Palamara et al., 1986; Ray and Downs, 1986; Hagan and Palloni, 1990) that he felt were more appropriate for testing labeling theory because they used general population samples. Each of these studies showed some support for the labeling proposition. While these are not methodologically perfect, it was suggested that more confidence should be placed in these than the previous three. In Bernburg's (2002) review, the strongest tests provided the most support for the perspective.

The three previous literature reviews seem to reach the same conclusion. That is, many empirical tests of secondary deviance are inadequate and may have led to its decline in popularity as a theory of criminal behavior. Despite these claims, labeling currently receives little attention and many criminologists would argue this is because of the lack of empirical support for the perspective. Examining past reviews leads us to a different conclusion. While it does not appear that labeling has received overwhelming support, researchers have argued that most tests are not appropriate (Tittle, 1980; Paternoster and Iovanni, 1989) and that the most rigorous tests tend to show more support for the perspective (Bernburg, 2002). At the same time, prior reviews have focused on a handful of studies aimed at testing the theory and no one has attempted to synthesize the full body of relevant work. Until this is done, we cannot be sure exactly what the prior research says about the effects of labeling.

The remainder of this chapter is divided into two sections. The first attempts to synthesize four decades of research on the relationship between sanctions and recidivism. The second contains a more thorough discussion of empirical tests that were the most attentive to theoretical propositions regarding potential contingent effects of labels as well as the mechanisms by which labels are claimed to work.

Quantitative Synthesis of Prior Research

Study Acquisition

Selection Criteria

Sixty-six empirical studies of the official sanction–recidivism relationship are reviewed here.[1] To qualify for inclusion in this assessment, the articles are not required to have the declared purpose of examining labeling theory, but rather only need to report at least one association between a measure of official sanctioning and recidivism. Because labeling theory has waned in popularity over the past twenty years, many of the studies reported here were not primarily aimed at testing the theory but nevertheless report associations between relevant variables. Indeed, many of these studies could be regarded as tests of special deterrence effects as much as tests of labeling theory. In selecting studies for inclusion in this review, the following criteria are applied:

1. Each study is required to measure at least one of the following official sanctions: arrest or police contact, conviction, contact with the juvenile justice system, or incarceration (either jail or prison).

There must also be a clear distinction concerning the specific type of sanction imposed. Studies using a general sanction measure, which, for example, may include anything from school sanctions to incarceration, are excluded.

2. Each study is required to measure actual recidivism. Studies examining the likelihood of future offending are excluded.

3. Each study has to be available in English.

Study Acquisition Methods

The sixty-six studies reviewed here were located in a systematic search of interdisciplinary internet databases, including Article First, WorldCat, the Criminal Justice Periodical Index, the National Criminal Justice Reference System, Cambridge Scientific Abstracts—Social Sciences, and the Web of Science and also from the bibliographies of previously retrieved labeling articles.

Findings

Before discussing the overall findings, the procedures used for deciding which estimates were included from each study will be discussed. Multiple findings from the same study were only counted if they were substantively different pairings of the independent (label) and dependent (recidivism) variables. Additional findings were included if they served to illustrate an important point, such as the differential impact a labeling event may have for certain types of offenses and offenders.

For example, if a study initially reported results of the official sanction–recidivism relationship for all initial crimes and also broken down by type (e.g., violent, property, and drug), then each estimate was counted so that this potential contingency could be examined. For the purpose of comparability, if the recidivism offense was recorded in this manner, only the estimate which did not differentiate crime type was used (only two studies broke down the estimates by recidivism offense). Multiple estimates were also counted if results were presented separately for relatively inexperienced and repeat offenders. These criteria for inclusion were selected because there were several studies that made these distinctions. It would have also been desirable to do the same for gender, race, and socioeconomic status, but this was not possible. While many studies control for race and socioeconomic status, most do not assess the labeling effect separately for those belonging to these different groups (for recent exceptions, see Bernburg and Krohn, 2003; Chiricos et al., 2007).

When different models were reported that varied only by the number of independent or control variables included, then the estimate from the most complete model was used. The more specific criteria listed below were also applied.

1. If findings were established by different statistical techniques in one study, then the method that seemed most appropriate for the hypothesis or the one the author presented as the best test was used.
2. If papers presented multiple follow-up periods for the same sample of individuals, then the estimate from the longest follow-up period was used.
3. Because controlling for potential mediators, such as employment or self-concept subsequent to the labeling event, could hide a portion of a label's effect, estimates from models including these potentially intervening variables are excluded. In each case a model without the intervening variable was presented, so no entire study was excluded for this purpose.
4. If a labeling variable included more than two categories (e.g., dismissal, conviction, and incarceration), then it was coded with respect to the most severe sanction (incarceration, in this case). If estimates were reported for different lengths of incarceration (rather than a continuous length variable), then the results for the longest and shortest sentences were compared.
5. Similarly, if a study provided multiple results for those with varying degrees of prior records, then the results were counted for the categories of least and most experienced. This is primarily presented as a dichotomy and does not present a problem.

The sixty-six studies yield 167 countable estimates of the official sanction–recidivism relationship. Overall, the labeling hypothesis receives more support than its logical opposite, specific deterrence (positive and significant findings indicate that the net effect of sanctioning is characterized more by deviance amplification than deterrence). Of the 167 total estimates of the official sanction–recidivism relationship, only 13.2 percent of the findings are negative and significant, 22.2 percent are negative of unknown significance or not significant while 30.5 percent are positive and significant and 34.1 percent are positive of unknown significance or not significant. Although the preliminary evidence here provides more support for secondary deviance than deterrence, there is more support for no effect (either deterrence or amplification) because the majority of findings are not statistically significant. To further assess the labeling evidence, I next examine the direction and significance of these relationships in different methodological (Tables 5.1 and 5.2) and substantive (Table 5.3) contexts.

Methodological Contexts

Different outcomes across studies may be partially attributable to variation in methodological procedures, including controls for criminal history, sample size, follow-up period, recidivism measure, and statistical method. Examining results across these methodological differences will allow us to see whether method matters and whether the strongest studies are in fact the most supportive (as suggested in prior reviews of the literature).

Controls for Criminal History

Prior deviance is generally assumed to be the most important potential confounding variable in studies examining secondary difference, and studies vary in ways of controlling for criminal history. Researchers use a variety of techniques to account for this relationship including random assignment to sanction, binary measures where either a prior record existed or not, counts which tabulate the total number of prior arrests or incarcerations, and weighted counts that take into account the frequency and severity of prior criminal acts. Because the relationship between prior and future behavior is strong, we should consider those studies with the most sophisticated controls (weighted counts) for prior behavior to be superior to those studies that have weaker or no controls at all. As Table 5.1 shows, approximately 44 percent of the relationships reviewed here do not control for criminal history. Of these, 29 percent are positive and significant. Estimates using a binary variable (a record exists or not) are only 13.3 percent positive and significant. Of the studies using a count measure, such as number of prior arrests, 36 percent are positive and significant. Of the studies using a weighted count that includes both frequency and severity of prior record, 29 percent produced positive and significant findings, out of a total of seven reported relationships (43 percent were positive and of unknown significance). Two studies examined here used random assignment to sanction; one yielded a significant negative outcome and the other a positive significant outcome.

While the pattern is not entirely clear, these findings appear to provide only mixed support for labeling theory. It is important to note that the categories with the best controls for prior behavior, random assignment

Table 5.1

Summary of direction and statistical significance for labeling and recidivism: Relationships under varying methodological conditions

	Total number of findings	Percent of findings					
		–ve significance	–ve NS	–ve?	+ve significance	+ve NS	+ve?
Total	167	13.2	19.8	2.4	30.5	26.9	7.2
Control criminal history							
None	73	9.6	19.2	4.1	28.8	28.8	9.6
Random assignment	2	50.0	0.0	0.0	50.0	0.0	0.0
Binary	15	33.3	26.7	0.0	13.3	26.7	0.0
Count	70	12.9	18.6	1.4	35.7	28.6	2.9
Weighted count	7	0.0	28.6	0.0	28.6	0.0	42.9
Sample size[a]							
1,000 or less	69	20.3	21.7	1.4	26.1	24.6	5.8
More than 1,000	25	4.0	16.0	0.0	48.0	28.0	4.0
Follow-up period[a]							
One year or less	14	14.3	28.6	0.0	14.3	21.4	21.4
More than one year	79	15.2	20.4	1.1	32.3	25.8	5.4
Recidivism measure[a]							
Self-report	15	0.0	0.0	0.0	73.3	6.7	20.0
Arrest/contact/report	52	15.4	30.8	1.9	21.2	28.8	1.9
Conviction	15	20.0	13.3	0.0	26.7	33.3	6.7
Incarceration	2	50.0	0.0	0.0	0.0	50.0	0.0
Charges filed	8	37.5	12.5	0.0	25.0	25.0	0.0
Unfavorable parole	2	0.0	0.0	0.0	100.0	0.0	0.0
Statistical method[a]							
Logistic regression	57	26.3	21.1	0.0	19.3	33.3	0.0
Other multivariate	31	0.0	22.6	3.2	48.4	9.7	16.1
Descriptive	6	0.0	0.0	0.0	66.7	33.3	0.0

[a]Includes only estimates that control for criminal history.
NS = Not Significant

Table 5.2
Summary of direction and statistical significance for labeling and recidivism:
Relationships among studies meeting multiple methodological criteria

	Percent of findings						
	Total number of findings	−ve significance	−ve NS	−ve?	+ve significance	+ve NS	+ve?
Control criminal history	94	16.0	20.2	1.1	31.9	25.5	5.3
Control criminal history, multivariate	88	17.0	21.6	1.1	29.5	25.0	5.7
Control criminal history, multivariate, large sample	25	4.0	16.0	0.0	48.0	28.0	4.0
Control criminal history, multivariate, large sample, follow-up > one year	18	5.6	11.1	0.0	55.6	27.8	0.0

NS = Not Significant

and weighted counts, contain a combined total of nine estimates. Future researchers should be attentive to this issue and use the most rigorous measure of criminal history possible. Criminal history is arguably the most important variable to control when examining labeling effects. Because of this, all findings discussed below only include studies that controlled for prior behavior in some manner. This reduced the total sample size from 167 to 94 estimates of the relationship.

Sample Size

In addition to variation in controls for prior record, the sample sizes varied greatly from fifty to nearly 100,000 cases. Studies with a larger sample size should be more likely to produce significant findings than those with only fifty individuals, for example. Small sample sizes lead to unstable and inefficient estimates. Because of this, more weight should be given to studies with the larger samples. Apparent support for labeling effects is found when studies are compared by sample size. The stronger estimates, those with samples of more than 1,000, produce 48 percent positive and significant findings and only 4 percent negative and significant. On the other hand, studies that consisted of 1,000 or less participants produce only 26 percent positive and significant findings and 20 percent negative and significant findings.

Length of Follow-Up Period

Follow-up periods also varied between studies, ranging from six months to ten years. Studies with a short follow-up period should be less likely to find support for the labeling hypothesis because an individual may not have had enough time to reoffend. Because labeling is a dynamic and developmental theory by nature, it could be argued that the use of longer follow-up periods would provide a more accurate test of the perspective. As expected, studies with longer follow-up periods (more than one year) show stronger support for labeling than those which used short follow-ups. While only 14 percent of the short follow-up studies have positive and significant results, 32 percent of those studies that tracked offenders for more than one year find a positive relationship between labeling and recidivism. Unfortunately, 21 percent of the studies with short follow-up periods do not report significance levels.

Recidivism Measure

There is also variation in the measurement of recidivism. Some researchers use self-report measures of criminal involvement, and others use official measures, such as arrest, conviction, or incarceration. We may expect self-report data to provide a more accurate test of deviance amplification because it will tap into subsequent unreported criminality as well as that which is officially recognized. Labeling theory argues that official intervention may increase the likelihood of reoffense, not necessarily apprehension, and only self-report measures allow us to examine criminal behavior unknown to authorities. It should be noted, though, that self-report data is not perfect. People may underreport their own deviant acts, and may do so in systematic ways relevant to labeling hypotheses. In particular, those who engage in the most deviant behavior may also underreport their involvement in deviant acts more so than those who engage in less deviance. This could artificially reduce support for labeling by concealing increases in deviant behavior following a sanctioning experience.

Self-report measures of reoffending produce findings more supportive of secondary deviance than any of the official measures, with 73 percent positive and significant. Additionally, none of these estimates were supportive of a deterrent argument. This is one of the only occasions when the majority of findings are actually in support of labeling theory. This may point to the fact that many individuals reoffend after being officially labeled, but may not get back into the system. By this rationale, we would also think that arrest would have more supportive findings because it is the first step of several in the system, and some individuals may never go past this initial police encounter. The data are less supportive when arrest is used as the recidivism measure, with only 21 percent positive and significant compared with 15 percent negative and significant. The results are similar for conviction.

Statistical Method

Finally, some variation across statistical methods is also found. Many researchers relied solely on descriptive statistics, such as frequencies and percentages, while others used multivariate techniques. Estimates based on multivariate techniques should be given more weight than those relying solely on descriptive statistics. Logistic regression, which is the most commonly used technique (two-thirds of the estimates), yields 19 percent positive and significant results and 26 percent negative and significant. Estimates produced by logistic regression, which is arguably the most appropriate statistical technique to use in assessing labeling theory, are actually more supportive of a deterrent than a labeling effect. Other multivariate techniques, which included ordinary least squares regression, survival analysis, structural equation modeling, among others, produce 48 percent positive and significant findings. Two-thirds of the estimates arising out of descriptive statistics, such as frequencies and percentages, were positive and significant.

One limitation to the above analyses is that the studies are examined only under one methodological criterion, other than criminal history, at a time. For example, if a study has a large sample but examines only bivariate relationships, it may not be the most well designed test. To examine this, Table 3 contains findings that have multiple design strengths. Beginning with controlling for criminal history, each set of findings adds an additional methodological criterion, and the sample size of estimates to be considered decreases. If the percent of findings in support of labeling theory increases as the methodological criteria are made more stringent, it will provide stronger support for the theory.

When only criminal history is controlled, 32 percent of the findings are in support of labeling theory. This sample is then reduced by including only those that also use multivariate statistical techniques and the support

Table 5.3

Summary of direction and statistical significance for labeling and recidivism:
Relationships under varying substantive conditions

	Total number of findings	−ve significance	−ve NS	−ve?	+ve significance	+ve NS	+ve?
				Percent of findings			
Official sanction[a]							
Arrest/contact	15	20.0	26.7	0.0	26.7	6.7	20.0
Conviction	12	8.3	0.0	0.0	58.3	33.3	0.0
Juvenile justice	6	0.0	16.7	0.0	83.3	0.0	0.0
Incarceration	31	6.5	16.1	3.2	22.6	45.2	6.5
Incarceration length	30	30.0	30.0	0.0	23.3	16.7	0.0
Population[a]							
Juvenile	24	4.2	12.5	0.0	58.3	8.3	16.7
Adult	70	20.0	22.9	1.4	22.9	31.4	1.4
Offense type[a]							
Not specified	45	13.3	15.6	0.0	44.4	17.8	8.9
Domestic violence	18	38.9	22.2	0.0	5.6	33.3	0.0
Drunk driving	6	0.0	16.7	0.0	16.7	66.7	0.0
Drugs	4	0.0	25.0	0.0	25.0	50.0	0.0
Violent	10	20.0	10.0	0.0	40.0	30.0	0.0
Property	11	0.0	45.5	9.1	27.3	9.1	9.1
Offender[a]							
Naïve	5	0.0	20.0	0.0	40.0	20.0	20.0
Experienced	5	0.0	20.0	0.0	0.0	60.0	20.0

[a]Includes only estimates that control for criminal history.
NS = Not Significant

decreased slightly to 30 percent in favor of labeling. When the sample is further reduced by requiring large samples ($n > 1,000$), the percent of positive and significant findings increases to 48 percent. Finally, when the requirement of a long follow-up period (greater than one year) is added, the majority (56 percent) of the findings are in support of labeling hypotheses. This is almost ten times greater than the support for specific deterrence indicated by negative significant results. It appears then that the strongest studies provide the most support for the perspective.

Substantive Contexts
  Label
  Variable patterns in labeling effects can also be seen along more substantive grounds. The type of label imposed, or punishment, ranges from recorded police contact to length of incarceration. The more severe sanctions should be more likely to lead to future offending. As Table 5.3 shows, among types of official sanctions, overwhelmingly the strongest support is found for juvenile justice intervention (83 percent positive and significant), though the sample size is quite small. The majority of findings for conviction (58 percent positive and significant) are also sup-portive of secondary deviance. Being arrested yields little support, with only 27 percent of the estimates positive and significant compared with 20 percent negative and significant. While incarceration was found to be more likely to have a labeling effect (23 percent) than a deterrent effect (7 percent), no support is found for labeling effects in relation to the length of incarceration. In fact, for this sanction, 23 percent of the findings are supportive of labeling, and 30 percent are supportive of a deterrent hypothesis. While labeling theory would predict that more severe sanc-tions, such as conviction and incarceration, would be more likely to lead to secondary deviance than mere arrest, it might also predict that longer periods of incarceration would be more likely to lead to reoffense. The findings here provide mixed support for this claim.

  Offender Age
  It could be argued that juveniles are more malleable and thus more likely to internalize a label than adults. If this is the case, then we should expect stronger labeling effects in studies using juvenile samples. As ex-pected, juveniles are more likely to recidivate after a labeling event than adults, with 58 percent of the findings positive and significant for juveniles and only 23 percent positive and significant for adults. Additionally, it appears that while adults have a nearly equal chance of a label leading

to deterrence (20 percent) as amplification, juveniles only experienced a deterrent effect in about 4 percent of the cases. There are at least two potential interpretations of this finding.

First, it is possible that juveniles' identities are more malleable than adults' and thus more subject to the negative consequences of stigmatization. If true, this would lend support to the labeling proposition that stigmatization may influence one's self-identity or structural opportunities. Another possibility, which would not support labeling theory, is that juveniles are more likely to reoffend than adults anyway because they are in the upward phase of the age–crime curve, while adults should be on the decreasing end of that continuum. Juvenile delinquency is expected to increase toward adulthood and peak around the late teens or early twenties regardless of sanction, and adult criminality is expected to decline with age.

Offense Type
Labeling effects may also vary by crime type. It has been argued for over thirty years that labelists need to start examining what individual characteristics, including crime type, condition the effects of a label (Tittle, 1975). While most studies examine any crime that leads to a label, others focus exclusively on a certain crime, such as domestic violence or drunk driving. While theorists have not specified if those engaging in certain types of crimes would be more affected by being labeled, this is an issue that should be explored.

While no offense type yielded a majority of findings in support of labeling theory, some differences can be noted. The strongest support is found for violent offenses (40 percent positive and significant) and property offenses (27 percent positive and significant). Studies examining drug or drinking and driving offenses yielded more support for labeling than deterrence, but were based on very small samples. In the case of domestic violence, much greater support was found for deterrence hypotheses than for labeling, where 39 percent of the estimates were negative and significant and only 6 percent were positive and significant. Domestic violence was the only crime type to produce more estimates in favor of deterrence than labeling. These findings seem to suggest that those involved in violent or property offenses are more likely to be negatively affected by legal intervention while those engaging in spousal abuse are less likely to experience such consequences. Future research could help further disentangle the relationship between crime type and labeling effects.

Offender Experience

Additionally, certain types of offenders may be more prone to labeling effects than others. The initial labeling event is probably the most consequential. While not fully developed, there is some consensus that naive offenders will be more vulnerable to the negative consequences of official sanctions (Paternoster and Iovanni, 1989). If this is true, then studies of first-time offenders should produce more findings supportive of labeling theory than those using samples of repeat offenders. Naive offenders yield 40 percent positive and significant findings, while experienced offenders produce no positive and significant estimates. However, estimates involving experienced offenders yielded 80 percent positive findings that were either not significant or the significance was not reported. Due to small sample sizes ($n = 5$ for each group), these findings should be interpreted with caution.

Statistical Analysis

Although at first glance it looks like there is some support for deviance amplification, especially when the strongest methodologies are employed, statistical analyses were performed to determine whether these apparent effects may be due to chance. Consistent with the table above, the results are from the reduced sample, excluding estimates that did not control for criminal history. First, the sign test,[2] which ignores statistical significance but tallies the number of findings in each direction, was conducted. If the null hypothesis is true, then we would expect the number of positive and negative findings to be equal. Providing support for labeling, the results indicated that the set of estimates contained significantly more positive findings than could be obtained by chance alone if the null hypothesis were true. The one-tailed test was significant at $p < .007$.

Next, the Adding Zs test[3] was performed because it not only takes account of the direction of each finding but also its significance level. This test addresses the shortcomings of the sign test by accounting for relationship strength. There is less than a .0001 chance that a set of findings this significant could be obtained by chance alone if the null hypothesis were true. This more rigorous test provided additional support for the relationship between sanctions and recidivism.

Although the studies examined here provide some support for labeling theory, it has been mentioned that, while they certainly have merit, most are not ideal tests of labeling theory. While most failed to examine either mediating or conditioning factors, for the most part, they controlled for important confounders (criminal history) and used multivariate techniques.

These previous studies provide a starting position for new studies to build upon and improve. It is rare that empirical tests of criminological theory are able to use the most ideal measures and research designs. At the same time, some studies come closer to this standard than others. For this reason, the examination of the cumulative evidence should be accompanied by the findings from the most theoretically informed studies, those that examined intervening mechanisms and/or potential contingencies of the relationship.

Examination of the Most Theoretically Informed Studies

It has been argued that prior tests of labeling theory that were instrumental in its demise failed to consider either the proposition that labeling effects may be contingent on individual characteristics or the process by which labels actually produce secondary deviance (Paternoster and Iovanni, 1989). This is less true of some recent research which has attempted to fill this void. Several studies that have done this will be discussed below.

Intervening Mechanisms

Some theorists argue that stigmatization can alter one's identity, others argue that labels may limit one's structural opportunities, such as education and employment, in society, and others argue that labels impact one's peer associations. Only a few studies to date have attempted to test the full process by which a label may have an effect. While recent empirical attention has focused on structural opportunities and peer groups as potential intervening mechanisms, early labelists argued that labels could have an effect on future behavior by changing one's self-concept.

Deviant Self-Concept or Identity

Early labeling theorists proposed that official assignment of the meaning of deviant or criminal to an individual can eventually lead that individual to take on an identity consistent with the meaning and continue to engage in such behaviors through a self-fulfilling prophecy (e.g., Becker, 1963; Matza, 1969). Yet, to date, few empirical studies have examined whether formal sanctions impact recidivism through one's identity.[4]

In an early exception, David Farrington (1977) examined the impact of criminal conviction on self-reported delinquency among a sample of approximately 400 working-class London boys using data from the *Cambridge Study in Delinquent Development*. The convicted youth were matched to those with similar levels of self-reported delinquency prior to the labeling event, and the labeled boys were found to have higher levels of subsequent delinquency. Farrington hypothesized that a hostile attitude towards the police (an indication of a deviant self-concept) may mediate the relationship he found between conviction and later delinquency. Indeed, he found that hostility levels were similar for labeled and non-labeled youths prior to the labeling event but were significantly higher among the labeled group in the interview after the conviction. Changes in hostility scores were significantly correlated with changes in delinquency, supporting the hypothesis that hostile attitudes toward the police mediated the relationship between criminal conviction and increased delinquency.

Using self-report data from a sample of both labeled and non-labeled junior and senior high school students in Virginia, Charles Thomas and Donna Bishop (1984) found a small positive relationship between having any contact with the police or juvenile court authorities and later delinquency, controlling for prior delinquency and informal sanctions. They constructed a delinquent self-concept scale to test the labeling proposition that formal sanctions may produce a change in self-identity. However, they found that while police contact is associated with an increase in delinquent identity, it only added one percent to the explained variance. They concluded that their study provided little support for labeling theory overall.

Blocked Access to Conventional Others

In addition to identity changes, labelists recognized that formal labels may create obstacles to conventional others that may assist in perpetuating a criminal career. When society stigmatizes an individual, he may be excluded from conventional others and either choose or be forced to socialize with those similarly labeled.

In addition to examining self-concept as a potential mediator, Farrington (1977) also examined the possibility that labeling increases the likelihood that a youth would associate with other delinquents, which would in turn increase delinquent behavior. However, he found that the number of delinquent friends actually decreased after conviction, contradicting the hypothesis that peer associations mediate the relationship between conviction and delinquency.

Using panel data on 870 seventh- and eighth-grade students from the *Rochester Youth Development Study*, Bernburg et al. (2006) hypothesized that the impact of juvenile justice intervention on subsequent delinquency is mediated by embeddedness in deviant groups. To measure criminal embeddedness, respondents were asked whether they had been members of a gang in the past six months and also how many of their friends participated in delinquent activities. Bernburg and colleagues found that involvement with the juvenile justice system is associated with subsequent serious delinquency and this relationship was substantially mediated by gang membership and peer delinquency.

Blocked Access to Mainstream Opportunities

Early labelists, such as Becker (1963) recognized that the exclusion from conventional routines and others may also impact mainstream opportunities, such as employment. More recently, this idea that official intervention can lead to blocked conventional opportunities has been integrated into a life-course perspective (Sampson and Laub, 1997). Specifically, Robert Sampson and John Laub's (1997: 147) age-graded theory of informal social control, "suggests a 'snowball' effect—that adolescent delinquency and its negative consequences (e.g., arrest, official labeling, and incarceration) increasingly 'mortgage' one's future, especially later life chances molded by schooling and employment." The lack of investment in these arguably beneficial social institutions then leads to continued criminal behavior.

Reanalyzing data from the *Cambridge Study in Delinquent Development*, Spencer De Li (1999) examined whether unemployment at ages sixteen to seventeen mediates the impact of a conviction between ten and thirteen years of age on subsequent delinquency. Indeed, using structural equation modeling he found that conviction prior to age fourteen has a direct positive effect on delinquency at ages fourteen to fifteen and has a continued, albeit indirect, impact on delinquency at ages eighteen to nineteen through increased unemployment at sixteen to seventeen years of age.

Using 605 male respondents in the *Rochester* study described above, Bernburg and Krohn (2003) tested the hypothesis that police contact or juvenile justice intervention impact early adulthood crime and that this relationship is mediated by educational attainment and unemployment. Indeed, they found that both police contact and juvenile justice intervention are positively associated with early adulthood criminality measures and employment and educational attainment partially mediate the relationship.

Some support was found for each theoretically expected mediator: changes in identity, peer associations, and structural obstacles. Future research on each potential mediator is clearly needed before definitive conclusions can be drawn. Empirically disentangling the process by which labels may impact subsequent behavior is an important task for both researchers and labeling theorists. In addition to having a variety of viewpoints on how labels work, there has also been a debate over the impact that individual characteristics may have on the sanction–recidivism relationship.

Potential Contingencies

Although it did not receive much attention until quite recently, some early labeling theorists proposed that the effect of a label may be contingent on personal characteristics. While these hypotheses were not as fully developed as others during the peak of labeling theory's popularity, much recent theoretical and empirical attention to the deviance escalating effects of formal labeling has focused on the proposition that the effect of a label may be contingent on personal characteristics (Paternoster and Iovanni, 1989; Sampson and Laub, 1997; Bernburg and Krohn, 2003; Chiricos et al., 2007). In addition to those characteristics included in the synthesis above, other personal traits, including race, class, stakes in conformity, and sex, have been hypothesized to impact one's susceptibility to the impact of a label. Although some of these areas have yet to be exposed to serious empirical testing, the results of existing studies will be discussed and recommendations for future research provided.

Race and Class

Both race and social class have been hypothesized to interact with labeling effects, but empirical evaluations of these claims are rare. Early labelists (Jensen, 1972; Ageton and Elliott, 1974; Harris, 1976) hypothesized that the effects of a formal sanction would vary by race and class in such a way that it would be less consequential for minorities and those of low social standing. More recently, scholars have argued the opposing position, that official labeling should have more negative consequences for those who are disadvantaged (primarily referring to minority and poverty status) (e.g., Sampson and Laub, 1997).

The small body of recent research that has actually examined race and class effects in labeling hypotheses has produced inconsistent findings. A series of domestic violence field experiments examined the impact of arrest on recidivism in four cities and found some support for labeling theory. Sherman et al. (1992) found that the interaction of race and arrest was not significant in predicting recidivism in Milwaukee. However, a study examining data pooled from four sites (including Milwaukee) involved in these studies found that the labeling effect of arrest on recidivism was 11 percent higher for blacks than whites (Berk et al., 1992). Studies of other offenses have similarly conflicting findings.

In addition to examining intervening mechanisms, Bernburg and Krohn (2003) also created interaction terms to determine whether sanctions are more consequential for youths who were black or living in households with an income below the poverty line. They found that the relationship between official intervention (police contact or juvenile justice intervention) and self-reported recidivism was stronger for blacks and on those who are impoverished in some (but not all) situations.

Ted Chiricos et al. (2007) attempted to tease out the situations in which labels may have their greatest impact. Taking advantage of a unique situation in Florida, they were able to examine the impact of felony conviction on recidivism for a sample of nearly 100,000 probationers, about half of whom were convicted of a felony while the others had "adjudication withheld." Overall, they found that adjudication was associated with higher levels of recidivism. In contrast to the prior studies, they found that the effect of adjudication was stronger for offenders who are white than for black and Hispanic offenders.

Stakes in Conformity

Related to disadvantage is the issue of stakes in conformity, which have also been suggested to impact labeling consequences. Sherman and colleagues (1992: 682) noted that there is disagreement over the relationship between stakes in conformity and labeling outcomes and they have referred to the opposing hypotheses as the greater vulnerability and less vulnerability versions. Those who support the greater vulnerability version expect that those who "care more about the opinions of conventional society" will be more vulnerable to negative consequences of formal labeling (Sherman et al., 1992: 682). According to the less vulnerability version, those who have strong informal social bonds, including marriage and employment, will be more insulated from the effects because they have "other social resources that overcome the impact of labeling" (Sherman et al., 1992). As with race, studies have supported both of the opposing hypotheses.

In a study on specific deterrence, Dejong (1997: 569) found that, "individuals with few bonds to society (job, family, education) are more likely to recidivate following a period of incarceration." Additionally, three of the domestic violence experiments found that arrest had a greater deterrent effect for employed offenders (Berk et al., 1992; Pate and Hamilton, 1992; Sherman et al., 1992). Two of the studies also found some evidence that arrest may increase reoffending among those who are unemployed (Pate and Hamilton, 1992; Sherman et al., 1992). Finally, Richard Berk et al. (1992) examined three-way interactions of race, employment, and arrest and found that the effect of arrest on recidivism was 47 percent higher for unemployed blacks than for employed whites. The interactions between marriage and race were not significant in any of the reports. While the results from the domestic violence studies may not be generalizable to sanctions other than arrest or perpetrators of other offenses, they provide guidance for offender characteristics that may warrant further examination.

Sex

The impact that race, class, and stakes in conformity has on labeling outcomes has received some attention over the years; however, sex has been substantially overlooked in this regard, even in the most recent research. Keane et al. (1989) proposed that those who are averse to risk will be more susceptible to deterrent effects while those who take risks will be more susceptible to labeling effects. And, "because of gender differences in orientations to risk, deterrence theory holds more for females, while the amplification argument is more salient for males" (Keane et al., 1989: 337). Indeed, for females they found a deterrent effect of police contact and for males they found an amplification effect. However, Chiricos et al. (2007) found that both men and women exhibited a labeling effect, and the impact of adjudication on subsequent felony reconviction was stronger for women than men.

Because of the inconsistent findings in studies examining potential contingencies of labeling theory, future work should continue to explore interactions between these individual traits and official labels or disaggregate the samples along these lines and perform separate analyses. The findings from such research would be important for both furthering theoretical development and informing policy.

Since 1975, Tittle (and others) has been requesting research to address both the intervening mechanisms and conditions under which a label has detrimental consequences. The foregoing studies have addressed some of these concerns. While conclusive remarks on the viability of the perspective or the hypotheses regarding individual traits or mediators are not possible, the most recent findings stand as a request for continued rigorous testing of labeling hypotheses. If these findings can be replicated with different data and populations, then we may see a resurgence of interest in the labeling paradigm.

Conclusions

Labeling proponents argue that being publicly defined as a deviant will increase the likelihood of future deviant behavior. Critics of the perspective argue that the empirical evidence generally does not support the notion of secondary deviance. A systematic examination of research findings that bear upon the question of whether labeling increases future deviance shows that while deviance amplification is not supported by a majority of the estimates, it receives more support than its antithesis, specific deterrence, under most conditions and when tested in the most appropriate manner. Overall, there were significantly more findings supportive of the proposition than against it.

It also appears that the impact of a labeling event may be more detrimental to certain types of people. In the systematic review, more support was found for juveniles than adults and those involved in violent and property crimes than perpetrators of domestic violence. A few studies described in more detail above also examined how other individual traits, such as race and ethnicity, socioeconomic status, stakes in conformity, and sex, may condition that impact of a label on recidivism. However, there are relatively few findings and they often produce inconsistent conclusions. Additional research is essential to test these labeling propositions. Future studies should also focus on testing hypotheses relating to the intervening mechanisms. Some support was found for changes in identity, peer associations, and structural obstacles, but definitive conclusions cannot be drawn until the findings are replicated.

Although some pronounced the perspective dead twenty years ago, labeling theory has received some renewed theoretical and empirical attention in recent years. A quantitative assessment of studies examining the impact of arrest, conviction, juvenile justice intervention, and incarceration on recidivism provides modest support for the hypothesis that official sanctions, in certain situations, may increase subsequent deviance. While the findings are still relatively inconclusive, potential for the perspective has been found. What we need to see now is a revival in empirical tests of labeling theory that are attentive to the primary flaws of the previous work. The policy implications are too great to leave these questions unanswered.

Notes

1. Studies included in the quantitative synthesis are marked by an * in the reference list.
2. $Z_{vc} = (N_p) - (1/2\ N)\ /\ 1/2\ \sqrt{N}$; where Z_{vc} = standard normal deviate for the overall series of findings, N_p = number of positive findings, and N = total number of findings (Cooper, 1998: 118).
3. $Z_{st} = (\sum Z_i)\ /\ \sqrt{N}$; where Z_{st} = standard normal deviate for the overall series of finding, Z_i = standard normal deviate for the ith finding, and N = total number of findings (Cooper, 1998: 120).
4. However, studies of identity and labeling have been conducted in the context of informal labels, such as parental appraisals (Heimer and Matsueda, 1994; Matsueda, 1992).

References

Ageton, S. S. and D. S. Elliott. "The Effects of Legal Processing on Delinquent Orientations." *Social Problems* 22 (1974): 87–100.

Babst, D. V., W. H. Moseley, J. Schmeidler, M. G. Neithercutt, and M. Koval. "Assessing Length of Institutionalization in Relation to Parole Outcome: A Study of Drug Users Paroled in the United States in 1968 and 1969." *Criminology* 14, no. 1 (1976): 41–54.

Becker, H. S. *Outsiders: Studies in the Sociology of Deviance.* New York: The Free Press, 1963.

*Berk, R. A., A. Campbell, R. Klap, and B. Western. "The Deterrent Effect of Arrest in Incidents of Domestic Violence: A Bayesian Analysis of Four Field Experiments." *American Sociological Review* 57, no. 5 (1992): 698–708.

Bernburg, J. G. *State Reaction, Life-Course Outcomes, and Structural Disadvantage: A Panel Study of the Impact of Formal Criminal Labeling on the Transition to Adulthood.* Albany: State University of New York, 2002.

*Bernburg, J. G. and M. D. Krohn. "Labeling, Life Chances, and Adult Crime: The Direct and Indirect Effects of Official Intervention in Adolescence on Crime in Early Adulthood." *Criminology* 41 (2003): 1287–318.

*Bernburg, J. G., M. D. Krohn, and C. J. Rivera. "Official Labeling, Criminal Embeddedness, and Subsequent Delinquency: A Longitudinal Test of Labeling Theory." *Journal of Research in Crime and Delinquency* 43, no. 1 (2006): 67–88.

*Chiricos, T., K. Barrick, W. Bales, and S. Bontrager. "The Labeling of Convicted Felons and Its Consequences for Recidivism." *Criminology* 45, no. 3 (2007): 547–82.

Cooper, H. *Synthesizing Research.* 3rd ed., vol. 2. Thousand Oaks, CA: Sage Publications, 1998.

*Dejong, C. "Survival Analysis and Specific Deterrence: Integrating Theoretical and Empirical Models of Recidivism." *Criminology* 35 (1997): 561–75.

*Farrington, D. P. "The Effects of Public Labeling." *British Journal of Criminology* 17 (1977): 112–25.

Gottfredson, D. M., M. R. Gottfredson, and J. Garofalo. "Time Served in Prison and Parole Outcomes among Parolee Risk Categories." *Journal of Criminal Justice* 5 (1977): 1–12.

*Hagan, J. and A. Palloni. "The Social Reproduction of a Criminal Class in Working-Class London, circa 1950–1980." *The American Journal of Sociology* 96, no. 2 (1990): 265–99.

Harris, A. R. "Race, Commitment to Deviance, and Spoiled Identity." *American Sociological Review* 41, no. 3 (1976): 432–42.

Heimer, K. and R. L. Matsueda. "Role-Taking, Role Commitment, and Delinquency: A Theory of Differential Social Control." *American Sociological Review* 59, no. 3 (1994): 365–90.

*Horwitz, A. and M. Wasserman. "The Effect of Social Control on Delinquent Behavior: A Longitudinal Test." *Sociological Focus* 12, no. 1 (1979): 53–70.

Jensen, G. "Delinquency and Adolescent Self-Conceptions: A Study of the Personal Relevance of Infraction." *Social Problems* 20 (1972): 84–103.

Keane, C., A. R. Gillis, and J. Hagan. "Deterrence and Amplification of Juvenile Delinquency by Police Contact." *British Journal of Criminology* 29, no. 4 (1989): 336–52.

Li, Spencer De. "Legal Sanctions and Youths' Status Achievement: A Longitudinal Study." *Justice Quarterly* 16 (1999): 377–402.

Matsueda, R. L. "Reflected Appraisals, Parental Labeling, and Delinquency: Specifying a Symbolic Interactionist Theory." *The American Journal of Sociology* 97, no. 6 (1992): 1577–611.

Matza, D. *Becoming Deviant*. Prentice Hall, 1969.

*Palamara, F., F. T. Cullen, and J. C. Gersten. "The Effect of Police and Mental Health Intervention on Juvenile Deviance: Specifying Contingencies in the Impact of Formal Reaction." *Journal of Health and Social Behavior* 27 (1986): 90–105.

*Pate, A. M. and E. E. Hamilton. "Formal and Informal Deterrents to Domestic Violence: The Dade County Spouse Assault Experiment." *American Sociological Review* 57, no. 5 (1992): 691–97.

Paternoster, R. and L. Iovanni. "The Labeling Perspective and Delinquency: An Elaboration of the Theory and an Assessment of the Evidence." *Justice Quarterly* 6, no. 3 (1989): 359–94.

*Rasmussen, D. W., B. L. Benson, I. J. Kim, and T. W. Zuehlke. *An Economic Analysis of Recidivism among Drug Offenders in Florida* (No. Project Grant Number 89-058, Florida House Appropriations Committee). Applied Research Program, 1990.

Ray, M. C. and W. R. Downs. "An Empirical Test of Labeling Theory using Longitudinal Data." *Journal of Research in Crime and Delinquency* 23 (1986): 169–94.

Sampson, R. J. and J. H. Laub. "A Life-Course Theory of Cumulative Disadvantage and the Stability of Delinquency." In *Developmental Theories of Crime and Delinquency*, edited by T. P. Thornberry, vol. 7. New Brunswick: Transaction Publishers, 1997.

*Sherman, L. W., D. A. Smith, J. D. Schmidt, and D. P. Rogan. "Crime, Punishment, and Stake in Conformity: Legal and Informal Control of Domestic Violence." *American Sociological Review* 57, no. 5 (1992): 680–90.

*Smith, D. A. and P. R. Gartin. "Specifying Specific Deterrence: The Influence of Arrest on Future Criminal Activity." *American Sociological Review* 54, no. 1 (1989): 94–106.

*Smith, D. A. and R. Paternoster. "Formal Processing and Future Delinquency: Deviance Amplification as Selection Artifact." *Law and Society Review* 24 (1990): 1109–31.

*Thomas, C. W. and D. M. Bishop. "The Effect of Formal and Informal Sanctions on Delinquency: A Longitudinal Comparison of Labelling and Deterrence Theories." *Journal of Criminal Law and Criminology* 75 (1984): 1222–45.

Tittle, C. R. "Deterrents or labeling?" *Social Forces* 53, no. 3 (1975): 399–410.

———. "Labelling and Crime: An Empirical Evaluation." In *The Labelling of Deviance: Evaluating a Perspective*, edited by W. R. Gove. Beverly Hills, CA: Sage Publications, 1980.

*Tolman, R. M. and A. Weisz. "Coordinated Community Intervention for Domestic Violence: The Effects of Arrest and Prosecution on Recidivism of Woman Abuse Perpetrators." *Crime and Delinquency* 41 (1995): 481–95.

*Ulmer, J. T. "Intermediate Sanctions: A Comparative Analysis of the Probability and Severity of Recidivism." *Sociological Inquiry* 71, no. 2 (2001): 164–93.

*Ventura, L. A. and G. Davis. "Domestic iolence: Court Case Conviction and Recidivism." *Violence Against Women* 11, no. 2 (2005): 255–77.

*Wooldredge, J. "Differentiating the Effects of Juvenile Court Sentences on Eliminating Recidivism." *Journal of Research in Crime and Delinquency* 25 (1988): 264–300.

6

The Impact of Juvenile System Processing on Delinquency

Anthony Petrosino, Carolyn Turpin-Petrosino,
and Sarah Guckenburg

Background

Justice practitioners have tremendous discretion on how to handle less serious juvenile offenders. Less serious juvenile offenders are those that commit offenses that are of moderate or low severity, and that often do not have or have a limited prior record of contacts with legal authorities. Police officers, district attorneys, juvenile court intake officers, juvenile and family court judges, and other officials can decide whether the juvenile should be "officially processed" by the juvenile justice system, diverted from the system to counseling or services, or released altogether. An *important policy question* is which strategy leads to the best outcomes for juveniles. Although some experts believe that entry or further "penetration" into the formal juvenile justice system can help deter future criminal behavior by juveniles, others believe that it could

Acknowledgments. The Norwegian Knowledge Centre for the Health Sciences and an unnamed U.S. organization provided funding for the review. We thank Charlotte Gill, David Wilson, Mark Steinmeyer and several peer reviewers for their comments on the Campbell Collaboration protocol (plan) and funding proposal. This chapter is based on a systematic review completed for the Campbell Collaboration (Petrosino et al., 2010).

lead juveniles to commit more crimes in the future, perhaps due to a "labeling" effect. A further consideration for policymakers is that release or diversion options may be cheaper than juvenile court processing, so that even a net gain of "zero" (no crime impact whatsoever) favors the release or diversion group in a cost-benefit analysis. The question on how to handle such offenders is not a trivial one. For example, in 2005 there were nearly 1.7 million delinquency cases processed at the intake stage by U.S. juvenile courts, and nearly 60 percent were formally processed, with 40 percent being diverted or otherwise "kicked out" of the system (Puzzanchera and Sickmund, 2008).

Given the juvenile justice system's dual goal of protecting public safety while rehabilitating juvenile offenders, it is not surprising that a strong argument for traditional processing can be made. For example, some officials believe that less serious offenses are a "gateway" to more serious offending, and should be dealt with intensively to prevent the juvenile from becoming a repeat offender. Some officials believe that the official system processing and subsequent handling by the juvenile court will deter or "scare" low-level offenders from future misconduct. Some officials also believe that the primary role of the juvenile (or sometimes family) court is to rehabilitate the child, and therefore believe it necessary that even low-level offenders be linked to treatment and services via the court system.

On the other hand, there are those who believe in a "minimalist" position: that low-level offenders should be handled in as non-intrusive a manner as possible. Researchers have warned of a possible "labeling" effect that may come from official processing of juveniles (e.g., Schur, 1973). For example, it is suggested that a petition results in an official label of the child as a delinquent, and significant others around the child will now begin to treat him or her differently. Such a labeled juvenile may receive increased police scrutiny and end up getting rearrested more often than juveniles who are not under the same surveillance. The same actions that resulted in the police turning a blind eye to misconduct may now result in an arrest. labeling is theorized to have other potential impacts, including economic or educational losses, and marginalization by significant others such as family and friends. There are other theories, apart from labeling, that could explain why further processing in the juvenile system may increase crime. For example, such processing could further expose youth to more deviant peers, resulting in a criminogenic effect (e.g., Dishion et al., 1999).

For less serious juvenile offenders, the question is whether it is better to process the child through the juvenile justice system, or to divert the child out of the system? To find out whether a policy alternative "works," we have to examine the scientific evidence on the question. What do prior assessments, or evaluations, of the outcome of this decision tell us? Does it support handling juvenile offenders formally through the system or informally through release or diversion programs?

Fortunately, there have been randomized experiments in the juvenile courts that can be gathered together in a systematic fashion to provide rigorous evidence about the impact of this decision on subsequent offending by juveniles. Since the 1960s, a series of randomized experiments have been done in the juvenile courts to test the efficacy of programs that diverted juveniles from official processing into more informal strategies. These experiments for the most part tested diversion programs that included counseling or other services. The control or comparison condition in most of these experiments has been the "traditional system processing" condition. By turning the experiment around, and treating traditional system processing as the "treatment" or "intervention" condition, and the diversion with services, or release (diversion without services) as the control condition, the impact of moving the juvenile into the formal court process or the impact of further "penetration" in the juvenile system can be rigorously tested.

Despite the fact that there have been a fair number of randomized controlled studies that included traditional system processing as a condition, there has not been an attempt to systematically gather only this experimental evidence and analyze it to determine what the crime deterrent impact is for traditional system processing on low-level juvenile offenders. There has been one prior meta-analysis that focused on juvenile diversion programs, with many of these programs comparing diversion to system processing. However, this review is now over twenty years old, including quasi-experiments of varying levels of rigor (as well as pre-post designs without a comparison group), and overall reported a positive effect size across these studies for diversion from the system of .26 (Gensheimer et al., 1986).

Methodology

For this project, we systematically identified, collected, and analyzed experiments that responded to the question: Does juvenile system processing reduce subsequent delinquency?

Criteria for Study Eligibility

For this project, we only included those studies that had the follow-ing characteristics: (1) used random or quasi-random (e.g., alternation) assignment; (2) randomly assigned juvenile delinquents (ages seventeen and younger) who have not yet been "officially adjudicated" for their current offense to juvenile system processing (e.g., "juvenile system processing," "traditional handling by the juvenile court," "traditional processing," or "regular petition and processing by the juvenile court")—or to an alterna-tive non-system condition; (3) included at least one quantifiable outcome measure of crime (e.g., arrest, conviction); and (4) the study report was published or available through July 2008, without regard to language.

Search Strategy for Identification of Relevant Studies

Our review was built upon earlier work done by David Weisburd, Sherman and Petrosino (1990) and Petrosino (1997), which identified a large number of randomized experiments in criminal justice. For ex-ample, Petrosino (1997) conducted electronic searches of bibliographic databases (e.g., *Criminal Justice Abstracts*); did visual hand searching of twenty-nine leading social science journals; made personal contact with reviewers and experimental researchers; published solicitations for reports in association newsletters; and chased down citations from exist-ing reviews and experimental literature. Despite the narrow eligibility criteria, several hundred trials were identified; retrieval methods ended after the first 300 trials were obtained. In that collection alone, which only covers experiments published or available through 1993, there were fifteen experiments that met the criteria for this review.

To augment the fifteen trials in our existing data file, we relied on two strategies (that have been most productive in prior projects) to identify relevant trials published between 1994 and 2008.

(1) *Electronic searches of bibliographic databases.* We searched forty-four electronic databases and two Internet search engines (*Google* and *Google Scholar*). After a series of pilot searches, we were most successful in searching the databases by combining three sets of keywords: (1) those associated with rigorous evalu-ation (e.g., controlled, randomly, and experiment); (2) the use of juvenile or delinquent and their derivatives; and (3) more focused keywords to identify components of the juvenile justice system (e.g., diversion, adjudication, processing, system, and court).

(2) *Existing reviews.* We searched through the bibliographies of over fifty prior reviews of research for references to potential experiments meeting our criteria.

As noted in the eligibility criteria, we did not exclusively seek English reports. We asked colleagues from Spain, Germany, Denmark, Israel, the Netherlands, and other nations for help in identifying any non-English studies. None were identified.

Our efforts resulted in a final sample of twenty-nine randomized experiments that included a comparison of juvenile system processing to either a release or a diversion program condition. (For more details about these twenty-nine studies, see Petrosino et al., 2010.)

Extracting Information from Each Study

Informed by our prior research (Petrosino, 1997), we designed a preliminary instrument to guide us in recording information from each study. The instrument included items in the following areas: (1) researcher and study characteristics (e.g., type of publication); (2) study methods and methodological quality (e.g., if randomization integrity was substantially violated or there was large attrition from the study sample); (3) treatment and control conditions data (e.g., type of condition and number of participants assigned to the condition); (4) participants in the trial data (e.g., race, gender, and prior record); and (5) outcome data (prevalence, incidence, severity, latency, and self-report).

How Decisions about Studies Were Made

It is important in a systematic review to be as explicit as possible about the procedures we followed and how we made decisions so readers can interpret and judge the work accordingly. For example, when we encountered studies that reported more than one comparison or control condition, our standard principle was to select the least intrusive or least harsh condition as the control group (i.e., diversion over diversion with services). Our rationale is that this would provide a control condition that presents the "strongest contrast" with the juvenile system processing condition. If special deterrence applies to the juveniles in these experiments, then a contrast between juvenile court processing and release (the harshest versus least harsh disposition) would be the ideal comparison to test that theory. Moreover, if labeling theory applies, the same comparison of juvenile court processing and release presents the best test of that theory. In addition, note that investigators may publish several articles on the same study. Our unit of analysis was the individual experiment and not the individual research article, and we extracted information from all documents to complete the coding instrument for one experiment. Most studies in our sample, however, issued just one report.

Moreover, each study is represented in the analyses by a *single effect size* to prevent the analysis from being compromised by non-independence (multiple effect sizes from one study). Our protocol indicated that we would partition the data by four types of crime outcome (prevalence, incidence, severity, and latency). The Appendix provides the outcome data from the twenty-nine included experiments, organized by prevalence, incidence, severity, and latency. Self-report data is included within these categories, but we ended up separating it out to provide another analysis. Only one study reported one latency measure, and so no meta-analysis of those data was conducted. Because the follow-up intervals were so disparate, with some studies reporting just one follow-up and a few studies reporting multiple follow-ups over many years, we decided to conduct the following analyses for each of the four crime outcomes[1]:

- *First follow-up effect*: the earliest post-intervention follow-up outcome reported in the study
- *Longest follow-up effect*: the post-intervention follow-up outcome that had the longest time interval
- *Strongest follow-up effect*: The post-intervention follow-up that reported the strongest effect for juvenile system processing.

There is still the issue, however, that multiple types of prevalence or incidence data might be reported at the same follow-up period (e.g., police data and petitions). When that occurred, we selected the outcome that represented the earliest point of contact in the juvenile justice system (i.e., usually police contact).

Statistical Procedures and Conventions

We report standardized mean differences (Cohen's *d*). Cohen's *d* provides the flexibility in that many types of outcome data can be used to estimate the standardized mean difference (e.g., the test statistic or probability level and sample size). We used the transformation formulae provided in Comprehensive Meta-Analysis (our software for analysis) or in Lipsey and Wilson (2001) to make these conversions.

We reported effect sizes assuming both fixed and random effects models for the global meta-analyses across the twenty-nine studies. We conducted one sensitivity analysis, examining the impact of two studies with substantial methodological problems on the overall results. We also conducted several exploratory moderator analyses to determine if variables such as the type of control condition or extent of prior record in the sample have any impact on the meta-analytic results. Of course, moderator analyses must be viewed with caution for two reasons. First, as moderator analysis is done, the number of studies remaining in the cells can drop precipitously. The analyses are based on very small numbers of studies in many instances. Second, as the number of analyses increases, the likelihood of a chance finding that a variable is moderating the result increases.

Results

Descriptive Analyses

The studies included in the review were published between 1973 and 2008, and included 7,304 juveniles across twenty-nine experiments reported over this thirty-five-year period. Also of note is that the time intervals for follow-up of outcomes ranged from 2 to 108 months. Studies reported between one and seven different types of crime outcomes.

Table 6.1 provides a summary of some descriptive data on the included experiments. Most studies were reported before 1990 (76 percent). Only 38 percent of the primary documents used to code the studies were published in peer review journals or books. Only two studies were conducted outside of the United States (Australia). In fact, nearly four in ten were conducted in the Midwest, largely because Michigan State University (MSU) researchers reported them.

Most of the studies had two or three study groups (79 percent). The intervention or treatment in this review was described as "processing" in nearly two-thirds (65.5 percent) of the experiments; other descriptions of the included treatments were "petition," "adjudication," or "appear before magistrate." The type of control condition was nearly evenly split across the review sample. Fifteen studies (51.7 percent) assigned juveniles to diversion with services, including such conditions as family counseling, restorative justice conferencing, or an education program. Fourteen studies (48.3 percent) assigned juveniles to diversion alone, such as counsel and release or outright release.

Table 6.1
Characteristics of included studies

Where were the studies conducted?	Midwest (USA)	11	37.9%
	West (USA)	7	24.1%
	South (USA)	4	13.8%
	East (USA)	3	10.3%
	Unknown (USA)	2	6.9%
	Outside USA	2	6.9%
Who did the studies?	Michigan State University	12	41.4%
	Others	17	58.6%
When were the studies conducted?	Before January 1990	22	76.0%
	After January 1990	7	24.0%
Where were studies reported?	Journals/books	11	37.9%
	Unpublished	18	62.1%
How many study groups were included?	Two groups	10	34.5%
	Three groups	13	44.8%
	Four or more groups	6	20.7%
What was the processing condition?	Traditional processing	19	65.5%
	Other	10	34.5%
What was the control condition?	Diversion with services	15	51.7%
	Diversion	14	48.3%
Was the assignment random or quasi-random?	Random	17	85.0%
	Quasi-random	3	15.0%
	Missing	9	
At what stage in the process did randomization occur?	Following police contact	9	37.5%
	After referral to program	8	33.3%
	Other	7	29.2%
	Missing	5	
What was the combined sample size of treatment and control groups?	1–100	6	21.4%
	101–200	9	32.1%
	201–300	6	21.4%
	301–400	3	10.7%
	401–500	1	3.6%
	501+	3	10.7%
	Missing	1	
What was the mean age of juveniles?	14.73 (7 cases missing)		
What was the average percentage of whites?	61.0% (10 cases missing)		

(*continued*)

Table 6.1 (*continued*)

What was the average percentage of males?	74.2% (7 cases missing)		
What was the level of prior offending?	High	8	34.8%
	Moderate	3	13.0%
	Low	9	39.1%
	None	3	13.0%
	Missing	6	
Did the study include specific or general offending types?	Specific	5	17.8%
	General	23	82.2%
	Missing	1	

The randomization procedures were not often described explicitly enough to determine how they were done. In the twenty experiments in which enough detail was provided, only 15 percent used quasi-random allocation procedures such as alternation. Randomization most often occurred following police contact or arrest (37.5 percent) or after referral to a diversion program (33 percent).[2] Most studies included 300 or fewer juvenile participants in the treatment and control condition (74.9 percent).[3]

The average age of participants across these twenty-nine experiments was—fourteen to fifteen years. Studies in the review sample were comprised of large percentages of white (61 percent on average) and male (74 percent on average) participants. Surprisingly, although most studies included juveniles with prior offending records rates as "low" or "none" (twelve studies, 52.1 percent), there were eight studies (34.8 percent) that included juveniles with prior offending records rated as "high." Only five studies (17.8 percent) targeted specific offending types (for the current or instant offense) such as shoplifters; the majority included juvenile offenders of all types.

Meta-Analysis

Prevalence

Twenty-seven of the twenty-nine included studies reported prevalence data that could be used in meta-analysis. Figure 6.1 presents the results (in a forest plot) for first post-treatment effect. Note that the average length of the first follow-up reported across these twenty-seven studies was ten to eleven months, ranging from two to twenty-four months. It should

Figure 6.1
Prevalence: First effect

Study name	Std diff in means	Std diff in means and 95% CI
Patrick & Marsh (2005)	0.278	
Severy & Whitaker (1982)	0.095	
Klein (1986)	-0.479	
Smith, et al. (1979)	0.000	
Baron & Feeney (1976) 602	-0.428	
Baron & Feeney (1976) 601	-0.253	
Dunford, et al. (1982) KC	0.093	
Dunford, et al. (1982) NY	-0.323	
Dunford, et al. (1982) FL	0.097	
Koch (1985)	-0.275	
Blakely (1981)	0.065	
Davidson II, et al. (1987)	-0.226	
Davidson II, et al. (1990)	-0.936	
Quay & Love (1977)	-0.244	
Bauer et al. (1980)	-0.512	
Quincy (1981)	-0.472	
Hintzen, et al. (1979)	0.999	
Smith, et al. (2004)	-0.050	
Povitsky Stickle, et al. (2008)	0.161	
University Associates (1986) OTSEGO	-0.192	
University Associates (1986) BAY	-0.027	
University Associates (1986) KALAMAZOO	0.029	
University Associates (1986) DETROIT	-0.050	
Curran, et al. (1977)	-0.635	
Sherman, et al. (2000) JPP	0.649	
McCold & Wachtel (1998)	0.368	
True (1973)	0.684	
Random	**-0.109**	

-1.00   -0.50   0.00   0.50   1.00

CRIME INCREASED ↑   CRIME DECREASED ↓

also be pointed out that prevalence data were all based on official records (e.g., police contact, arrest, bookings, petitions, court contacts, etc.).

Fifteen of the twenty-seven effects are negative in direction (the effect size is located to the left of zero) for juvenile system processing, meaning that the intervention has a *criminogenic or crime-increasing* effect. Eleven reported a decrease in subsequent crime (the effect size is located to the right of zero), and one study reported an absolute zero effect (both groups had the same prevalence rate and sample size). The overall effect size across the studies is –.11, assuming a random effects model and –.18 assuming a fixed effects model.

Figure 6.2 presents the effect sizes (in a forest plot) across the twenty-seven studies for the longest time interval reported in the study. The mean of the longest follow-up across the twenty-seven studies is twelve to thirteen months, which is not dramatically different from the average first follow-up (ten to eleven months). This is because most studies either reported just one follow-up interval or two follow-up intervals that were not very far apart (e.g., six months and twelve months). The range of the longest time interval follow-up across these twenty-seven studies was four to thirty-six months.

Eighteen of the twenty-seven effects are now negative in direction (eight are positive, with one effect equaling zero). The standardized mean

Figure 6.2
Prevalence: Longest effect

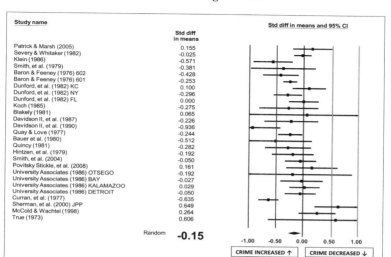

difference, assuming random effects, has increased to –.15 (and remains at –.18 assuming a fixed effects model). This increase is likely due to the three studies that initially reported a positive impact for juvenile system processing at first follow-up and reported a negative impact at the longest follow-up interval.

Our final analysis with the prevalence data was a "proof of concept" analysis. From all the prevalence outcomes, we computed the strongest effect (i.e., the effect size with the largest reported positive effect for juvenile system processing). As Figure 6.3 shows, fifteen of the twenty-seven studies reporting the "strongest effects" for system processing were still negative in direction. The overall effect size was very similar to those reported for the first post treatment effect in Figure 6.2 (–.10 for random effects model; –.15 for fixed effects model).

Incidence

Prevalence data captures how many or the percentage of each treatment group that fails or succeeds according to the outcome of interest. Another important question to policymakers is whether juvenile system processing reduces the total number of offenses by the group (i.e., the mean number of offenses per person in the group). This is especially important in understanding whether intervention impacted high-rate

Figure 6.3
Prevalence: Strongest positive effect

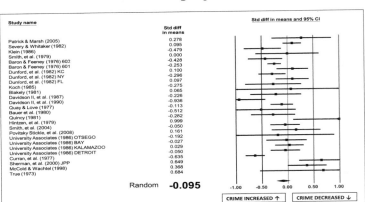

offenders (i.e., juveniles who go on to commit more than one offense after being exposed to processing).

Unfortunately, only seven experiments reported data that we could use to compute effect sizes for incidence measures. Because five of these seven studies only report incidence measures at more than one interval, the outcomes for first effect, longest effect, and strongest effect are very similar. Figure 6.4 presents the results for the first effect for juvenile system processing. It should be pointed out that these incidence data were all generated from official data from police or courts. The average follow-up period to measure the incidence data for these seven studies was nine to ten months.

As indicated, processing has an even larger negative effect for juvenile system processing than on the prevalence measures, at least according to these seven experiments. As Figure 6.4 indicates, six of the seven incidence measures are negative in direction. The overall effect size is −.23 when assuming a random effects model and −.21 when assuming a fixed effects model.

Severity

Another important question for policymakers is whether or not a system intervention like juvenile system processing reduces the seriousness of offending. That is, an intervention may not impact the number of offenders who commit new offenses (prevalence) or the number of offenses committed by each person (incidence), but could be considered effective if it reduced the severity or harm caused by those new offenses.

Figure 6.4
Incidence: First effect

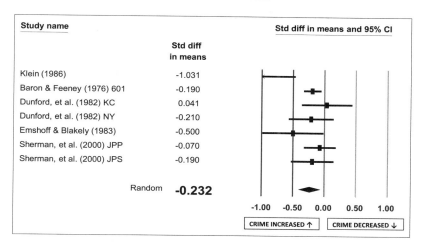

Unfortunately, only nine experiments reported severity data. As with incidence data, very few experiments reported more than one follow-up of a severity outcome measure, so that the effect sizes for the first effect, longest effect, and strongest effect were very similar. Figure 6.5 presents the strongest effect for juvenile system processing for the nine experiments that reported such data that could be used in a meta-analysis. Again, these data were generated from official crime measures such as police contact or arrest. The average length of follow-up across these nine studies was twenty-four months. This is because one study reported its only severity measure at 108 months follow-up.

As Figure 6.5 indicates, of the nine experiments, five are negative and four are positive in direction. However, the overall effect size is again negative in direction, with –.13 assuming a random effects model, and –.20 when a fixed effects model is assumed.

Self-Report Data

Because only one study reported a latency or "time to failure" outcome, our final analyses of crime data came from self-report data. One issue could be that juvenile system processing has a "labeling" effect and official crime measures such as police contact reflect that. One way to examine this is to look at self-reported crime by the juveniles in the studies. Only five experiments, however, captured self-report data that

Figure 6.5
Severity: First effect

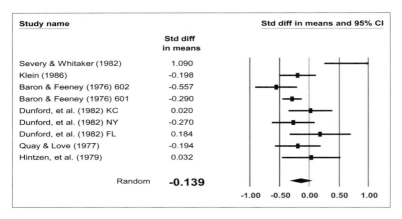

Figure 6.6
Self-Report: First effect

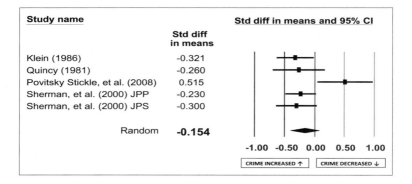

could be used in the meta-analysis. The average length of follow-up for these five studies is eleven months. As Figure 6.6 indicates, in four of these five studies, the first effect for juvenile system processing is negative in direction. The overall effect size is –.15 assuming a random effects model and –.23 assuming a fixed effects model.

Sensitivity Analysis

Although our review sample is comprised of experiments that randomly (or in three studies, quasi-randomly) assigned participants, there are many things that can go wrong in evaluation research, including experiments. The two most common methodological factors that can compromize the findings in the types of experiments reported here are randomization failure and attrition. Although a small number of experiments reported randomization or attrition problems, only two studies were determined to have significant methodological problems because of breakdowns that would potentially undermine the reported findings.

In the study conducted by Wendy Povitsky-Stickle et al. (2008), youths were randomly assigned to traditional processing or to a diversion program featuring a "teen court." Randomization was done before juvenile participants (and their parents) agreed to participate. Therefore, a large number of juveniles were dropped from the initial randomization sample. In the Bethlehem, Pennsylvania restorative justice experiment, youths were randomly assigned to traditional processing or a diversionary program featuring victim conferencing (McCold and Wachtel, 1998). However, over half of youths assigned to the diversionary program refused to participate and were officially processed.

Sensitivity analyses are one method that reviewers can use to determine the impact of studies that report methodological compromises on the overall meta-analysis findings. To conduct such analyses, reviewers drop certain studies to determine how removing them affects the overall findings. Using prevalence data at first, longest and strongest effects (for the twenty-seven studies that reported such data), we dropped the studies conducted by Paul McCold and Benjamin Wachtel (1998) and Wendy Povitsky-Stickle et al. (2008) to determine how that impacted effect size. Table 6.2 presents the results for this analysis, comparing the effect sizes assuming random and fixed effects models for all twenty-seven studies versus the remaining twenty-five studies (after the two aforementioned studies are dropped from the meta-analysis).

Table 6.2
Sensitivity analysis dropping two studies

Type of analysis	Type of effects model assumed	First effect	Longest effect	Strongest effect for system processing
All 27 studies	Random	−.11	−.15	−.10
	Fixed	−.17	−.18	−.15
Dropping two studies	Random	−.14	−.18	−.13
	Fixed	−.19	−.20	−.17

As Table 6.2 indicates, the effect sizes remain negative and increase about −.02 to −.03 in magnitude when the two studies are dropped, regardless of which effects model is assumed. However, despite this, the inclusion of these two particular studies when using the sample of twenty-seven studies does not substantively impact the overall conclusions.

Moderator Analyses

Juvenile system processing, at least given the experimental evidence presented here, appears to have consistently negative effects on crime measures of prevalence, incidence, and severity, as well as that measured by self-report. However, the results are not universal across every study and some experiments do report a positive impact for system processing. In addition, the size of the effect varies across the studies. In such cases, moderator analyses (examining how the effect varies across dimensions of the studies) can be helpful in illuminating these differences. Because prevalence data were reported in such a way that it could be used in meta-analysis by twenty-seven of the twenty-nine included studies, we rely on prevalence data reported at the first follow-up time interval for these moderating analyses. We have also limited our initial set of moderating analyses to five. We should also again note that the average follow-up time interval for first prevalence outcome measurement is between ten and eleven months.

Table 6.3 provides the results for five moderating analyses. Because analyses conducted assuming random effects models are considered more conservative, we report those and place those effect sizes computed in parentheses while assuming fixed effects models.

An important moderator is the type of control group that juvenile system processing is being compared to. There are two basic alternative groups in these experiments: (1) groups in which juveniles are diverted from the system to receive "services" ("diversion with services"); and (2) groups in which juveniles are diverted from the system and are simply released to receive no services (e.g., "counsel and release"). As Table 6.3 indicates, there are fourteen experiments that compare juvenile system processing with diversion and thirteen experiments that have a diversion with services alternative group. The overall effect for juvenile system processing is slightly negative when compared to "doing nothing," with effect sizes of −.04 (random) and −.05 (fixed). When system processing is compared to "doing something," the effect sizes are larger and remain negative, with −.16 (random) and −.28 (fixed).

Table 6.3
The results of moderating analyses

Moderator	Characteristic	Effect size— Random (Fixed)
Type of control group	Diversion Alone ($n = 14$)	−.04 (−.05)
	Diversion with Services ($n = 13$)	−.16 (−.28)
Did Michigan State University researchers conduct the study?	Yes ($n = 12$)	−.20 (−.16)
	No ($n = 15$)	−.03 (−.17)
Was the experiment reported before or after 1990?	Before 1990 ($n = 21$)	−.17 (−.20)
	1990 and Beyond ($n = 6$)	.09 (.09)
Was the report published or unpublished?	Published ($n = 11$)	−.18 (−.11)
	Unpublished ($n = 16$)	−.06 (−.19)
What was the extent of the study sample's prior record?	High ($n = 8$)	−.29 (−.27)
	Moderate ($n = 2$)	−.30 (−.30)
	Low ($n = 9$)	−.06 (−.13)
	None ($n = 3$)	.31 (.22)

Researchers and Ph.D. students from MSU, generally under the supervision of Professor William Davidson, conducted twelve of the experiments in the review sample. Davidson was part of a team that developed a particular approach to juvenile diversion that included behavioral contracting and child advocacy (the Adolescent Diversion Program). Given the long program of research that he and others established at MSU, they generated a number of the randomized trials in this review sample (over 40 percent). To explore the influence of MSU studies on the sample, we compared effect size for the twelve MSU experiments with the fifteen non-MSU studies that comprised the remaining twenty-seven reports in this prevalence, first-effect analysis. Table 6.3 indicates that, like the control group moderator analysis, all of the effects are negative in direction. However, the effect size for juvenile system processing in non-MSU studies varies widely depending on whether a fixed (−.17) or random effects (−.03) model is assumed. System processing in the twelve studies reported by William Davidson and his colleagues at MSU had a larger negative effect regardless of which effects model is assumed (−.20 assuming a random effects model and −.16 assuming a fixed effects model).

Because this systematic review did not have eligibility criteria to limit it to more recent studies, experiments that were conducted and reported from 1973 through 2008 were included. This exploratory moderating analysis examines the effect for juvenile system processing in studies reported before January 1, 1990, and those reported after January 1, 1990. We should note that only six experiments were reported in 1990 or later; twenty-one of the twenty-seven studies reporting prevalence data that could be used in meta-analysis were conducted before 1990.

As Table 6.3 also indicates, the effect size varies according to the year of publication. For those studies reported before 1990, the effect size is –.17 assuming a random effects model and –.20 assuming a fixed effects model. However, for the six studies reported in 1990 or beyond, the effect size for juvenile system processing is positive in direction, at .09 assuming either a random or fixed effects model. It should be noted, however, that the two studies that experienced the greatest threats to the experimental design were more recent studies (McCold and Wachtel, 1998; Povitsky-Stickle et al., 2008), and both reported large and positive effects for juvenile system processing. When these two studies are removed from the analysis, leaving just four post-1990 studies, the positive results dissipate (zero assuming a random effects model and –.01 assuming a fixed effects model).

This systematic review included searches for reports published in peer-reviewed journals and books as well as reports located in the grey or fugitive literature (e.g., dissertations, conference papers, government reports, technical reports, etc.). This provides an opportunity to explore the difference in effect size between published and unpublished reports. It should be noted that eleven studies in this analysis were published in peer-reviewed journals or books and sixteen were reported in the fugitive literature. As Table 6.3 indicates, the overall effect sizes for juvenile system processing as reported in both published and unpublished studies are negative in direction. However, the magnitude of that negative effect is larger for published findings than for unpublished reports. For published findings, the effect size is –.18 assuming a random effects model and –.11 assuming a fixed effects model. For unpublished studies, the effect is .06 assuming a random effects model and –.19 when assuming a fixed effects model.

Although the reports did not have an extensive amount of information on prior record, some studies did permit us to rate the extent of the sample's prior record of offending into four categories: none, low, moderate, or high. The distinctions between the categories are that if one-third or less of the study sample has a prior offense (in addition to the current offense), we rated that as "low." If the report indicated that between one-third and two-thirds of the study sample had a prior record, we rated that as "moderate." If the report indicated that over two-thirds of the study sample had a prior record, we rated that as "high." Obviously, these are subjective criteria but they provide one method to ascertain the influence of how extensive the prior record of study participants was and how that might influence the magnitude of the effect size for juvenile system processing. For example, it might be that juvenile system processing is more effective with more serious juveniles (who have a prior record) than those who have not been in trouble before. Or perhaps the inverse is the case. Table 6.3 also presents the effect sizes for the four categories of the extensiveness of the individual study sample's prior record. It should be noted that twenty-two studies reported enough data to allow us to rate the extensiveness of prior record in the studies, with eight rated as "high," two as "moderate," nine as "low," and three as "none." As Table 6.3 indicates, the effect sizes for juvenile system processing are larger and negative in direction when the extensiveness of prior offending in the study sample is rated as "high" or "moderate." For example, when the sample is rated as having a "high" amount of prior offending, the effect size is $-.29$ assuming a random effects model and $-.27$ for fixed effects. For the two "moderate" rated studies, the effect size is exactly $-.30$ regardless of which effects size model is assumed. Although the effect sizes for the nine "low" rated studies are still negative in direction, it reduces in size to $-.06$ when assuming the random effects model and $-.13$ when assuming the fixed effects model. We should note that the two studies dropped in the sensitivity analysis involved samples rated as having "low" degree of prior offending. When they are dropped here, the effect sizes are $-.15$ (random) and $-.18$ (fixed). Finally, in the three studies that included first-time offenders only (no prior offending record), juvenile system processing has positive and much larger effects (.31 assuming a random effects model and .22 assuming a fixed effects model).

Conclusion

This review, examining the results of twenty-nine randomized controlled trials, finds that juvenile system processing has an overall negative impact on crime. This was consistent across measures of prevalence, incidence, severity, and self-report, and consistent when looking at the first or longest time interval that the crime measure was reported. In fact, even when giving juvenile system processing the benefit of the doubt and looking only at the strongest positive effect for processing, a negative impact across all crime outcomes was reported. The effects are even more negative for juvenile system processing when the two trials experiencing significant randomization or attrition issues are removed from the analysis.

Moderating analyses indicated that effect sizes were more negative for processing in studies that compared it to a diversion program or provision of services than in those trials that compared processing to simple release ("doing nothing"). Effect sizes were also larger and more negative in direction for older studies (before 1990), those conducted by MSU researchers, and those reported in published documents. An interesting moderating variable was the extent of prior recorded offending in the study sample. When the study sample was rated as having a low, moderate, or high amount of prior offending, system processing had consistently negative effects. However, for the three studies that were rated as having no prior record because they were comprised of first-time offenders, system processing had a positive crime-reduction effect.

Research Implications

One common question in response to a review that reports an overall negative impact for a policy or practice intervention is "why?" What is the mechanism responsible for negative or crime enhancing effects for juvenile system processing? It is possible, of course, that labeling is still the key ingredient, but the meta-analysis of five experiments that included self-report data indicated that system processing also had an overall negative impact on crime when measured by self-report data. Although moderating variable analyses can shed light on this, there were insufficient data reported in the studies that would allow researchers to unpack the key ingredients that would help explain why system processing had consistently negative impacts on juveniles.

Because the investigators conducting experiments that were collected for this review were more interested in the effects of the diversion program (diversion was the "treatment" group), scant information is reported on the juvenile system processing condition. In fact, many of the trials simply labeled the condition as "official processing" or "traditional processing" with no further details. Better descriptions of the control conditions in randomized trials are needed in such experiments to permit a better assessment of exactly what the treatment is being compared to. In our review, in which we were ultimately concerned with the juvenile system processing condition (it became our "treatment" group), data on the eventual outcomes in the process would have been helpful. For example, how many of the juvenile cases that were officially processed ended up being dismissed? It is possible that system processing is not a deterrent because most cases end up being dismissed or assigned to a weak or informal probation condition. The diversion program may actually end up being a stronger deterrent because juveniles may view the condition as being more onerous or intrusive.

Implications for Policy

Given the overall negative results for juvenile system processing across these studies and outcome measures, jurisdictions should review their own policies regarding the handling of a juvenile coming to the attention of legal authorities. First, although the results are not uniform across the twenty-nine experiments, the main effect shows that system processing results in more subsequent delinquency. Rather than providing a public safety benefit, processing a juvenile through the system appears to have a negative or backfire effect. This was especially true in those studies that compared system processing with a diversion program or services. Even if the diversion program were more expensive than system processing, which may not be likely, the crime reduction benefit associated with the diversion program would likely persuade any cost-benefit analysis to favor the implementation of diversion programs.

But, as the moderating analysis indicated, even those studies that compared juvenile system processing with "doing nothing" averaged a slightly negative impact. Even if the impact were zero, given that the evidence indicates that there is no public safety benefit to system processing, and its greater costs when compared to release, even the most conservative cost-benefit analyses would favor release over system processing. One could argue that interventions achieve other important goals, but other than crime reduction, we are not sure what other potential benefits of system processing should be measured. The studies included here all too infrequently examined the impacts of system processing on education and other measures.

None of the findings here provide guidance on what the juvenile system should do with an individual juvenile offender. This review captured aggregate data from twenty-nine experimental studies. It is most appropriate for guiding larger local, state, and national policies regarding juveniles. This systematic review does not specifically identify the particular offender that could benefit from further processing in the juvenile justice system.

It should be noted that these experiments compared system processing with a diversion program or simple release. Thus, the data from these studies do not support a policy of establishing diversion programs for juveniles that normally would not have been officially processed (i.e., also called "net-widening").

Appendix
Study outcomes for included experiments

Study (Year)	Prevalence	Incidence	Severity	Latency
Patrick and Marsh (2005)[4]	Recidivism: 12 m: 8% E (7/83) v. 13% C (9/68) 36 m: 43% E (34/79) v. 50% C (34/68)	None	None	None
Severy and Whitaker (1982)[5]	Referrals to court: 6 m: 21% E (377) v. 24% C (475) 12 m: 33% E (377) v. 32% C (475)	Mean referrals to court:[6] 6 m: .29 E (377) v. .54 C (475, no SD) 12 m: .35 E (377) v. .61 C (475, no SD)	Escalation from minor to serious: 6 m: E .05% (377) v. C 3.7% (475) 12 m: E 1.3% (377) v. C 5.1% (475)	Mean days to referral 6 m: E 161 (377) v. C 158 (475, no SD) 12 m: E 294 (377) v. C 289 (475, no SD)
Klein (1986)	Re-arrests: 6 m: 48% E (39/81) v. 28% C (23/82) 15 m: 63% E (51/81) v. 37% C (30/82) 27 m: 73% E (59/81) v. 49% C (40/82) Self-report delinquency: 6 m: 35% E (81) v. 35% C (82) 12 m: 62% E (81) v. 45% C (82)	% w/2 or more arrests 6 m: E 29% (5/81) v. 6% C (24/82) 15 m: E 41% (13/81) v. 16% C (34/82) Self-reported delinquency 9 m: E 29.96 (SD 17.82, N = 81) v. C 24.53 (SD 16.00, N = 82)	Self-reported severity 9 m: E 5.23 (sd. 43, N = 81) v. C 5.13 (SD = .57, N = 82)	None

(continued)

Appendix (continued)

Study (Year)	Prevalence	Incidence	Severity	Latency
Smith et al. (1979)	Re-arrests: 6 m: E 35% (N=26) v. C 35% (N=29); 12 m: E 62% (N=26) v. 45% C (N=29)	None	None	None
Baron and Feeney (1976) 602 study[7]	Rebookings: 7 m: E 38% (105) v. C 22% (111)		Criminal rebookings only: 7 m: E 36% (105) v. C 17% (111). Drug/felony rebooking: 7 m: E 25% (105) v. C 12% (111)	None
Baron and Feeney (1976) 601 study[8]	Rebookings for status or criminal: 12 m: E 46% (526) v. C 35% (674)	Multiple recidivism (2+ offenses): 12 m: E 32% (526) v. C 25% (674)	602 (criminal only) rebookings: 12 m: E 23% (526) v. C 15% (674)	None
Dunford et al. (1982)[9] Kansas City	All arrests: 6 m: E 41% (44/107) v. C 45% (43/95); 12 m: E 52% (56/107) v. C 57% (54/95)	% w/2 + arrests (all):[10] 6 m: E 17% (18/107) v. C 18% (17/95); 12 m: E 27 (29/107) v. C 28% (27/95)	%w/felony arrests 6 m: E 22% (23/107) v. C 22% (21/95); 12 m: E 22% (28/107) v. C 24% (23/95)	None

Dunford et al. (1982) New York	Misd/Felony arrests only: 6 m: *E* 37% (40/107) *v. C* 36% (34/95) 12 m: *E* 36% (49/107) *v. C* 47% (45/95) All arrests: 6 m: *E* 26% (40/152) *v. C* 17% (32/193) 12 m: *E* 34% (52/152) *v. C* 23% (45/193) Misd/Felony arrests only: 6 m: *E* 26% (40/152) *v. C* 17% (32/193) 12 m: *E* 34% (52/152) *v. C* 23% (45/193)	Multiple arrests (all): 6 m: *E* 14% (22/152) *v. C* 10% (20/193) 12 m: *E* 24% (37/152) *v. C* 17% (33/193)	Felony arrests: 6 m: *E* 15% (23/152) *v. C* 10% (19/193) 12 m: *E* 21% (32/152) *v. C* 16% (30/193)	None
Dunford et al. (1982) Orange county	Arrests: 6 m: *E* 11% (24/216) *v. C* 13% (28/216) 12 m: *E* 18% (38/216) *v. C* 18% (38/216) Misd/Felony arrests only: 6 m: *E* 11% (23/216) *v. C* 12% (27/216)	None	Felony arrests: 6 m: *E* 4% (8/216) *v. C* 5% (11/216) 12 m: *E* 8% (17/216) *v. C* 7% (16/216)	None

(continued)

Appendix (*continued*)

Study (Year)	Prevalence	Incidence	Severity	Latency
Koch (1985)	12 m: E 17% (36/316) v. C 17% (37/216) Offenses: 4 m: E 14% (78) v. C 9% (86)	Mean offending rate:[11] 4 m: E .14 (78, no SD) v. C .12 (86, no SD)	None	None
Blakely (1981)[12]	Police contacts/court appearances: 6 m: E 18% (2/11) v. C 20% (3/15)	Mean police contacts: 6 m: E .68 (11, no SD) v. C .23 (15, no SD) Mean petitions: 6 m: E 1.04 (11, no SD) v. C .23 (15, no SD)	Mean severity police contacts: 6 m: E .49 (11, no SD) v. C .36 (15, no SD) Most severe police disposition: 6 m: E .40 (11, no SD) v. C .18 (15, no SD) Mean severity petitions: 6 m: E .02 (11, no SD) v. C .01 (15, no SD) Most severe court disposition: 6 m: E 1.87 (11, no SD) v. C .18 (15, no SD)	None

(continued)

Davidson et al. (1987)[13]	Petitions: 24 m: *E* 62% (60) v. *C* 52% (29)	None	None	None
Davidson et al. (1990)[14]	Petitions: 24 m: *E* 68% (27) v. *C* 28% (102)	None	None	None
Quay and Love (1977)[15]	Arrests: Variable *E* 45% (173/436) v. *C* 40% (59/132) All arrests To 300 days: *E* 30% (436) v. *C* 40% (132) Post-program only: Variable *E* 45% (136/436) v. *C* 32% (59/132, *z* = 3.78)	Mean arrests: Variable *E* 1.00 (436, no SD) v. *C* .86 (132, no SD)	Against the person arrests: Variable *E* 11% (436) v. *C* 8% (132) none	None
Bauer et al. (1980)	Recidivism: 24 m: *E* 16% (33) v. *C* 7% (99)	None	None	None
Emshoff and Blakely (1983)	None	Mean police contacts: 6 m: *E* .98 (126, no SD) v. *C* .96 (47, no SD) *F* test for incarceration favors *C* (*F* = 3.83)[16]	None	None

Appendix (*continued*)

Study (Year)	Prevalence	Incidence	Severity	Latency
Quincy (1981)[17]	Offenses: 3 m, chi = 4.75 ($E = 59$, $C = 31$, favors C) 6 m, chi = 1.76 ($E = 59$, $C = 31$, favors C) Petitions: 3 m, chi = .94 ($E = 59$, $C = 31$, favors C) 6 m, chi = .41 ($E = 59$, $C = 31$, favors C)	Self-reported delinquency: 6 m: F test for composite ($E = 59$, $C = 31$; $F = 1.40$)	None	None
Hintzen et al. (1979)	Recidivism (referrals): 6 m: E 6% (2/36) v. C 27% (9/34) 12 m: E 25% (8/32) v. C 31% (11/35) 24 m: E 42% (27/65) v. C 29% (18/61) 36 m: E 54% (35/65) v. C 46% (28/62)[18] Arrests as adults only: 108 m: E 15% v. (28/65) C 14% (26/62)		Felony arrests: 108 m: E 6% (12/65) v. C 6% (12/62)	

(continued)

	Misdemeanors only: 108 m: E 14% (26/65) v. C 13% (25/62)			
	Burglary arrests (Juvenile arrests only): 36 m: E 14% (9/65) v. C 13% (8/62)			
	Burglary arrests (Adult): 108 m: E 3% (6/65) v. C 4% (7/62)			
Smith et al. (2004)[19]	Recidivism: 12 m: E 34% (124) v. C 32% (134)	None	None	None
Povitsky-Stickle et al. (2008)	Recidivism: 18 m: E 26% (51) v. C 32% (52)	Mean arrests: 18 m: E .53 (52, no SD) v. C .75 (51, no SD) Mean self-reported del 18 m: E 1.16 (33, SD .25) v. C 1.31 (42, SD .32)	None	None
University Associates (1986) Otsego, Crawford, Cheboygan	Petitions: 12 m: E 20% (15) v. C 15% (13)	Self-reported delinquency: 4 m: E 17.85 (13, no SD) v. C 8.92 (12, no SD)	None	None

Appendix (*continued*)

Study (Year)	Prevalence	Incidence	Severity	Latency
University Associates (1986) Bay County	Petitions: 12 m: *E* 30% (71) v. *C* 29% (76)	12 m: *E* 36.38 (13, no SD) v. *C* 21.17 (12, no SD) Self-reported delinquency: 4 m: *E* 24.47 (60, no SD) v. *C* 21.97 (65, no SD) 12 m: *E* 31.23 (60, no SD) v. *C* 19.92 (65, no SD)	None	None
University Associates (1986) Kalamazoo	Petitions: 12 m: *E* 25% (149) v. *C* 26% (174)	Self-reported delinquency: 4 m: *E* 15.90 (131, no SD) v. *C* 14.25 (146, no SD) 12 m: *E* 20.52 (131, no SD) v. *C* 16.82 (146, no SD)	None	None
University Associates (1986) Detroit	Petitions: 12 m: *E* 34% (124) v. *C* 32% (135)	Self-Reported delinquency:[20] 4 m: *E* 15.87 (115, no SD) v. *C* 19.42 (128, no SD) 12 m: *E* 19.50 (115, no SD) v. *C* 16.27 (128, no SD)	None	None
Curran et al. (1977)[21]	Petition/New offense: 12 m: *E* 63% (288) v. *C* 35% (306)	None	None	None

(continued)

Sherman et al. (2000) Juvenile property offenders	Offending: 12 m: *E* 78% (115) v. *C* 92% (124)	Offending rate: 12 m: *E* .068 v. *C* .067 (t = .573, d = .07) Mean reconvictions 12 m: *E* .69 (114, SD 2.1) v. *C* 1.02 (124, SD 2.68), d = .14 Self-Reported property crime: 12 m: *E* 21 (115) v. *C* 38 (124), t = 1.318, d = .23	Self-Reported violent crime: 12 m *E* 14 (115) v. *C* 20 (124), (t = .662, d = .16)	None
Sherman et al. (2000) Juvenile Shoplifters	Change in monthly offending: 12 m: *E* 81% (62) v. *C* 120% (73)	Monthly offending rate: 12 m: *E* .065 (62) v. *C* .046 (73), t = 1.095, d = .19 Mean reconvictions: 12 m: *E* .82 (62, SD 1.52) v. *C* .57 (73, SD 1.71), d = .15 Self-Reported property: 12 m: *E* 26 (62) v. *C* 67 (73), t = 1.361, d = .30	Self-reported violent: 12 m: *E* 3 (62) v. *C* 16 (73) t = 1.528, d = .51	None

Appendix (*continued*)

Study (Year)	Prevalence	Incidence	Severity	Latency
McCold and Wachtel (1998)[22]	Recidivism: 6 m: E 12% (107) v. C 21% (188) 12 m: E 25% (79) v. C 35% (143)	None	None	None
True (1973)	Re-offending: 2 m: E 33% (6) v. C 63% (8) 4 m: E 50% (6) v. C 75% (8)	None	None	None

Notes

1. We also conducted analyses with a "standardized one year follow-up," i.e., the outcome closest to twelve months. However, we found the difference in effect sizes between the one-year and longest follow-up for the prevalence data to be negligible. For incidence, severity, and self-report data, so few follow-up periods were included so that first effect, longest effect, and strongest effect meta-analyses yielded very similar estimates.

2. In these trials, assignment was then made to processing or to stay in the diversion program.

3. This represents the total number of the juveniles in the processing condition and the control condition we used in the meta-analysis. This would not reflect the total study sample if multiple comparison groups were involved that were not collapsed into a single comparison group, for example.

4. Other recidivism data were reported but not broken down for treatment versus comparison groups.

5. Note that this study was also included in Dunford et al.'s (1982) National Evaluation of Diversion projects, but the results are slightly different in that cross-site study.

6. Three-way F tests are reported for these data: at 6 m, $F = .7$ and at 12 m, $F = .48$ (2, 128 df). There is no F for the ITT analyses for latency.

7. Data are provided that combine outcomes at referral arrest (that gets youth into program) and any subsequent arrest.

8. Data presented on number of bookings for new offenses within 12 m per 100 cases handled; and net reduction from year one to year two, and combined referral offense and subsequent offense data.

9. Time × self-reported delinquency interactions reported for all sites but only statistically significant findings on the ten subscale items reported.

10. Multiple arrests also reported for felony only, and for misdemeanor-felony only.

11. F test for self-reported delinquency across three groups is .62 (2, 232). Koch also reported an ITT and TOT analysis and found no difference.

12. Blakely also conducted adjusted analyses for time at risk, but three group F tests run. Also presented self-reported delinquency, but three-group F used.

13. Davidson et al. did state they performed a 6 × 4 F test on self-reported delinquency with no significant condition or interaction effects.

14. Davidson et al. (1990) conducted similar analysis with self-reported delinquency as in 1987 and reported no significant finding.

15. Quay and Love (1977) also report TOT analysis that shows significant impact for treatment completers. They also conduct F test that combines referral type by mean offenses.

16. Emshoff and Blakely (1983) reported a two-group F for incarceration by combining the two treatment conditions.

17. Quincy (1981) did report three-month to six-month comparisons for both groups.

18. There is one conflicting number in the report (with one table showing C with 42 percent rather than 46 percent recidivism).

19. Smith et al. (2004) also report a non-significant F test for interaction for condition by time.

20. University Associates (1986) reported a non-significant three-way F test for self-report data.

21. Curran et al. (1977) reported many other analyses, but they did not include breakdown for experimental versus control groups.

22. We combined the violent and property offender analyses that had been reported separately by McCold and Wachtel (1998).

References

Baron, R. and F. Feeney. *Juvenile Diversion through Family Counseling*. Washington, DC: Government Printing Office, 1976.

Bauer, Michelle, Gilda Bordeaux, John Cole, William S. Davidson, Arnoldo Martinez, Christina Mitchell, and Dolly Singleton. "A Diversion Program for Juvenile Offenders: The Experience of Ingham County, Michigan." *Justice and Family Court Journal* (1980): 53–62.

Blakely, Craig H. "The Diversion of Juvenile Delinquents: A First Step toward the Dissemination of a Successful Innovation." PhD diss., Michigan State University (Psychology), Ann Arbor, MI.

Curran, J. T., R. Bonn, B. Johnson, C. Grenchanik, K. Moss, and M. Colitti. *Nassau County Probation Department Operation Juvenile Intercept Evaluation. Final Report*. New York: John Jay College of Criminal Justice, 1977.

Davidson II, William S., Robin Redner, Craig H. Blakely, Christina M. Mitchell, and James G. Emshoff. "Diversion of Juvenile Offenders: An Experimental Comparison." *Journal of Consulting and Clinical Psychology* 55, no. 1 (1987): 68–75.

Davidson II, William S., Robin Redner, Richard L. Amdur, and Christina M. Mitchell. *Alternative Treatments for Troubled Youth. The Case of Diversion from the Justice System*. New York: Plenum, 1990.

Dishion, T. J., J. McCord, and F. Poulin. "When Interventions Harm: Peer Groups and Problem Behavior." *American Psychologist* 54, no. 9 (1999): 755–64.

Dunford, F. W., D. W. Osgood, and H. F. Weichselbaum. *National Evaluation of Diversion Projects: Executive Summary*. Washington, DC: US Government Printing Office, 1982.

Emshoff, James G. and Craig H. Blakely. "The Diversion of Delinquent Youth: Family-Focused Intervention." *Children and Youth Services Review* 5 (1983): 343–56.

Gensheimer, L. K., J. P. Mayer, and R. Gottschalk. "Diverting Youth from the Juvenile Justice System: A Meta-Analysis of Intervention Efficacy." In *Youth Violence: Problems and Prospects*, edited by S. J. Apter and A. Goldstein, 39–57. Elmsford, NY: Pergamon, 1986.

Hintzen, Rachel, Keith Inouye, and Beryl Iramina. *Research Report. A Three Year Follow-Up Study of Project '75*. Manoa, Hawaii: University of Hawaii, School of Social Work, Social Welfare Development and Research Center, 1979.

Klein, Malcolm W. "Labeling Theory and Delinquency Policy: An Experimental Test." *Criminal Justice and Behavior* 13, no. 1 (1986): 47–79.

Koch, Randy J. "Community Service and Outright Release as Alternatives to Juvenile Court: An Experimental Evaluation." PhD diss., Michigan State University, Ann Arbor, MI.

Lipsey, M. W. and D. B. Wilson. *Practical Meta-Analysis*. Applied Social Research Methods Series (Vol. 49). Thousand Oaks, CA: Sage Publications, 2001.

McCold, P. and J. Wachtel. *Restorative Policing Experiment: The Bethlehem Pennsylvania Police Family Group Conferencing Project*. Washington, DC: US Department of Justice, National Institute of Justice, 1998.

Patrick, S. and R. Marsh. "Juvenile Diversion: Results of a Three Year Experimental Study." *Criminal Justice Policy Review* 16, no. 1 (2005): 59–73.

Petrosino, A. J. "What Works? Revisited Again: A Meta-Analysis of Randomized Experiments in Rehabilitation, Deterrence and Prevention." Doctoral diss., University Microfilms, Ann Arbor, MI, 1997.

Petrosino, A. J., C. Turpin-Petrosino, and S. Guckenburg. "Formal System Processing of Juveniles: Effects on Delinquency." *Campbell Systematic Reviews* (2010): 1.

Povitsky-Stickle, W. P., N. M. Connell, D. M. Wilson, and D. C. Gottfredson. "An Experimental Evaluation of Teen Courts." *Journal of Experimental Criminology* 4, no. 2 (2008): 137–63.

Puzzanchera, C. and M. Sickmund. *Juvenile Court Statistics 2005. Report.* Washington, DC: US Department of Justice, Office of Justice Programs, Office of Juvenile Justice and Delinquency Prevention, 2008.

Quay, H. C. and C. T. Love. "The Effect of a Juvenile Diversion Program on Rearrests." *Criminal Justice and Behavior* 4, no. 4 (1977): 377–96.

Quincy, Ronald L. 1981. "An Evaluation of the Effectiveness of the Youth Service Bureau Diversion Concept: A Study of Labeling Theory as Related to Juvenile Justice System Penetration." PhD diss., Michigan State University, Ann Arbor, MI.

Schur, E. *Radical Nonintervention: Rethinking the Delinquency Problem.* Englewood Cliffs, NJ: Prentice-Hall, 1973.

Severy, L. J. and J. M. Whitaker. "Juvenile Diversion—An Experimental Analysis of Effectiveness." *Evaluation Review* 6, no. 6 (1982): 753–74.

Sherman, L. W., H. Strang, and D. J. Woods. *Recidivism Patterns in the Canberra Reintegrative Shaming Experiments (RISE).* Canberra, Australia: Australian National University Press, 2000.

Smith, P., M. Bohnstedt, and T. Tompkins. "Juvenile Diversion Evaluation—Report of an Experimental Study." In *Pretrial Services Annual Journal,* edited by D. Alan Henry, 118–40. Washington, DC: Pretrial Services Resource Center, 1979.

Smith, E. P., A. M. Wolf, D. M. Cantillon, O. Thomas, and W. S. Davidson. "The Adolescent Diversion Project: 25 Years of Research on an Ecological Model of Intervention." *Journal of Offender Rehabilitation* 27, no. 2/3 (2004): 29–48.

True, D. A. "Evaluative Research in a Police Juvenile Diversion Program." PhD diss., University of Oregon, Ann Arbor, MI.

University Associates. *Diversion in Michigan. Final Report.* Lansing, MI: Michigan State University, University Associates, 1986.

Weisburd, D., L. W. Sherman, and A. J. Petrosino. *Registry of Randomized Criminal Justice Experiments in Sanctions.* Unpublished Report, Rutgers University, University of Maryland and Crime Control Institute, 1990.

7

Experiments in Criminal Sanctions: Labeling, Defiance, and Restorative Justice

Lawrence W. Sherman

What effect does punishment have on the punished? The best answer to this question is "it depends." Sometimes punishment causes less future crime by the punished. Sometimes it causes more. Sometimes punishment makes no difference. That much is well-established (Sherman, 1993). But *why* these effects vary so greatly across similar tests with different samples remains largely unknown. Even *when* or *with whom* these different effects will occur remains largely unpredictable.

One reason we know so little is that the most prominent behavioral theories of criminal sanction effects account for only *one* possible effect of punishment: the one they predict. Deterrence doctrine explains why punishment reduces crime by the punished, as the "specific deterrence" hypothesis predicts. Labeling theory explains why sanctions increase crime, as the "labeling" hypothesis predicts. Neither deterrence nor labeling theory, however, can offer compelling explanations for observed failures of their own predictions. That also leaves them helpless to predict when sanctions will have different effects on individual criminality.

Acknowledgments. This essay was prepared with the support of the Regulatory Institutions Network, College of Asia and the Pacific, Australian National University, and the Australian Research Council. The author is indebted to Heather Strang, Malcolm Mearns, Linda Gosnell, and John Braithwaite for their work on the RISE Project.

More recent theories are designed to predict variable effects of punishment. That is, they offer a multi-dimensional framework for predicting when punishment will reduce or increase offending. While they still lack substantial evidence, they are at least addressing the wide range of offender reactions to the same kinds of punishments. These theories frame criminal sanctions as a complex social interaction, about which many nuanced questions must be asked. Does it matter, for example, *how* offenders are punished, or how *much* they are punished, or whether they escape punishment entirely? How much does the certainty, severity, or celerity (speed) of any punishment affect the future behavior of those punished? Is future offending affected by the perceptions that punished people have about the *fairness* with which punishment is generally dispensed? Does a punished offender's sense of belonging to, or exclusion from, a society modify the extent to which punishment reduces or increases future offending? Why do criminal sanctions often appear largely irrelevant in relation to more powerful causes of people committing criminal acts?

These questions are among the most important issues in criminology. They lie at the nexus of the science of law breaking and the science of reactions to law breaking (Sutherland, 1924). Yet they have been very hard to answer, for reasons of both measurement and causal inference. The problem of *measurement* is that many of the nuances of how punishments are delivered and received are difficult to observe and document. They consist partly of how criminal sanctions are dispensed, and partly of the reactions offenders have to agents of criminal law and their actions, as well as the emotions punishment evokes in offenders. The problem of *causal inference* is the difficulty of separating the effect of punishments from other causes of criminal behavior. If, for example, living in a high-crime area causes more police patrol, that can increase the risk of punishment for each offense, or even for no offense (Stinchcombe, 1963). Yet people in high-crime areas may also be more likely to commit crimes regardless of whether they are punished.

In recent decades, criminology has received more answers to these questions from research using better measurement, and with stronger evidence for inferring causation. Unfortunately, it is rare that both kinds of enhancement are combined in the same studies. The best measurement of how people perceive the agents of criminal law (e.g., Tyler, 1990) has been used in studies that offer only a weak basis for inferring causation, as distinct from correlations, of offending and criminal sanctions. Conversely, the best designs for inferring causation (e.g., Sherman and

Smith, 1992) have been unable to measure the most critical dimensions of offender perceptions and emotions.

Thus while our theories may be better, our predictions are still inadequate. To a large extent, we remain unable to predict when punishment will backfire and when it will work. Achieving better predictions is likely to require both more powerful causal inference and better measurements of causal processes. A major advance in causal inference can start with greater use of longitudinal randomized experiments, in contrast to observed correlations at single points in time. A major advance in measurement would be to gather more information from (consenting) offenders while they are experiencing punishment processes, including interviews or even biological measures.

The goal of this essay is to map out these main strengths and weaknesses of the available and possible evidence on the effects of punishment on the punished. It begins by describing the three main theories of those effects, and their demanding requirements for measurement of causal processes. It then examines the measurement of those processes in the most powerful tests of sanction effects: the evidence from randomized field experiments. It first considers the power of causal inference from randomized experiments. It then considers the challenges of measurement of causal mechanisms within any research design, but especially within experiments. The chapter concludes with proposals that can help us fill in the "black box" of causal processes when criminal sanctions are randomly assigned. These proposals can be combined as a long-term research strategy for building closer links between predicting and explaining criminal sanction effects.

Three Reasons for Sanctions to Backfire—or Succeed

The hypothesis that penal sanctions are a *cause* of crime, rather than a deterrent, is central to three different streams of criminological theory. Each stream predicts that punishment will *increase* crime by those who are punished, rather than deterring it. Each stream predicts the opposite of the effects predicted by the utilitarian "rational choice" doctrines of Cesare Beccaria, Jeremy Bentham, and their progeny. This much they hold in common. They differ not in what they predict, but in why they predict it.

The three different causal mechanisms they offer to explain the same effects are (1) perceptions of *identity* (labeling theory), (2) perceptions of *legitimacy* (procedural justice and defiance theory), and (3) perceptions of *integration* into group membership (which is central to restorative justice theory). At the same time, each theory offers an implicit explanation of why punishment might succeed in reducing crime, as well as why punishment may fail to have any impact at all. That explanation is the absence of the conditions cited that explain or predict criminogenic effects of punishment. Each of these three mechanisms is presented from both sides of their logic in the three sections below.

It is important to note, however, that these theories are not the only reasons punishment may affect future crime. Meeting gang members in prison, for example, may be a turning point for future affiliation with gangs (Jacobs, 1978), causing crime for reasons unrelated to the three theories cited below. Conversely, losing ties to co-offenders after serving a prison term by being sent to live in a different city may reduce the chances of repeat offending (Kirk, 2009). The three theories discussed here are selected because of their association with the labeling tradition, rather than from a comprehensive review of the effects of punishment on crime.

In order to understand and compare each of these three theoretical perspectives, it is useful to imagine a footrace. In this race, three runners start at exactly the same line, then run exactly the same distance on perfectly level ground. Any alteration of those conditions would make the race unfair. Similarly, if we would compare the capacity of these three theories to fit the facts of punishment effects, we must imagine research designs that provide measures of causal mechanisms that have equal validity in measuring the theoretical *constructs* (Cook and Campbell, 1979) or mechanisms they each propose. For that reason, each theory is briefly summarized, with an emphasis on the theoretical constructs they imply should be measured in empirical research.

Identity: Labeling Theory

The oldest of the three streams is labeling theory, which is actually a mix of theories on both crime and punishment. A labeling theory of repeat offending makes the primary causal mechanism the offender's self-labeling based on their perceptions of their own *identity* as a criminal (Lemert, 1951). A second stream of theory, in contrast, explains why some people and not others are punished (Becker, 1963; Stinchcombe, 1963; Piliavin and Briar, 1964; Black, 1970). That is, it explains official labeling of people by governmental authorities as offenders, regardless of how those people view themselves. In this chapter, I focus on the labeling theory of offending, as distinct from the labeling theory of punishment. Thus our focus is on offenders' self-labeling and identity, and not the selection bias of authorities.

Labeling theory was in its prime in the 1960s, when ideology was often more important to criminology than evidence. The ideology was rebellious, with good causes for rebellion: racial segregation in the United States, apartheid in South Africa, class and racial inequalities in criminal punishment, police brutality, and (in the United States) police killings of citizens. Labeling was also empathetic, with an effort to make the powerful understand how the world looks from the perspective of powerlessness. In their attempt to "walk a mile in the shoes" of some very oppressed people, labeling theorists imagined a demoralized offender *internally* accepting the self-stigma of a label as "criminal."

This hypothesis was derived from the intellectual tradition of George Herbert Mead (1913), who suggested that people derive identity from social interactions. He described our identity as the "looking glass self." Mead's social psychology predicted that we see ourselves as others see us, and act accordingly. Social interactions, in this framework, provide a mirror in which we see ourselves. This view is over-simplified if described as a perfect correlation, which Mead never intended. If people treat us as if we are smart, then we may be more likely—but not guaranteed—to see ourselves as smart. If people treat us as if we are dumb, then we may be more likely to see ourselves as dumb. But just as we may look different every time we look into a mirror, we may find other people treat us differently in different situations, with different kinds of people present, different tasks at hand, and different social and economic contexts.

Critics of the labeling approach (Taylor, et al., 1973) focused primarily on its determinism. They rejected the idea that people would be willing to accept the labeling of the state, even with the hint of defiance implied by the causal mechanism of labeling: "if they say I'm a criminal, then I will really prove them right!" Alvin Gouldner (1970) derided this view of offenders as requiring a view of the offender as a "man on his back." The competing explanation of "techniques of neutralization" (Sykes and Matza, 1957) rebutted labeling theory, in favor of a strategy of counter labeling: "it is society that is wrong," the offender contends, "not me."

This debate was not driven very much by evidence. Rather, it was largely a clash of theories competing on the basis of ideology, intuition, and logical claims. Some of it was based on rich qualitative evidence from ethnographic accounts (e.g., Whyte, 1943). None of it, so far, has met the standards of a fair-race competition based on equal empirical standards. So let us be clear about the minimum standards for comparing causal mechanisms.

Standards for Testing Theories

As Karl Popper (1968) suggests, theories cannot be proven; they can only be falsified. Thus labeling theory, like any other theory of punishment effect, must be tested in a way that makes the test *possible to fail*. It can only be compared to other theories when they are given an equal chance to be falsified by a test. This means that there must be specific measures of changes in the offender's self-identification that will show whether or not the offender accepts the societal label as a criminal and decides to commit more crime based upon that acceptance. If it is not possible to construct such measures, then labeling fails to meet Popper's definition of a theory. Whether or not it is possible is the question to which we return in the third section of this essay.

Legitimacy: Defiance and Procedural Justice

The newest of the three streams is defiance theory, which cites offender *emotions* about the *legitimacy* of punishment as the primary mechanism causing increases or persistence in crime after punishment (Sherman, 2003; 2010). This approach builds heavily on procedural justice theory (Tyler, 1990), as well as reintegrative shaming theory (Braithwaite, 1989) and the contextual theory of shame, emotions, and violence by Thomas Scheff and Suzanne Retzinger (1991). The three central propositions of the initial statement of defiance as a *dependent* variable (an effect) were these (Sherman, 1993: 460):

Defiance occurs under four conditions, all of which are necessary.

1. The offender defines a criminal sanction as unfair.
2. The offender is poorly bonded to or alienated from the sanctioning agent or the community the agent represents.
3. The offender defines the sanction as stigmatizing and rejecting a person, not a law-breaking act.
4. The offender denies or refuses to acknowledge the shame the sanction has actually caused him to suffer.

The initial statement of defiance identified two alternative conditions under which offenders would define sanctions as unfair (Sherman, 1993: 460):

1. The sanctioning agent behaves with disrespect for the offender, or for the group to which the offender belongs, regardless of how fair the sanction is on substantive grounds.
2. The sanction is substantively arbitrary, discriminatory, excessive, undeserved, or otherwise objectively unjust.

These building blocks then predicted three reactions to punishment that offenders define as unfair (Sherman, 1993: 461). Point 2 in the following quotation can be seen as a "Defiance effect" of punishment causing more crime by the punished person:

1. When poorly bonded offenders accept the shame an unfair stigmatizing sanction provokes, the sanction will be *irrelevant* or possibly even deterrent to future rates of offending.
2. When poorly bonded offenders deny the shame they feel and respond with rage, the unfair stigmatizing sanction will *increase* their future rates of offending. This unacknowledged shame leads to an emotion of angry pride at defying the punishment. That pride predisposes the defiant offender to repeat the sanctioned conduct, symbolically labeling the sanctions or sanctioners, and not the offender's own acts, as truly shameful and morally deserving of punishment. . . .
3. The full shame-crime sequence does not occur, however, when a well-bonded offender defines a sanction as unfair. . . .

In the restatement of defiance theory (Sherman, 2010), defiance is also presented as an *independent* variable, which predicts the increase or persistence in offending as follows:

1. "Defiance" must be defined more broadly as a moral intuition (Sunstein, 2008) of an obligation or justification to defy the status quo, and not just as an effect of the administration of justice. That effect is included in the range of behavior that Defiance can explain as a general theory of criminology.
2. Defiance is therefore an independent variable, an emotional state of "angry pride," vengeance, sorrow, empathy or cold determination to disagree that can cause behaviour against the status quo.

The complexity of these mechanisms could make them much harder to measure than the simper formulation of labeling theory. Yet the constructs themselves may be closer to the surface of offenders' discourse about how they are feeling. These are also matters to which we return below in the discussion of measuring causal mechanisms.

The related theories of procedural justice and legitimacy are also derived from moral sentiments, intuitions, or "feelings" that some would call emotions. Tom Tyler (1990) and his colleagues (e.g., Tyler and Huo, 2002) have a longstanding series of measures for elaborating on some of the elements of defiance theory, but making the perceptions of fair treatment central to the theory. In this framework, it may not be necessary to probe an offender's emotions; it may be sufficient to say that in the absence of fair treatment, offenders did not feel obligated to obey the law. This is not about anger; it is about a failure of the state to persuade its citizens to comply with a rule of law for the state's sake, as well as the citizens'.

Group Membership: Reintegration and Restorative Justice

As a central component of defiance theory, John Braithwaite's (1989) theory of reintegrative shaming is embedded in the more elaborate requirements of defiance. Yet parsimony is a virtue in theory building. Reintegrative shaming, like labeling, has the virtue of a simpler formulation of the causal mechanism, at least in its initial (1989) formulation. That mechanism is what Braithwaite calls the "family model" of discipline and compliance: hate the sin but love the sinner. Reject the conduct as unacceptable, but do not reject the person from membership in the social group. Shame the act, but not the actor. Make the actor feel ashamed of committing the act, but not of themselves as a person. Always make them feel proud of their membership in the social group, and reinforce their identity as a member of that group by praise and encouragement for the good traits and acts of the actor.

In order to predict increases in crime caused by punishment, Braithwaite develops the concept of "stigmatic shaming." This concept allows the theory to predict increases in offending from punishment suggesting hate for the sinner as well as the sin, punishments excluding the offender from the social group, and punishments that generally fail to reintegrate a group member who has broken the rules. This prediction depends, theoretically, on the concepts of "reintegrative shaming" and "stigmatic shaming" remaining mutually exclusive. In order to falsify the theory, one could first show empirically that these concepts are not mutually exclusive. Then one could show that even with reintegrative shaming, crime could be increased by any attempt to cast shame on an offense.

In predicting the conditions under which punishment increases crime, Braithwaite (1989) places stigmatic shaming in the driver's seat. Punishment causes crime not by self-image, as labeling has it, but by exclusion and severed social bonds. Punishers can avoid more crime, Braithwaite predicts, by punishing in an inclusionary way, by building and enhancing bonds to mainstream society. In this formulation, stigmatic shaming replaces labeling as a competing explanation for the same prediction. It also offers a corresponding explanation for why punishment may also succeed in causing less crime, when it is observed to do so.

In his theory of restorative justice, Braithwaite (2002) emphasizes that converse prediction to stigmatic shaming theory. Maintaining the theoretical distinction between stigma and reintegration, restorative justice conferencing (RJC) theory embraces a wide range of policy initiatives from around the world as illustrative of either "restorative values" or "restorative processes." The restorative values support attempts to reintegrate people because those attempts reflect a shared belief in the goodness of that goal. The restorative processes are the concrete actions that actually push offenders towards reintegration, whether or not they succeed. Both these ideas go beyond the family model of discipline, into a range of ways for people to come together in response to a crime. The crime victim(s), offender(s), their families and supporters create a mission-focused community in order to democratically—by consensus if possible—determine what should be done about a specific crime, and who should do what.

Restorative justice, like reintegrative shaming (but unlike labeling), is therefore a theory that predicts the *variable* effects of a sanction on future offending by a sanctioned criminal. It predicts that there will be less frequent or serious offending when restorative justice is used than when it is not. Like procedural justice, it is stated in the opposite logical form from labeling or defiance. The latter theories predict *more* future harm from the presence of something *bad* about punishment. Restorative justice predicts *less* future harm from something *good* about punishment: reintegration.

In order to falsify reintegration theory, a test would need to show that the RJC process had occurred, and that it caused more (or no less) future harm than when RJC had not happened. Unlike pure reintegrative shaming theory, this test allows the measurement of causal mechanism to focus on the observable RJC process, as distinct from the offenders' emotions or identity.

Causal Inference and Randomized Experiments

The best way to test a theory is with a good experiment. A good experiment on theories of criminal sanction effects needs four things: (1) a statistically powerful sample size and research design (Cohen, 1988; Weisburd, 1993), (2) random assignment (Boruch, 1997) of visible criminal sanctions (versus less visible, qualitatively different, or no sanctions), (3) valid measurement of causal hypotheses inside the "black box" of "micro-mediation" (Cook and Campbell, 1979), and (4) reliable measurement of future criminal behavior. Few, if any, experiments in criminal sanctions have ever fully met all four of those standards. Most of those that come close are discussed elsewhere in this volume. This section highlights some of the evidence, plus some newer experiments, to distill what we do and don't know about the effects of criminal sanctions on criminal behavior.

Its purpose is to set the stage for proposals for improving the measurement of causal constructs, presented in the next section.

This substantive review of randomized experiments does not claim mutual exclusivity of any experiments for any of the theories reviewed above. Many experiments can and should be included as part of the evidence base for more than one theory, because the results are consistent with the theory's predictions. The fact that this remains possible is testament not to the power of causal inference from randomized experiments, but rather to their lack of measurement of causal mechanisms.

Why Randomized Experiments?

The answer to this question has been offered elsewhere at length (Farrington, 1983; Cook and Campbell 1979; Sherman et al, 1997). A brief summary of the answer must refer to the idea of competing explanations. Observational research, in which the study does not manipulate any of the many potential causes of a phenomenon, may be unable to rule out several competing explanations. Suppose that people who eat more vegetables live longer than people who don't (a prediction). Yet we would not know from that observation whether eating more vegetables *causes* increased longevity (an explanation). The correlation between vegetables and longevity can be "spurious" in the sense that some third factor may cause both longevity and a preference for vegetables. Observational research cannot rule out such competing explanations unless they have perfectly specified the theoretical structure of any outcome, such as life expectancy. Perfect specification is a tall order. Most people concede that it is impossible to achieve, despite continuing efforts to do so.

Once a potential cause can be *manipulated* in a study, it can rule out all competing explanations. If the presence versus absence of a potential cause can be made to vary independently of all other factors normally affecting that variable, then anything correlated with it can be seen as causal impact. We may thus "infer" causation, to a measured extent (called an "effect size") of changes in the outcome caused by the manipulated variable. The logical power of eliminating competing theories is so great that some observers make a sloganeering claim about causal inference: that there is "no causation without manipulation."

Creative statisticians have recently proposed a variety of ways in which one potential cause can be manipulated as an "instrument" without random assignment (see, e.g., Angrist, 2006). Yet random assignment by a research team arguably still remains at least the "bronze standard" of causal inference (Berk, 2005). While other kinds of research designs yield useful insights about labeling and sanction effects, this chapter is designed to focus just on what we know from the research using the bronze standard.

The focus on randomly assigned criminal sanctions gets us half-way to our goal. It gives us prediction, but not explanation. It shows what the causal effect is, but not how it works. It says that doing Treatment A to Group B1 (called the experimental group) causes Outcome C to happen, on average, in comparison to doing Treatment Not A to Group B2 (called a control group)—in one or endless ways. But it does not tell us whether doing A to B1 triggers a labeling process, a defiant reaction, a reintegration, or many other possible processes that occur between the criminal sanction and the future criminal behavior.

The remainder of this section summarizes some of the leading experiments that provide causal inference about the effect of sanctions on future crime. These experiments then provide the basis for the next section's assessment of measures of explanatory mechanisms proposed by the three streams of theory.

Experiments Testing Labeling

The prediction of more crime caused by sanctions (relative to no sanctions) has been tested in many randomized experiments. Petrosino and his colleagues (2010) have contributed a systematic review of twenty nine of those tests involving juvenile offenders—those that randomly assigned either diversion from criminal justice "system processing" or inclusion in it. Other juvenile tests have assigned different kinds of processing, such as Anne Schneider's (1990) random assignment of restitution during processing in juvenile court; these experiments included one random assignment of time behind bars versus no incarceration.

Adult offenders have also been employed in randomized field tests of labeling theory predictions. One randomized experiment in Switzerland compared adult offenders convicted of relatively minor offenses who were assigned to go to prison or perform community service (Killias et al., 2000). Six U.S. experiments randomly assigned adults to be arrested or cautioned for arrest in minor domestic violence cases (see Sherman, 1992). Four restorative justice experiments in Australia randomly assigned the creation of a criminal record (Strang et al. 2012).

These forty-one randomized experiments are not a complete list of all experiments randomly assigning criminal sanctions (see also Weisburd, 1993). They do comprise, however, of a substantial illustration of the range of offenses and offenders that have been used to test "labeling theory," broadly defined. While some of these experiments can be considered tests of other theories, all of them randomly assigned either the *use* or *intensity* of criminal sanctions.

The results of these experiments suggest two patterns. One is that the juvenile experiments generally show less offending with no labeling than when criminal sanctions are imposed (see Sherman, 1997: Table 8.5.b). There are exceptions, but the Petrosino et al. (2010) review generally compels this conclusion across both primary outcome measures of offending: the percentage of offenders with one or more new arrests (prevalence) and the number of such new arrests (incidence). This is despite the fact that in one of the key Australian experiments they included (see Strang et al., 2012), a later analysis based only on convictions (rather than arrests) showed a very different result. The later study found a strong deterrent effect of prosecution relative to diversion—the opposite of the labeling hypothesis. Petrosino et al. (2010) included in their calculation (accurately based on the initial analysis posted online by Sherman, Strang and Woods in 2000). Schneider's comparisons of Boise, Idaho juveniles who received jail versus restitution also failed to show any higher rates of offending for those sentenced to jail. But when juveniles receiving sanctions creating a criminal record are compared with juveniles treated in ways that avoid that label, the results are consistent with the theory.

However, this is not so for adults. The pattern for adult offenders is results that are far less consistent than results of juvenile diversion studies. In several of these studies, the results even change over time—a pattern that is not consistent with labeling theory predictions. In the Swiss experiment, the initial findings showed that people who were assigned to jail had more recidivism than people assigned to community service (Killias et al., 2000). Yet in a multi-year follow-up, Martin Killias (2010) reported that the effects had reversed: those who had been imprisoned had lower recidivism rates than those who were sent to community service.

Similarly, in the Milwaukee domestic violence experiment (Sherman et al. 1991), the effects of arrest on repeat offending reversed over time. Contrary to the labeling theory prediction, the effect of arrest on domestic violence was to reduce repeat offending over the first six months; after that the pattern reversed to show a long-term escalation of offending caused by arrest. The end result was what labeling theory predicted should have happened right away—an increase in offending following the arrest experience. Because labeling implicitly predicts an immediate change in identity, it is inconsistent with a delayed increase in offending, after an initial deterrent effect. Thus the Milwaukee experiment can also be seen as a falsification of labeling theory.

More generally, the effects of criminal sanctions on adults are unpredictably diverse. Both restorative justice and domestic violence experiments show this variation. In two adult experiments comparing prosecution with a criminal record to diversion to restorative justice, Heather Strang et al. (2012) report opposite effects. For adults arrested for drinking and driving, prosecution caused substantially less recidivism than diversion, thus falsifying the labeling effect. For adults (and juveniles) arrested for violence, diversion had substantially less recidivism than prosecution—a finding consistent with labeling theory.

The effects of arrest on adult domestic violence show even more dispersion of results. In Minneapolis, Miami, and Colorado Springs, arrest for domestic violence deterred official measures of repeat offending, thereby falsifying labeling theory (Sherman, 1992). In Omaha, Milwaukee, and Charlotte, arrests did not deter domestic violence, which was also a falsification of labeling. Yet in Milwaukee, Omaha, and Miami, a subgroup analysis showed that arrest increased recidivism among unemployed offenders, while reducing it among employed offenders.

It may well be that labeling theory is correct for some kinds of offenders and not others. Yet nothing in the theory makes that prediction. As a one-size-fits-all theory, it is ill-equipped to account for these variable results. Yet at least the theory preceded the experiments. In the next section, we may see an unfair advantage with a theory that grew out of the same experiments.

Experiments Testing Defiance and Legitimacy

The prediction of more crime being caused by a defiant reaction to punishment has been tested by some of the same experiments included in the tests of labeling theory above. The subset of those experiments testing defiance and legitimacy is more selective. The criterion for inclusion in this section is some measurement of the factors these theories predict will alter the probability of sanctions deterring or escalating crime. While Tyler's (1990) procedural justice theory preceded the experiments, Sherman's (1993) defiance theory was based on them. Thus a better test of this line of theory is what *followed* the introduction of the theory, when it was tested in the Australian restorative justice experiments.

The tests of defiance theory, by design, fit the facts of the experiments from which it was derived. In the comparison of sanction effects on offenders with weak versus stronger bonds to social institutions, all three (of the six) domestic violence arrest experiments with social bonding data found a consistent pattern (Sherman, 1992, 1993). Those suspects who were unemployed or unmarried were made *more* likely to recidivate by arrest. Those who were made *less* likely to recidivate by arrest were those who were employed, married, or both. This pattern was observed across three different sites with three different predominant ethnic groups—although with a stronger moderating effect of marriage than of employment. In Miami-Dade, the predominant ethnic group was Hispanic, who by law could only be included in the arrest on probable cause if they were married. In Milwaukee, the predominant ethnic group in the experiment was African American, with both marriage and employment predicting the effect of arrest. In Omaha, the predominant ethnic group was white, with employment the best predictor of the effect of arrest. Even at the neighborhood level in Milwaukee, the effect of employment and single-parent households as a proportion of the population predicted the effect of arrest.

The more impressive tests of defiance theory are the results of experiments conducted after the theory was published. These tests offer both confirmation and some falsification of defiance theory, at least in the absence of better measurement. In Canberra, the effects of diversion from prosecution for Aboriginals into RJCs were highly criminogenic (Sherman et al., 2006). This may be due to the fact that they experienced the conferences as more of a labeling process than prosecution in court. Nonetheless, labeling theory was falsified, and the defiant effect of prosecution was not found relative to diversion. These findings were limited to the property and violent crime experiments, in which white offenders had completely different reactions from the Aboriginals.

In the Canberra drinking–driving experiment, Tyler et al. (2007) reported that among those offenders surveyed who experienced RJCs as being more procedurally fair than prosecution, there was lower recidivism. But among *all* cases randomly assigned to RJCs, there was a *higher* rate of recidivism than among those who were sent to court and acquired a criminal record (Strang et al., 2012). In this case, the evidence is more ambiguous than with the Aboriginal offenders, who are clearly more generally alienated from white society (on a wide range of measures) than the nearly 100 percent white adult sample of the drinking–driving experiment. In some ways, the Tyler finding supports procedural justice theory. Yet the conclusion suggests that the theory may depend more on the predispositions of the offenders than on the nature of the criminal sanctions—or at least on the interaction of the two.

Experiments Testing RJC

A different way to examine the three theories is to compare them while holding constant key characteristics of the randomly assigned sanctioning experience. That strategy can be achieved by considering all twelve of the randomized experiments in face-to-face RJC. These tests provide a highly consistent test of Braithwaite's (2002) theory of restorative justice across 3,000 cases on three continents (Strang et al. 2012), both with and without criminal records being created in cases assigned to an RJC treatment. These experiments were consistent across several dimensions. First, the same trainers trained all of the people conducting the conferences. Second, most of the people facilitating the conferences were police officers. Third, in every experiment, the conference facilitators asked offenders and victims for consent prior to random assignment, creating high levels of completion of treatments as assigned. Fourth, in every experiment the comparison was to identical cases in offense type and stage of the criminal process for which RJCs were not made available. Fifth, all but one of the twelve randomized trials had a personal victim of the offender in the conference, the exception being the drinking–driving experiment.

These experiments also had differences, however, that were created by design. There were four experiments that compared prosecution to diversion; two that compared diversion with and without RJC; and six that added RJC to conventional justice for a comparison to that justice without RJC. There were four experiments composed exclusively of juvenile offenders and eight with adult offenders. There were four experiments in which RJC occurred after a guilty plea but before sentencing; two in which RJC occurred after sentencing (one in prison sentences and the other in community sentences); and six in which RJC occurred prior to or instead of prosecution. Seven of the samples included at least some violent crimes, while five were 100 percent violent. Six included some property crimes, while four were 100 percent property.

The major limitation of these experiments is that most of them had relatively low-statistical power—the ability to detect a true difference as not likely to have been due to chance (Cohen, 1988). All of the experiments did achieve the minimum David Farrington (1983) threshold of at least fifty cases per treatment group. Yet the probability of detecting a statistically significant difference of a *small* effect size was generally far below 80 percent, the conventional minimum for a two-tailed statistical test (meaning either negative or positive results would be of interest).

This risk is even greater with a more conservative measure of repeat offending: convictions rather than arrests. Joanna Shapland and her colleagues (2008) applied this measure to seven of the experiments, all of which found fewer reconvictions after random assignment to RJC than to the control groups. Not one of these individual findings was statistically significant on that measure. On the other hand, the combined meta-analysis of the seven tests showed that the mean effect size, while small, was clearly significant ($p = .01$) (Shapland et al., 2008: Figure 2.6, p. 27). Shapland et al. (2008: 64) reported that the cost-effectiveness of the RJC was also very large, at over eight times more cost of crime prevented by RJC than the cost of delivering RJCs.

Thus despite the weak *power* of the RJC tests, a high level of *consistency* is evident in the findings of reductions in repeat offending. In addition to the weighted meta-analyses, the raw vote count makes a strong statement in relation to a Bayesian perspective on repeated results. In ten of the twelve randomized experiments, offenders assigned to RJC have less repeat offending than the controls. And in ten of the eleven tests of RJC with a personal victim scheduled to attend each meeting with the offenders, the intention-to-treat with RJC group had less offending than the offenders assigned to the control condition. This consistency can be deemed to exceed the evidence for both labeling and defiance theory.

Comparing Three Theories with Experimental Evidence

The "consistency" results of a race among the three theories of interest may be judged on the basis of answers to three questions. First, we can ask how the evidence on predicted effects of RJC compares to the predicted effects of labeling theory. Second, we can ask how the predicted effects of RJC compare to the predicted effects of defiance theory. Third, we can ask how the predicted effects of labeling compare to the consistency of predictions of effects based on defiance theory.

1. Labeling Theory versus Restorative Conferencing

The twelve randomized experiments in RJC were assembled under a Campbell Collaboration protocol for a systematic review (Strang and Sherman, 2005). It is therefore appropriate to compare their results to the Petrosino et al. (2010) review of twenty-nine juvenile diversion experiments, which was also prepared under the peer-reviewed systematic review processes of the Campbell Collaboration. The Petrosino team's meta-analysis of twenty seven of the twenty-nine experiments found that eleven of the twenty-seven (41 percent) randomized trials reported higher rates of *prevalence* of repeat offending among the juveniles diverted from prosecution than among the juveniles who were processed formally. By contrast, only four of the twelve (25 percent) randomized trials of RJC showed increases in offending prevalence with the treatment predicted to reduce offending (Strang, 2013). This comparison is consistent with the conclusion that reintegration theory is more often accurate in predicting repeat offending results than labeling theory. This conclusion is even more solid when we recall that two of the labeling tests are also included in the RJC meta-analysis.

That conclusion, however, is not found by using offending *frequency*, rather than the prevalence (percentage) of one-or-more repeat offences, as the criterion measure of prediction. In the Petrosino team's test of labeling theory, the increased recidivism frequency prediction of prosecution over diversion was falsified in only one of the seven experiments reporting frequency data. While the RJC results are falsified in only one out of ten experiments with personal victims present, and in two of twelve with or without victims present, the RJC evidence is not much more consistent than the frequency evidence on labeling theory. Its main advantage is that there are five more tests of offending frequency for reintegration theory (twelve versus seven, or 71 percent more) than for juvenile diversion experiments.

It is also important to note that in the Petrosino team's comparison of prevalence rates with the *longest time period* available in each of the twenty-seven randomized controlled trials of juvenile diversion, the average effect was a small but statistically significant reduction in repeat offending from diversion—just as labeling theory predicts. Yet the evidence still ran the other way in eight of the twenty-seven tests (30 percent), or slightly more than the 25 percent of tests of offending prevalence that falsified reintegration theory.

Nonetheless, there are good theoretical reasons to prefer the prevalence results to the frequency results. While public policy analysis can properly focus on the total amount of harm (including frequency) caused by offenders sanctioned in different ways, labeling theory is by definition a prediction of prevalence, not frequency. Labeling predicts how an individual responds to a sanction. Its prediction is that more people will keep offending if they are labeled than if they are not. Labeling does not present any clear theoretical mechanism for the frequency of offending. It merely focuses on persistence in offending. On that basis, the combination of initial and longest offending prevalence effects of diversion can be compared to the two-year standard period effects of RJC. This comparison gives RJC at least marginal superiority over labeling. Only two of twelve tests falsified the RJC predictions, versus eleven (or eight) of twenty-seven tests falsifying labeling theory. While this conclusion could change with the accumulation of more evidence, it is at least a template for using experiments to assess theoretically based predictions of outcomes—if not of underlying causal mechanisms.

2. Defiance Theory versus Restorative Conferencing

A comparison of underlying theoretical mechanisms, however, is essential in comparing RJC and defiance theory. In this comparison, as in labeling and RJC, both theories predict the same outcomes from the same tests. But in this comparison, fully 100 percent of the randomized tests of defiance theory after it was developed are found in the RJC experiments. Fortunately, the measurement needed to distinguish between the essential theoretical arguments is available in the RJC experiments. This evidence is found in the offender interviews, including the recently completed ten-year follow-up of the randomly assigned cases (Strang et al., 2011). These cases come from four experiments: proactive arrests for driving with excessive blood alcohol content ($N = 900$), arrests of young people up to age thirty for violent crimes ($N = 121$ persons), arrests of persons under age eighteen for property crimes against personal victims ($N = 249$ persons), and arrests of persons under age eighteen for shoplifting in stores employing security guards ($N = 143$ persons).

The ten-year follow-up interviews built upon two earlier waves of interviews, one immediately after the conclusion of the court process or the RJC, and the other two years later. The cumulative response rates to at least one of the three interviews was 88 percent for the drinking–driving experiment, 83 percent for the violence experiment, 89 percent for the personal victim property crime experiment, and 87 percent for the shoplifting experiment. In future analyses, all three waves of interviews will be employed to provide estimates of the theoretical mechanisms inside the "black box" of offender reactions to their randomly assigned treatment paths. The present discussion is based only on the ten-year follow-up, in order to simplify the comparison. It does so, however, at the cost of lower response rates than from the cumulative evidence. These ten-year findings draw on a 62 percent response from drinking–driving arrestees, 56 percent response from violent crime arrestees, 60 percent response from the personal property crime arrestees, and 59 percent from the shoplifting arrestees. These response rates are less than ideal for testing theories, but they at least apply equally to both theories being compared.

The comparison is based on the randomly assigned "intention to treat," which varied substantially across the four experiments in determining the treatment actually completed. Many arrestees, for example, failed to appear in court, despite the legal requirement for them to do so. As for the arrestees assigned to attend a police-led RJC, the completion rates were 86.4 percent for drinking–driving, 77.1 percent for violent crime, 65.8 percent for personal property crime, and 87.5 percent for shoplifting. These completion rates track the differences across experiments in the social class of the offenders, which roughly approximates the measure of "bondedness" by offenders. The drinking–driving and shoplifting experiments had the best bondedness and highest RJC completion rates, while the violence and property crime experiments had less bonded arrestees (see Strang et al., 1999) by a variety of measures, as well as the lower completion rates.

As a test of treatment policy, it should be stressed that compliance rates were very high. Australian Federal Police delivered the randomly assigned policy across both treatment arms to 98.8 percent or more in all four experiments. But as a test of reintegration theory, the (lower) completion rates of RJCs are a more important issue for the integrity of theory testing. The further complication here is that defiance theory bases its prediction on the mere absence of court prosecution, whereas reintegration theory requires that an RJC experience must actually occur.

Yet for the purposes of theory testing, the data displayed in Table 7.1 offer both a strength and a weakness in this fact: the Year-10 respondents reported far higher completion rates for RJCs than were documented for the overall samples. In every one of the four experiments, respondents reported at least 89 percent attendance at the conferences if they had been randomly assigned to one—a rate that must still be compared to the records of attendance for each respondent to estimate the error rate of recall. The strength of this reported attendance rate is that the experience of RJC may be more closely linked to the test of reintegration theory in comparison to defiance. The weakness is that the respondents probably constitute a biased sample of the entire experimental population, with the bias in the direction of those who completed an RJC more likely to have responded than those who did not.

With these limitations in mind, Table 7.1 compares the effect size (standardized mean difference or Cohen's d) of the two-year after-only conviction rate of the arrestees by the randomly assigned intention to

Table 7.1

10-Year offender interview responses and 2-Year conviction effects in the Canberra RISE Project

Offense type	RJC effect size on 2-Year post-test Conviction rates	Percent of assigned RJC completed by 10-Year sample (%)	RJC effect size on defiance measure (anger)	RJC effect size on reintegration measure (repair)	Theories with which results are most consistent
Drinking–Driving	+.07	96.4	–.50	+.50	Neither defiance nor reintegration
Shoplifting	–.15	91.7	–.24	+.70	Reintegration
Violence	–.28	91.7	–.48	+.71	Reintegration
Property	+.14	89.1	–.04	+.13	Neither defiance nor reintegration

treat in each experiment with the effect size (Hedges' g, or a modified Cohen's d) of two measures of "black box" causal mechanisms taken from the 10-Year follow-up interviews. One measure is used to indicate a mechanism of defiance theory—the degree of the arrestee's anger at the official treatment they receive. The other measure can be used to indicate a measure of the offender's perceived reintegration into mainstream society—the extent to which they were able to "make up" for the crime for which they had been arrested, and had not denied their guilt.

The interpretation of the table is problematic for several reasons. The primary issue is the measurement of the two-year, after-only conviction outcomes, which is based on the entire randomly assigned sample. These effect sizes are thus based on a different population than the effect sizes derived from the 10-Year follow-up interviews. As noted above, about one-third of all the randomly assigned arrestees failed to complete the 10-Year interviews. Whether the inclusion of those missing respondents, in theory, would alter the effect sizes in the causal mechanism columns is unknown. Yet the table at least illustrates the ways in which experiments that measure intermediate causal mechanisms can compare and assess competing theories.

On the basis of only the data displayed in Table 7.1, reintegration theory provides a better fit to the experimentally derived facts than defiance theory. This conclusion stands despite the failure of both theories (as well as labeling theory) to predict the effects of diversion from prosecution in two of the four experiments. In both the drinking–driving and the property crime experiments, the conviction rate was higher in the group assigned to RJC than in the group assigned to prosecution in court. That result alone demonstrates the complexity of the causes of post-sanction offending, in which the impact of criminal sanctions on some kinds of offenders is minor compared to other causes of crime. That conclusion applies to both well-bonded people with low-offending rates (in the drinking–driving experiment) and to poorly bonded people with high-offending frequency (in the personal property experiment).

It is important to recall, however, that the findings from these two experiments that falsified all three theories under review—labeling, defiance, and reintegration—are completely anomalous in relation to the ten other randomized trials of RJC. There may well be some distinctive combination of the parameters of these two tests that make their results diverge so far from the ten other tests (Strang et al. 2012). These could include the offender characteristics in the samples selected by police for the randomized trial, the offense types selected, the largely non-incarcerative sanctioning in Canberra courts for these offense types, and the unique dynamics of Aboriginal offenders in relation to Australian police (Sherman et al. 2006). It is for that reason that we can fairly place more emphasis on comparing the theoretical mechanisms within the two experiments that offer results consistent with the eight other tests of RJC that found less crime with RJC than without it.

Table 7.1 shows two things in this theoretical comparison. One is that they fail to falsify defiance theory in the two experiments for which RJC reduced post-test convictions. In the violence and shoplifting experiments, arrestees assigned to prosecution in court were, as predicted by defiance theory, more angry at their treatment—after ten years!—than the offenders assigned to an RJC. This is especially compelling in relation to RJC theory, given the absence of a personal victim from the conferences in the shoplifting experiment. No Mom or Pop store owner was in the room (unlike in some of the personal property cases) talking about the harm they have suffered from shoplifting. It follows that an absence of stigma from a criminal record and court appearance should be a more compelling explanation for the shoplifting results than for the violence results, where the personal victim was almost always present at the RJCs.

The second thing the two reduced-conviction experiments show is that reintegration is a better explanation than defiance for the outcome.

The effect size of the reintegration measure ("the conference/court case allowed you to make up for what you did") was large and equivalent (Cohen's $d = .70$ or .71) in both of those experiments. The effect size of the defiance measure ("the conference/court case just made you feel angry"), however, was much weaker: a "small" ($d = .24$) effect for the shoplifting experiment and a "moderate" effect ($d = .48$) for the violence experiment. This does not mean that defiance theory is irrelevant to explaining the results of the experiment. Both defiance and reintegration may have been operating conjointly in the offenders' emotional reactions. Yet for what the interview responses are worth, they clearly suggest more resonance with the idea of reintegration causing *less* crime than with the idea of illegitimacy of the legal process causing *more* crime.

3. Labeling versus Defiance

The evidence supporting labeling theory in the Petrosino et al. (2010) review of diversion experiments is strong in relation to predictions. Yet the entire body of evidence on labeling effects is very weak on explanations. Almost none of them, for example, include offender interviews to reveal the "black box" between sanctions imposed and future offending. The Reintegrative Shaming Experiment (RISE) data from the Year-10 follow-up can thus be seen as a relatively rare opportunity to compare labeling theory to defiance theory on the basis of causal mechanisms.

One question in the Year-10 RISE interview suggests a reasonable test of labeling theory: "Looking back now, do you feel yourself bothered by thoughts that you were unfairly or critically judged by people?" While no one question can capture all of the dimensions of labeling theory, this item seems to fall much closer to the labeling construct than the question of anger that indicates defiance. This item allows subjects to report feeling "bothered," like a person who feels powerless. A second question on anger allows subjects to report that they responded more aggressively to the treatment they received, at least in their emotions. Comparing the four experiments for their effect sizes on the two questions may shed some light on a comparative assessment of defiance versus labeling.

For two of the experiments, both labeling and defiance theories are falsified. In both the drinking–driving and personal property crime samples, diversion from prosecution did no better in post-test convictions than prosecution in court. This is a substantial result in the case of drinking–driving, in which prosecution almost always meant a loss of driver's license for at least six months. More important for labeling theory, prosecution and conviction of drunk drivers were reported in the Canberra Times, and employers often learned of the conviction in this way. This means that for the adult drinking–driving offenders, a powerful test of labeling theory defeats its prediction.

For the other two experiments, defiance clearly defeats labeling, at least by this comparison (Strang et al., 2011). The labeling effect size of the "feeling" by violent crime arrestees who were prosecuted in court was only small ($d = .20$), compared to the moderate and more than doubled effect size of their treatment causing anger ($d = .48$). In the shoplifting experiment, the prosecution effect was small for defiance ($d = .24$), but almost zero for labeling ($d = .03$). Thus in both experiments, the effect size of differences between the prosecuted and not-prosecuted groups on the anger question is substantially larger than the effect size of their answers to the "feeling bothered" question.

The point of this comparison, again, is not to suggest any definitive conclusion about the relative success of defiance and labeling theories in explaining differences in outcomes of the same sanctions. Rather, the point is to illustrate the kinds of testing that must be developed in randomized experiments in order to advance and refine criminological theory. This point is the focus of the final section of this essay, which also draws on the RISE data in illustrating the potential of qualitative data in testing theories of criminal sanction effects.

Causal Mechanisms and Better Measurement

In order to measure the causal mechanism of sanction effects theories, it is necessary to track the dynamic process by which offenders do (or do not) react to the treatments they receive at the hands of legally empowered officials. Whether or not they incorporate a label into their identity, or react with anger, or feel reintegrated into society after repairing the harm they have caused, whatever they are thinking and feeling is in principle measureable. And as the economist Frank Knight reportedly said, "If you can't measure it, measure it anyway."

By "dynamic" I mean potentially rapid changes in emotions or self-definition in response to sanctioning or its threat. One example, measureable with tragic clarity, is the high rate of suicide in police lockup cells immediately after arrest, or overnight while awaiting a court appearance. Something in the offender's identity seems likely to have changed so quickly that the life worth living one moment was no longer worth living behind bars. Was it shame? The depression of defeat in a battle with the law? The despair of loss of liberty, perhaps for years to come? All of these mechanisms are possible to measure, at least by interview.

Similarly, the measurement of the dynamic process of reacting to sanctioning experiences would require interviews or observations at a range of points in sanctioning experiences, including

- just before a crime is committed versus right afterwards;
- when suspects are stopped, questioned, or searched by police;
- at a point shortly before an arrest occurs;
- immediately after arrest, but before being confined in a jail cell;
- after a criminal interrogation;
- during pre-trial incarceration;
- during appearances in court or in diversion programs;
- immediately after prosecution is dismissed or a jury acquits;
- during sentences served in custody or in the community; and
- after sentences are served and offenders are no longer under court supervision.

The difficulty of such measurement should not be underestimated. Yet that is no reason to ignore its importance. The testing of quantum theory in physics required the construction of an experimental station called the Hadron Large Collider, at a cost to European taxpayers of 8,000,000,000 Euros. The difficulty of raising the money and building the experimental station cannot be underestimated. Nonetheless, it happened. Whether experiments of comparable difficulty can occur in criminology is not a matter of theory, but of cost and politics.

The most expensive single project in the history of Australian criminology provides one benchmark. With a population of only some 20 million people—fifteen times smaller than the United States—Australia invested some $5 million in the RISE project in the 1990s. In U.S. terms, at fifteen times the size, that would be the equivalent of $75 million, or almost twice the size of the most expensive U.S. project in criminology (the Project on Human Development in Chicago Neighborhoods, funded jointly by the MacArthur Foundation and the U.S. National Institute of Justice at an initial budgeted cost of $40 million). What RISE has been able to produce, so far, is not nearly as much as it can produce with the Year-10 survey data, once all the data are made publicly available for scholarly analysis. These data will certainly not provide definitive answers to the key questions of sanctioning theories. They will, however, provide important lessons on how to continue to improve the measurement of causal mechanisms in the consequences of sanctioning. That, in turn, should help to improve the accuracy of predictions of sanction effects. These predictions could then be made by people in a wide range of professions to the betterment of society. Judges, police, legislators, and scholars could all employ better predictions of sanction effects to reduce crime and harm to victims.

At minimum, these predictions can be improved by the greater understanding that is gained from interviews of offenders in the context of randomized experiments. Yet such interviews are still the exception rather than the rule. As Geoffrey Barnes and Jordan Hyatt (2012) report, a systematic review of sixty-three randomized experiments reveals that only 16 percent of them even discussed the theory of the intervention being tested. Even more important, only 14 percent of them collected data on offender perceptions of the treatments. While the RISE studies certainly contain both features, they also raise issues about which kinds of measures are needed to advance theoretical understanding of sanction effects.

Two kinds of measures in particular merit further discussion in this section. One is the kind of measurement that is available to a small extent in the RISE data, and could have been profitably increased in scope. That measurement is the qualitative descriptions of emotions and experiences offenders gave to interviewers in the Year-10 interviews. The other kind of measure is the neuroscientific study of brain structure and function at different stages of the sanctioning processes. No such measure, such as functional magnetic resonance imaging (fMRI) has yet been gathered in any criminological field experiment, but could feasibly be collected with sufficient funding and planning.

Conclusion: Improving Theory and Prediction

Our knowledge of labeling, defiance, and restorative justice is improving, but is still not good enough. It is improving by the increased use of randomized experiments to compare the offending behavior outcomes of different sanctions for different kinds of offenses and offenders. It is improving by the increased use of interviews with offenders randomly assigned to different kinds of sanctioning. It is still not good enough, however, in designing measures that can falsify theories, or allow comparative assessments of competing (or complementary) theories.

Some might argue that simply increasing the supply of randomized experiments of sanction choices will improve prediction. That is no doubt a necessary condition for better choices of sanctioning policies. But it may not be a sufficient condition for either policies or theories. Improving explanation may be just as valuable for improving prediction as increasing the evidence on sanctions and outcomes.

What we need more of now is evidence from inside the "black box" of micro-mediation, the causal mechanisms by which sanctions affect behavior. These mechanisms cannot be limited to the late twentieth-century theories of criminogenic sanctioning. It would be far more useful, as well as scientific, to broaden the range of theories tested to include the full range of deterrence and incapacitation mechanisms. This would mean, at minimum, the development of experiments in certainty, celerity, and severity of punishment on the punished. Such experiments should be supplemented by measures of causal mechanisms within each sanctioning treatment condition. It is then, and only then, that our understanding of sanction effects on future criminal behavior will begin to take more systematic form, spreading its explanatory cover over a wide range of offenses, offenders, their trajectories and social contexts.

References

Angrist, J. D. "Instrumental Variables Methods in Experimental Criminological Research: What, Why and How." *Journal of Experimental Criminology* 2, no. 1 (2006): 23–44.

Barnes, G. C. and J. M. Hyatt. "Randomized Experiments and the Advancement of Criminological Theory." *Measuring Crime and Criminality: Advances in Criminological Theory* 17 (2012): 201.

Becker, H. S. *Outsiders: Studies in the Sociology of Deviance.* Glencoe, IL: Free Press, 1963.

Berk, R. A. "Randomized Experiments as the Bronze Standard." *Journal of Experimental Criminology* 1, no. 4 (2005): 417–33.

Black, D. J. "The Social Organization of Arrest." *Stanford Law Review* 23 (1970): 1087.

Boruch, R. *Randomized Experiment for Planning and Evaluation.* Beverly Hills, CA: Sage, 1997.

Braithwaite, J. *Crime, Shame and Reintegration.* Cambridge, MA: Cambridge University Press, 1989.

———. *Restorative Justice and Responsive Regulation.* Oxford, NY: Oxford University Press, 2002.

Cohen, J. *Statistical Power for the Behavioral Sciences,* 2nd ed. NJ: Erlbaum Associates, 1988.

Cook, T. D. and D. T. Campbell. *Quasi-Experimentation: Design and Analysis for Field Setting.* Boston, MA: Houghton Mifflin, 1979.

Farrington, D. P. "Randomized Experiments on Crime and Justice." *Crime and Justice* 4 (1983): 257–308.

Gouldner, A. W. *The Coming Crisis of Western Sociology,* vol. 504. New York: Basic Books, 1970.

Jacobs, J. *Stateville: The Penitentiary in Mass Society.* Chicago: University of Chicago Press, 1978.

Killias, M. Paper presented to the Stockholm Criminology Symposium, 2010.

Killias, M., M. Aebi, and D. Ribeaud. "Does Community Service Rehabilitate Better than Short-Term Imprisonment? Results of a Controlled Experiment." *The Howard Journal of Criminal Justice* 39, no. 1 (2000): 40–57.

Kirk, D. S. "A Natural Experiment on Residential Change and Recidivism: Lessons from Hurricane Katrina." *American Sociological Review* 74, no. 3 (2009): 484–505.

Lemert, E. M. *Social Pathology: A Systematic Approach to the Theory of Sociopathic Behavior.* New York: McGraw-Hill, 1951.

Mead, G. H. "The Social Self." *Journal of Philosophy, Psychology and Scientific Methods* 10 (1913): 374–80.

Petrosino, A., C. Turpin-Petrosino, and S. Guckenburg. "Formal System Processing of Juveniles: Effects on Delinquency." *Juvenile and Family Court Journal* 57, no. 2 (2010): 1–10.

Piliavin, I. and S. Briar. "Police Encounters with Juveniles." *American Journal of Sociology* 70 (1964): 206–14.

Popper, K. R. *The Logic of Scientific Discovery.* London: Routledge, 1968.

Scheff, T. and S. Retzinger. *Emotions and Violence: Shame and Rage in Destructive Conflicts.* Lexington, MA: Lexington Books, 1991.

Schneider, A. L. *Deterrence and Juvenile Crime: Results from a National Policy Experiment.* New York: Springer-Verlag Publishing, 1990.

Shapland, J., A. Atkinson, H. Atkinson, J. Dignan, L. Edwards, J. Hibbert, and United Kingdom. *Does Restorative Justice Affect Reconviction? The Fourth Report from the Evaluation of Three Schemes*, 89. London: Ministry of Justice, Publication No. ISBN 978-1-84099-200-7, 2008.

Sherman, L. W. "Defiance, Compliance and Consilience: A General Theory of Criminology." In *Handbook of Criminological Theory*, edited by E. McLaughlin and T. Newburn. London/Thousand Oaks, CA: Sage, 2010.

———. "Defiance, Deterrence, and Irrelevance: A Theory of the Criminal Sanction." *Journal of Research in Crime and Delinquency* 30 (1993): 445–73.

———. *Policing Domestic Violence: Experiments and Dilemmas.* New York: Free Press, 1992.

———. "Reason for Emotion: Reinventing Justice with Theories, Innovations and Research—The 2002 American Society of Criminology Presidential Address." *Criminology* 41 (2003): 1–38.

Sherman, L. W. and D. A. Smith. "Crime, Punishment and Stake in Conformity: Legal and Informal Control of Domestic Violence." *American Sociological Review* 57, no. 5 (1992): 680–90.

Sherman, L. W., D. Gottfredson, D. MacKenzie, J. Eck, P. Reuter, and S. Bushway. *Preventing Crime: What Works? What Doesn't? What's Promising? A Report to the United States Congress (NCJ 171676).* Washington, DC: US Department of Justice, Office of Justice Programs, 1997.

Sherman, L. W., J. D. Schmidt, D. P. Rogan, P. R. Gartin, E. G. Cohn, D. J. Collins, and A. R. Bacich. "From Initial Deterrence to Longterm Escalation: Short-Custoday Arrest for Poverty Ghetto Domestic Violence." *Criminology* 29, no. 4 (1991): 821–50.

Sherman, L. W., H. Strang, G. C. Barnes, and D. Woods. "Race and Restorative Justice: Differential Effects for Aboriginals and 5 Race and Restorative Justice: Differential Effects for Aboriginals and Whites in the Canberra RISE Project." Paper presented to the American Society of Criminology, Los Angeles, 2006.

Stinchcombe, A. L. "Institutions of Privacy in the Determination of Police Administrative Practice." *American Journal of Sociology* 69 (1963): 150–60.

Strang, H., G. Barnes, J. Braithwaite, and L. Sherman. *Experiments in Restorative Policing: A Progress Report.* Canberra: Australian National University, 1999. http://www.aic.gov.au/rjustice/rise/index.html#papers.

Strang, H. and L. W. Sherman. *Protocol for a Campbell Collaboration Systematic Review: Effects of Face-to-Face Restorative Justice for Personal Victim Crimes.* Oslo, Norway:

Campbell Library, Campbell Collaboration, 2005. http://www.campbellcollaboration. org/library.php.

Strang, H., L. Sherman, D. Woods, E. Mayo-Wilson, and B. Ariel. *Effects of Restorative Justice Conferences on Offenders and Victims. Draft Campbell Collaboration Review.* Cambridge: Cambridge University, Jerry Lee Centre for Experimental Criminology, 2013.

Sutherland, Edwin H. *Principles of Criminology.* Chicago: University of Chicago Press, 1924.

Sunstein, C. "Some Effects of Moral Indignation on Law." *Vermont Law Review* 33 (2008): 405.

Sykes, G. and D. Matza. "Techniques of Neutralization: A Theory of Delinquency." *American Sociological Review* 22 (1957): 664–70.

Taylor, I., P. Walton, and J. Young. *The New Criminology.* London: Routledge, 1973.

Tyler, T. R. *Why People Obey the Law.* New Haven, CT: Yale University Press, 1990.

Tyler, T. R. and Y. J. Huo. *Trust in the Law: Encouraging Public Cooperation with the Police and Courts*, vol. 5. NY: Russell Sage Foundation Publications, 2002.

Tyler, T. R., L. Sherman, H. Strang, G. C. Barnes, and D. Woods. "Reintegrative Shaming, Procedural Justice, and Recidivism: The Engagement of Offenders' Psychological Mechanisms in the Canberra RISE Drinking-and-Driving Experiment." *Law & Society Review* 41, no. 3 (2007): 553–86.

Weisburd, D., A. Petrosino, and G. Mason. "Design Sensitivity in Criminal Justice Experiments." *Crime and Justice* 17 (1993): 337–79.

Whyte, W. F. *Street-Corner Society: The Social Structure of an Italian Slum.* Chicago: University of Chicago Press, 1943.

Part III
Specific Empirical Tests

8

Effects of Official Intervention on Later Offending in the Rochester Youth Development Study

Marvin D. Krohn, Giza Lopes, and Jeffrey T. Ward

Effects of Official Intervention on Later Offending

Throughout its extensive history, labeling theory has experienced its share of popularity, as well as disenchantment among criminologists and deviance scholars. While enjoying its intellectual peak in the 1960s, the perspective's early developments can be traced back to the 1930s. By the 1980s the approach had received sustained and severe criticisms aimed both at its lack of theoretical specificity and empirical support (Hirschi, 1980; Tittle, 1980). In recent years, however, there has been a revived interest in the perspective.

Emerging from this long history are two interrelated reasons why intervention to misbehavior, especially official intervention, is seen as having a problematic effect on individuals' future behavior. Steeped in the tradition of symbolic interactionism, labeling someone deviant, delinquent, or criminal is seen to have an effect on self-identity, ultimately resulting in subsequent behavior that is consistent with the newly formed self-image. In addition to the potential cognitive impact of the label, intervention is also seen as limiting interactions with those who are seen as conventional and restricting educational and work-related opportunities which, in turn, increase later deviant behavior. Discursive and theoretical statements concerning the impact of labels have generally incorporated both strains.

However, empirical research on the labeling process tends to stress either one or the other pathway.

In this paper we focus particularly on our own recent research on the impact of the label on limiting opportunities and interactions in the conventional arena. We then follow Bruce Link (1987) in rejoining these strains, presenting some preliminary findings from the Rochester Youth Development Study (RYDS). We begin by briefly exploring the historical roots of the labeling approach.

Early Developments and Theoretical Foundations

Labeling's main tenets were first articulated in the work of Frank Tannenbaum (1938), whose interests in issues dealing with the rule of law and its autonomous capacity—or power—to shape social life ranged from advocacy of agrarian reform in South America (1929), to race relations in the South (1946) and in the Nazi regime (1951). Tannenbaum's attention to the penal system and criminal issues (1922, 1938) was perhaps prompted by the economic, social, and political context of the 1930s—specifically the widespread distrust in the government, brought about by the Great Depression and the emergence of totalitarian regimes in Europe—as well as his own brushes with the law. Character-ized as "a criminal menace" by New York's *World*, Tannenbaum's orga-nized march of 1,000 unemployed men into Harlem churches seeking food and shelter led to his year-long imprisonment in 1914 (Foner, 1965: 444).

In his *Wall Shadows: A Study in American Prisons* (1922), he began to sketch his views on the negative ramifications associated with the label-ing of offenders. "The prison," Tannenbaum (1922) argues, "is a great equalizer, [in that] all men are fit for it; all they need done is to break the law" (pp. 154–55). Once an offender is "stamped as a criminal" and imprisoned, he adds, one's "every interest, every ambition, every hope, [. . .] all his work and contacts" are cut away, and the offender loses his/her original identity and is forced to reprocess it as to include a newly acquired criminal label (Tannenbaum, 1922: 154–55).

The novelty of Tannenbaum's work comes from his emphasis on this "stamping" or "tagging" process through which an individual becomes a deviant, following his/her involvement in an initial maladjustment to social norms whose meaning has been dramatized by society. In *Crime and the Community* (1938), Tannenbaum further develops this notion, specifically in the context of criminal justice treatment of juveniles. Thus, he suggests that criminals are created by a societal reaction process to deviance, which separates an individual from conventional society and pushes him/her further into a deviant career:

> The first dramatization of the "evil" which separates the child out of his group for specialized treatment plays a greater role in making the criminal than perhaps any other experience. It cannot be too often emphasized that for the child the whole situation has become different. He now lives in a different world. He has been tagged. A new and hitherto non-existent environment has been precipitated out for him.
>
> The process of making the criminal, therefore, is a process of tagging, defining, identifying, segregating, describing, emphasizing, making conscious and self-conscious; it becomes a way of stimulating, suggesting, emphasizing, and evoking the very traits that are complained of (Tannenbaum, 1938: 19–20).

Drawing heavily on the symbolic interactionist notions of *self* (Cooley, 1902; Mead, 1934), as well as the *definition of the situation* (Thomas, 1923), Tannenbaum explains how the redefinition of an "innocent maladjustment" into a delinquent act can have a profound impact on the youth's identity and thereby his/her subsequent behavior.

Nearly two decades later, these propositions were further developed by Edwin Lemert, whose concepts of *primary* and *secondary deviance* have become central in the labeling perspective. According to Lemert (1951), primary deviance is sporadic deviant behavior, often situational in nature, which is rationalized, excused, or even tolerated by conventional members of society. He subsequently added that primary deviance has "only marginal implications for the psychic structure of the individual" and, as such, it "does not lead to symbolic reorganization at the level of self regarding attitudes and social roles" (Lemert, 1967: 17). Secondary deviance, in its turn, is a pivotal, engulfing deviant activity to which a person has become committed and which is primarily triggered by (mostly severe) societal reaction. In this sense,

> it refers to a special class of socially defined responses which people make to problems created by the societal reaction to their deviance. These problems are essentially moral problems which revolve around stigmatization, punishments, segregation, and social control. Their general effect is to differentiate the symbolic and interactional environment to which the person responds, so that early or adult socialization is categorically affected. They become central facts of existence for those experiencing them, altering psychic structure [and] producing specialized organization of social roles and self-regarding attitudes (Lemert, 1967: 40).

Though reactions to deviance can arise in private, non-official social settings (e.g., in the family), since labeling's inception, scholars have emphasized how *official* reactions to deviance tend to successfully transform one's identity as to reflect largely his/her criminal activities.

Along these lines, Harold Garfinkel (1956) has suggested that such changes in identity typically emerge from successful "status degradation ceremonies," or "communicative work that is directed to transforming an individual's total identity into an identity lower in the group's scheme of social types" (p. 423). These ceremonies, he added, are most effective when closed by an official act that marks the actor's separation from a place in the legitimate order, such as public denunciations and legal verdicts.

The works of these early labeling theorists were revisited in the 1960s, when the perspective reached mainstream appeal, subsequently followed by sharp criticism in the 1970s and 1980s, and renewed interest in the past two decades. We turn our attention to these theoretical developments in the following section.

Labeling Redux: Peak, Demise, and Revival

The socio-political context of the 1960s afforded labeling a unique intellectual momentum which shed light on at least two important aspects of research on deviance, in general. For one, labeling studies published at that time emphasized the politicization and social construction of deviance, particularly in respect to rule creation and enforcement. During the immediate post-war period, crime and deviance had been primarily explained as a product of individual psychology or traits. In this sense, criminology, as established then, tended to favor authoritative definitions of deviance. Labeling theorists introduced certain relativism into studies of deviance, calling for a shift from questions addressing the motivation and behavioral patterns of offenders to actual definitional issues of rule-making and breaking. In 1963, for example, Howard Becker laid out a critique to hitherto uncontested norm-based or consensual definitions of deviance, and argued that what constitutes a deviant act is, instead, socially defined and essentially based in power relations. Certain social groups, he proposes, *"create deviance by making the rules whose infraction constitutes deviance*, and by applying those rules to particular people and labeling them outsiders" (Becker, 1963: 9, *emphasis in original*). Furthermore, theoretical works developed during the sixties built on the foundational labeling statements by taking into account the mediating mechanisms through which changes in identity are said to take place, and on how those changes affect subsequent deviant behavior. Most of these theoretical contributions took place in the mental health field and were later incorporated into criminology. Labeling's contemporary studies

(Sampson and Laub, 1997; Bernburg and Krohn, 2003) owe their development partly to those discussions, which are briefly covered below.

Even though original works in labeling had focused mainly on offenders —particularly juveniles—as an epitome of deviant behavior, by the 1960s the discussion had captured the attention of sociologists interested in extending labeling propositions to mental health issues. Following Erving Goffman's seminal contributions in *Asylums* (1961) and *Stigma: Notes on the Management of Spoiled Identity* (1963), and drawing heavily on the contributions made by Edwin Lemert (1951) and Howard Becker (1963), labeling theory gained further appeal with the publication of Thomas Scheff's *Being Mentally Ill: a Sociological Theory* (1966). In the book, Scheff describes the underlying social processes which lead to chronic mental illness and provides a detailed account of the contingencies that shape societal reaction.

It could be argued that the most problematic of Scheff's assertions—and the one visibly fueling critiques of his work—was the notion that labeling, especially official labeling as conferred by hospitalization and formal treatment, was in itself the direct etiology of mental disorders. Moderating Scheff's claims and elaborating on the actual mechanisms through which deviance amplification takes place, Link, Cullen, Elmer Struening, Patrick Shrout, and Bruce Dohrenwend (1989) proposed a modified labeling theory, "which claims that even if labeling does not directly produce mental disorder, it can lead to negative outcomes" (p. 400).

"Modified" Labeling Theory

Interest in the labeling perspective was revitalized through the work on mental illness by Link. Link (1982: 202) correctly suggests that the focus of prior research on labeling has been on the creation and maintenance of deviant behavior. This research either examined the direct impact of intervention on subsequent behavior or the indirect effect through a change in self-concept. Link argues that prior research underemphasized the effect that the intervention has on other arenas of a person's life such as education, work, and income. If, indeed, labeling affects these other arenas, the person would likely be under increased environmental stress, have reduced access to social supports, and increased self-devaluation (Link, 1982: 213).

In the first of a series of articles exploring the implications of his argument, Link (1982) examines the impact of having been a mental patient on both income status and work status. Controlling for psychiatric impairment, education, occupation, and marital status, Link finds that having been a patient is significantly related to the acquisition of income and to having a disadvantaged work status.

Using the same data set, Link (1987) explored the role of self-devaluation. He divided the sample into five groups that included first-treatment contact patients, repeat-treatment contact patients, formerly treated community residents, untreated community cases, and community residents with no evidence of severe psychopathology. A scale measuring beliefs that mental patients would be discriminated against and devalued was administered to all groups. For those groups that had been labeled, Link found that this scale was related to demoralization, income loss, and unemployment—although the salience of beliefs about devaluation was less among those former patients who had been labeled earlier rather than later. For non-labeled groups, the scale was not related to those outcomes. Link interpreted the results as being indicative that the label's effect is consistent with Lemert's concept of secondary deviance. The label—and the attendant recognition that the mentally ill are devalued and discriminated against—leads to a devaluation of self and to problematic income and employment outcomes.

Link and colleagues (1989) more fully articulated their perspective, referring to it as a "modified labeling theory." According to this modified version, mental patients engage in adaptive social strategies following treatment, which can lead to negative consequences for social support networks, employment stability, earning power, and self-esteem (see, e.g., Link et al., 1991). In response to an official label, people will act in three alternative ways. They will try to keep the label a secret, they will withdraw from social interaction, or they will try to educate others in hopes of warding off stigmatization. Importantly, the responses to the official label may result in the withdrawal from social networks and from seeking life chances in the areas of education and employment. This will result in fewer opportunities in the conventional arena and make the labeled individual more vulnerable to negative outcomes.

Besides these adaptive coping strategies that ensue from psychiatric treatment, Link had previously claimed that the detrimental effects of a psychiatric label in social functioning can also emerge at the inception of the treatment process. Grounded on the notions of stigma as "loss of status" (Goffman, 1963; Cumming and Cumming, 1965) and on the social distance tradition, Link (1987) argued that "[w]hen people enter psychiatric treatments and are labeled," their beliefs about how others respond to mental patients, generally anticipated as negatively, "become personally applicable and lead to self-devaluation and/or the fear of rejection by others" (p. 92). In other words, he stressed, "official labeling can transform a person's beliefs about the devaluation and discrimination of mental patients into an *expectation of rejection*," which ultimately leads to negative consequences, such as capacity to obtain jobs, earn income, and so forth (Link, 1987: 97).

Link et al. (1989) partially examine their theory. They find that individuals have negative conceptions of mental patients which patients internalize once they are diagnosed as such. These conceptions lead them to have support networks with people whom they can trust and not with people who are outside their immediate household. They conclude that their findings indicate that labeling and stigma are consequential in the lives of psychiatric patients.

Link's research established a need to revisit labeling and focus particularly on the variables that are suggested to mediate the relationship between official intervention and problematic outcomes, including the increased probability of mental illness. Link et al. (1989) recognize that although they have found that official intervention increases the likelihood of stigma and outcomes such as employment and income, they have not established the additional link between official intervention and subsequent mental illness through those mediating variables.

Labeling and Crime

Link's research on mental health labeling did not go unnoticed by delinquency scholars who thought that the dismissal of the theory, as called for by its critics in the 1970s and 1980s, was premature. In a wide ranging review of the literature on the labeling perspective, Raymond Paternoster and LeeAnn Iovanni (1989) chastised those who declared the labeling perspective dead based on research that they characterized as inherently flawed; more specifically, they maintained that prior empirical tests have failed to capture the perspective's complexities and "grossly misrepresented hypotheses that are more caricature than characteristic of the theory" (p. 360). They further stated that the complex causal model proposed by the "modified labeling theory" (Link et al., 1989) allowed for an analysis of the mechanisms intervening between the ascription of a mental illness label and subsequent behavior. Consistent with Link's emphasis, they urged that criminology look for the intervening links and the contingencies of the labeling process and they suggested that the problematic impact of labeling may be seen as being due to a weakening of the social bond to conventional society.

Focusing on the mechanisms that intervene between official interven-tion and behavioral outcomes serves to underscore the developmental nature of the labeling process. The emergence of the life course perspec-tive (Elder, 1985, 1994; Sampson and Laub, 1993, 1997; Thornberry and Krohn, 2001, 2005; Benson, 2002; Farrington, 2005) provided a theoreti-cal framework with which Robert Sampson and John Laub (1993, 1997) could explain the impact of official intervention on the social bond and, in turn, the continuation of criminal behavior. To describe the impact of events early in life on subsequent processes and outcomes, Sampson and Laub introduced the term "cumulative disadvantage." Robert Merton had introduced the concept of cumulative advantage to describe how the reward system in science favors those who have established reputations; initial success increases the probability of future success (Merton, 1968, 1988). Sampson and Laub seized Merton's concept and applied it to the difficulties in acquiring the necessary skills and opportunities to obtain resources to foster a successful life course. Cumulative disadvantage was used to describe how early events such as official intervention could affect a number of interactions, behaviors, and intermediary outcomes, leading to an accumulation of deficits that decrease the probability of life chances. From this perspective, official intervention is seen as a transi-tional event that can lead to cumulative deficits, ultimately affecting the life course trajectories of youth. Sampson and Laub (1997) summarized the hypothesized impact of labeling:

> Cumulative disadvantage is generated most explicitly by the negative structural con-sequences of criminal offending and official sanctions for life chances. The theory specifically suggests a "snowball" effect—that adolescent delinquency and its negative consequences (e.g., arrest, official labeling, and incarceration) increasingly "mortgage" one's future, especially later life chances molded by schooling and employment . . . The theoretical perspective in turn points to a possible indirect effect of delinquency and official sanctioning in generating future crime (pp. 147–48).

Sampson and Laub (1997) used the data originally collected by Glueck and Glueck to partially examine their theory. The Gluecks had collected longitudinal data on 500 male delinquents who had been incarcerated and 500 male non-delinquents who had not been. They examined the impact of the length of incarceration on job stability at ages seventeen, twenty-five, and thirty-two. They found that the longer incarceration the youth experienced, the less job stability they enjoyed, even after controlling for a number of factors including crime and drug use. Moreover, they found that the effect of incarceration on subsequent criminal behavior is not significant when job stability is controlled. They interpreted these findings as suggesting that incarceration cuts off opportunities to establish a bond to conventional society later in life and, thereby, increases the probability of continued criminal behavior. They conclude that ". . . even if the direct effect of incarceration is zero or possibly even negative (i.e., a deterrent), its indirect effect may well be criminogenic (positive) as structural labeling theorists have long argued" (Sampson and Laub, 1997: 150).

Although Sampson and Laub only examine length of incarceration and use a problematic sample, their findings certainly suggest that it is important to focus on outcomes other than just crime and drug use and to determine if variables such as education and employment mediate the effect of official intervention on criminal behavior. Perhaps more importantly, Sampson and Laub's work illustrated the importance of examining the labeling perspective within a life course framework.

Our own work on labeling takes up the baton laid down by Sampson and Laub, as we have continued to examine the impact of official intervention on life chances and subsequent criminal behavior (Bernburg, 2002; Bernburg and Krohn, 2003; Bernburg et al., 2006; Lopes et al., 2012). To that end, we have utilized prospective longitudinal panel data collected from a general school population sample. The breadth of these data, coupled with its richness and relatively long and interspersed time span has allowed us to address, at least partly, several methodological limitations regarding labeling's empirical tests that were identified during the theory's revival in the late 1980s.

In their thorough assessment of labeling research, Paternoster and Iovanni (1989) noted that a large proportion of the studies conducted until then was methodologically flawed and hence yielded few reliable conclusions. Though empirical tests of the perspective have generally improved since labeling's revival, we will briefly discuss a few methodological shortcomings as they contributed considerably to the premature dismissal of the theory and, to some extent, continue to be found in the literature. Below we touch on the following four key research limitations: reliance on nonrandom samples, limited attention to the intermediate processes triggered by labeling which ultimately lead to subsequent deviance, insufficient examination of the conditioning effects of offender characteristics, and narrow focus on short-term effects of official intervention.

Limitations of Prior Research

Most studies examining the criminogenic effect of official labeling more often than not draw on nonrandom samples such as samples derived exclusively from police records or other sources of formal reaction.

In these cases, the absolute effects of labeling—or the comparison between non-labeled individuals and those who have gone through official intervention—are left out. The focus instead is on official labeling's relative effects; that is, the potential differential impact of dissimilar types of labels (e.g., probation versus incarceration) on secondary deviance.

A significant theoretical implication results from this methodological shortcoming. As Paternoster and Iovanni (1989) point out, "[t]o say that one type of label has little additional effect on secondary deviance in relation to another is *not* to say that it has *no* deviance-generating effects at all" (pp. 385–86). In fact, empirical tests of labeling which utilize samples from general populations tend to provide consistent support for the theory, suggesting that an official label, affixed through an arrest and/or other formal sanctions, positively affects subsequent delinquency in adulthood, net of delinquent behavior earlier in life (Farrington, 1977; Farrington et al., 1978; Palamara et al., 1986; Ray and Downs, 1986; Hagan and Palloni, 1990; Stewart et al., 2002; Bernburg and Krohn, 2003; Johnson et al., 2004; Bernburg et al., 2006).

Another limitation of the empirical assessments of labeling theory is the relative inattention paid to the stigmatizing and exclusionary effects that act as intervening mechanisms in the deviance amplification process. According to the perspective, a labeling event can trigger changes in personal identity and exclusion from conventional opportunities and conventional others. These processes, in turn, can lead to further entrenchment in deviant behavior.

Some research has been conducted on how labeling limits access to and success in conventional life arenas, particularly education and employment. The stigmatizing effect of a labeling event as experienced in school—a social environment where youth spend a substantial amount of time—has been shown to shape further reactions of school administrators and teachers. In this sense, the perception of a youth as a "troublemaker" by school officials, brought about in part by the knowledge of youth's experience with the police and the juvenile justice system, encourages disciplinarians to use suspensions, transfers, and involuntary "drops" to "get rid of" such students (Bowditch, 1993: 493). Research has demonstrated that if the school is aware of youths' involvement in the juvenile justice system, those students are more likely to drop out (Bernburg, 2002). Finally, consistent with these observations, labeling has been found to decrease the likelihood of success in the educational arena (DeLi, 1999; Bernburg, 2002; Bernburg and Krohn, 2003; Sweeten, 2006; Hjalmarsson, 2008).

In terms of employment opportunities, official intervention has been found to impact the likelihood of finding/maintaining stable employment. For one, a criminal record or previous incarceration negatively affects the chances of getting a job, as potential employers are reluctant to hire those applicants (Schwartz and Skolnick, 1962; Buikhuisen and Dijksterhuis, 1971; Boshier and Johnson, 1974; Pager, 2003; Irwin, 2005). Additionally, research on the job histories of individuals who have experienced official intervention has consistently found that they are less likely to secure stable employment (Freeman, 1991; Western and Beckett, 1999; Bernburg and Krohn, 2003; Davies and Tanner, 2003). In a recent study, for instance, Nadine Lanctôt, Stephen Cernkovich, and Peggy Giordano (2007) found that incarceration in adolescence increased socioeconomic disadvantage and job instability. These deficiencies may, in turn, be related to economic sustainability (Sampson and Laub, 1993; Laub and Sampson, 1994).

Unlike research on exclusion from or diminished opportunities in conventional arenas (e.g., education and employment), which has for the most part captured scholars' interest fairly recently, the impact of (mostly informal) social reactions on self-concept and subsequent deviance has received slightly more attention over time. Matsueda and colleagues (Matsueda, 1992; Heimer and Matsueda, 1994; Bartusch and Matsueda, 1996; Heimer, 1996; Matsueda and Heimer, 1997) find support for a symbolic interactionist approach to delinquency, which examines the conception of self (as delinquent or rule-abiding) as a reflection of the appraisals by others and as a mechanism of social control through role-taking processes. Among the findings, firstly, reflected appraisals of self as "rule violator" were related to future delinquency and predicted by prior delinquency. Secondly, and along the lines of the looking-glass self notion, adolescents' reflected appraisals were predicted by corresponding appraisals by parents. Thirdly, the effects of parental appraisals on delinquency were found to operate indirectly, through youths' reflected appraisals, therefore corroborating the idea that one tends to assume the role impinged by others' expectations.

The social contexts and individual-level characteristics upon which formal labels are contingent have long been identified as a gap in the labeling research (Tittle, 1980; Paternoster and Iovanni, 1989). In this sense, the differential effects of labeling with respect to gender, race, and poverty, for example, has emerged as a recurrent, yet still understudied, theme (Chiricos et al., 2007).

In terms of the conditional effects of minority and poverty statuses, two opposing hypotheses have been articulated within a labeling framework.

First, it has been argued that those who are already socially and economically disadvantaged are more impervious to the effects of a criminal label, due to their reduced stakes in conformity (Ageton and Eliott, 1974; Harris, 1976; Jensen, 1980). Alternatively, other scholars have suggested that minorities and impoverished groups are more susceptible to the effects of labeling, particularly formal labeling, because such labels may be "enhanced by negative stereotypes that are already associated with these youths in mainstream culture" (Bernburg and Krohn, 2003: 1290; see also Sampson and Laub, 1997).

Though both hypotheses have found some corroboration in the literature, empirical tests tend to validate the latter more substantively. For instance, Mike Adams, James Johnson, and T. David Evans (1998) found that the effect of subjective labeling on delinquency is larger among African Americans as opposed to whites. In addition, field experiments on police response to minor domestic violence events also found that the effect of arrest on subsequent violence is contingent on the perpetrator's employment status (Berk et al., 1992; Pate and Hamilton, 1992; Sherman et al., 1992).

The fourth limitation of prior research is a narrow focus on the relatively short-term effects of official intervention. The bulk of research has focused on the consequences of contact with the juvenile justice system during the teenage years. Some research has examined the impact of adult incarceration on a limited time period after release. Few studies have followed respondents from their teens to the age at which adult roles and statuses should be established.

As noted above, researchers are beginning to address these limitations. The advent of the life course perspective coupled with the increase in the number of studies using prospective longitudinal panel designs with general populations have been important in this regard. The remainder of this chapter focuses on the findings from one such research project, the RYDS, which has explored issues concerning the impact of official intervention on various criminal and non-criminal outcomes.

RYDS Research on Labeling

Led by Jon Bernburg (2002; Bernburg and Krohn, 2003; Bernburg et al., 2006), we have begun to explore a number of hypotheses that are derived from what is referred to above as a "modified labeling theory" with data from the RYDS. The RYDS is a longitudinal panel study of 1,000 youth who were approximately fourteen years old and enrolled in the Rochester Public School system at Wave 1. We oversampled males

(75 percent versus 25 percent females) in high crime areas in order to obtain a sample that would be at high risk for serious criminal behavior. The sample reflects the characteristics of school children in Rochester, New York. It is comprised of 68 percent African Americans, 17 percent Hispanics, and 14 percent Caucasians. The sample is disproportionately economically disadvantaged.

During the first phase of the study we interviewed students and one of their parents or guardians every six months over nine waves (eight waves for parents or guardians). After a two-year break in data collection, we interviewed our target subjects and one of their parents or guardians on a yearly basis for three waves when they were approximately twenty to twenty-three years old. In Phase 3 of the study, we re-interviewed just our target subjects twice when they were approximately twenty-nine and thirty-one years old. Thus, we have fourteen waves of data spanning the ages of approximately fourteen to thirty-one years.

The RYDS data provide a number of advantages in examining a modified labeling approach. The wide measurement space that includes information on police contact, juvenile justice involvement, and incarceration, as well as a number of theoretically relevant outcomes (criminal and non-criminal) provides the necessary variables to examine many hypotheses derived from the theory. The sample is obtained from a general school population, including youth who were and were not involved in criminal behavior and who did and did not have contact with the juvenile justice system. Having data on these respondents through their adolescent years up to the age of thirty-one affords an examination of what happens to youth who experience official intervention over a longer time period than most previous studies have been able to assess. Because the study was designed to oversample youth at risk for serious criminal behavior, we have a sufficient number of respondents who have experienced some official intervention to obtain meaningful results.

Bernburg and Krohn (2003) began their investigations of the labeling perspective by focusing on the potential social structural mediators (e.g., educational attainment and unemployment) of official intervention (e.g., police intervention and juvenile justice intervention) during the early teenage years on outcomes when subjects were in their early twenties. In that study only males were used because fewer females had experienced official intervention and even fewer continued to commit criminal activities in their early twenties. The model they examined is depicted in Figure 8.1. Official intervention in adolescence (ages 13.5 to 16.5) is predicted to lead to a lower probability of graduating from high school.

Figure 8.1
Hypothesized effects of official intervention in adolescence on crime in early adulthood (adapted from Bernburg and Krohn, 2003)

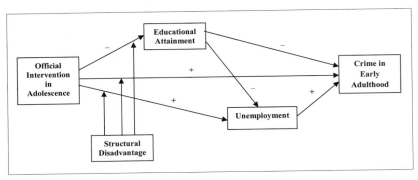

In turn, educational attainment is predicted to have both a direct effect and an indirect effect through unemployment on crime in early adulthood (serious crime, drug selling, and general crime). Unemployment (number of months unemployed when subjects are aged nineteen to twenty-one) is also predicted to have a direct effect on crime in early adulthood. In addition to the indirect effects through both educational attainment and unemployment, official intervention is predicted to directly affect crime in early adulthood.

Other than the main effects depicted in the model, Bernburg and Krohn (2003) also examined whether the effects were contingent on social structural location of the subjects. Specifically, they examined whether being labeled has a greater effect for those who are structurally disadvantaged (e.g., African American and poverty status).

The results vary slightly depending on which measure of official intervention is used to predict which crime outcome. However, clear support is found for the overall premise that official intervention leads to problems obtaining education. Failing to obtain a high school diploma increases the probability of non-stable employment, and instability in employment, in turn, leads to a greater probability of crime. Official intervention, whether measured by police contact or juvenile justice involvement, had direct effects in three out of the four estimated models. Only when police intervention was used to predict general crime were just indirect effects through education and non-employment found.

Additionally, Bernburg and Krohn (2003) found that the effect of police and juvenile justice intervention on crime is stronger among males from poverty backgrounds, and the effect of juvenile justice intervention is stronger among African Americans. They suggest that people from disadvantaged backgrounds may not have the necessary resources to resist the effects of deviant labeling.

Bernburg and Krohn's (2003) study provides a number of advantages over prior work on the impact of labeling. For one, it employed a prospective longitudinal design allowing for a temporal distinction in the variables that is consistent with the theoretical argument of a labeling process. Secondly, the sample is from a general population with sufficient cases to provide reliable estimates. Finally, in addition to the main effects, the effect of structural disadvantage on the relationship between official intervention and the outcomes was examined.

Bernburg et al. (2006) continued the examination of the potential mediators of the relationship between official intervention and subsequent criminal behavior. In that article, they explore the impact of labeling on social interactions. Goffman (1963) stated that contact between those who are stigmatized and those who are not, the "normal" people, is often uneasy. In fact, Goffman (1963) further argues that "the very anticipation of such contacts can . . . lead normals and the stigmatized to arrange life so as to avoid them" (p. 13). Link's (1982; Link et al., 1989) modified labeling theory contains a similar argument suggesting that the expectation of social rejection isolates labeled individuals from conventional interactions as well as conventional opportunities. Bernburg et al. (2006) suggest that the consequence of such anticipated (and actual) rejection is the seeking of associations that share the stigma of being labeled deviant. Thus, they predict that official intervention should increase the likelihood of embeddedness in criminal groups and that such embeddedness will mediate the effect of juvenile justice intervention on criminal behavior outcomes.

Using the first four waves of the RYDS data, Bernburg et al. (2006) examine a model (Figure 8.2) that reflects the above argument. That is, formal criminal intervention is predicted to increase the probability of deviant networks at Time 2 and the probability of subsequent delinquency at Time 3. Intervention is also predicted to have an indirect effect on Time 3 delinquency through Time 2 deviant networks.

Juvenile justice intervention was measured as a dichotomy, with "1" equal to some involvement with the police or other aspects of the juvenile justice system and "0" equal to no involvement. Two measures of deviant groups were employed. The first is gang membership, coded "1" if they were a member of gang in Waves 2 or 3 and "0" if they were not.

Figure 8.2
Causal structure among formal criminal intervention, association with deviant networks, and delinquency (adapted from Bernburg et al., 2006)

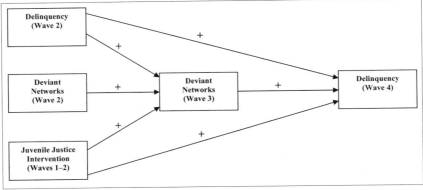

The other measure of deviant groups was peer delinquency, a scale indicating the degree to which subjects had friends who participated in delinquent behavior. A measure of serious delinquency was used as the dependent variable (Wave 4).

Bernburg et al. (2006) find substantial support for their theoretical model. Both measures of deviant networks are significantly related to serious delinquency. Whether gang membership or peer delinquency is used, deviant networks significantly reduce the effect of juvenile justice intervention on both serious delinquency measures, although a direct effect of juvenile justice intervention remains. This is a particularly important finding given that Bernburg et al. control for both prior delinquent behavior (serious delinquency and drug use) and either gang membership or peer delinquency.

The theoretical significance of these findings, coupled with the findings from Bernburg and Krohn (2003), is the recognition that the label has consequences that are far more reaching than its impact on self-concept and subsequent delinquency. The effect of official intervention on subsequent delinquent behavior may, at least partially, be indirect through its impact on life chances and type of associations.

While these findings are important, they are limited because they examine somewhat short-term outcomes. The Bernburg et al. (2006) study focuses on associations and behaviors taking place at the age of approximately fifteen, while Bernburg and Krohn (2003) examine outcomes at the age of approximately twenty-two. Do the effects of official intervention reverberate into later adulthood when life course opportunities become somewhat set? Recent analyses using the RYDS data are beginning to explore this question.

Lopes et al. (2012) take full advantage of the lengthy follow-up period of the RYDS to explore longer consequences of official intervention. The fourteen waves of the RYDS data collection span the ages of approximately fourteen to thirty-one. By the time subjects reach the age of thirty, the overwhelming majority will have completed whatever education they are going to obtain (this is particularly true given an economically disadvantaged sample). In addition, we would expect that whether they have a job at that age and whether they require welfare assistance will be indicative of the direction that their work history and financial future will take.

Recognizing that non-criminal and criminal outcomes are both important in determining a person's life course, Lopes et al. examined four outcomes, two non-crime outcomes (welfare dependency and unemployment) and two crime outcomes (general crime and drug use). The findings indicate that if youth are arrested during their adolescent years, they will be more likely to be arrested as young adults (ages twenty to twenty-two). In turn, arrest in young adulthood decreases life chances when subjects reach the age of about thirty. Specifically, having been arrested in adolescence has indirect effects through young adult arrest on both being more likely to receive welfare and being less likely to be employed.

Not surprisingly, arrest in adolescence is also indirectly related to drug use through young adult arrests. In addition, if adolescents are arrested, they are more likely to use drugs in young adulthood and the use of drugs, in turn, increases the probability that they will commit more general crime at the age of thirty. It is important to note that these indirect effects of arrest in adolescence are independent of other variables such as adolescent delinquency, drug use, family poverty, and education, which are held constant in both adolescence and young adulthood. It is also worth stressing that the effects of arrest in adolescence are being evidenced for both crime and non-crime outcomes up to sixteen years after they occurred.

Although they were unable to differentiate in time, unemployment, and welfare status from criminal behavior and drug use, Lopes et al. did investigate whether adolescent arrest indirectly affected the criminal behavioral indicators through welfare and unemployment. Neither unemployment nor welfare status at Wave 13 were directly related to a combined Waves 13 and 14 measure of drug use and crime.

Continuing Examination of the Modified Labeling Approach

Our own research, as well as studies by other scholars, has demonstrated that the importance that Link and others placed on examining the indirect effects of labeling on subsequent crime is certainly warranted. However, the above research has not explored an important part of Link's theoretical approach. Recall that Link suggested that official intervention had an impact on self-devaluation and self-removal from conventional arenas because people who are labeled would assume that conventional society would reject them, and they, in turn, would opt out of pursuing conventional goals and opportunities. Other than Link's work (Link et al., 1987), there have been few studies that have examined this argument. The RYDS data set does have a measure of self-devaluation that we can incorporate with official intervention and non-crime intermediary processes to explain criminal behavior. Our examination of this model is in its incipient stages and any conclusions derived from it have to be considered very tentative, but for illustration purposes we present some preliminary findings.

The theoretical model that we examine is depicted in Figure 8.3. Following Link et al. (1989), we predict that official intervention will lessen participation in conventional activities, reduce self-esteem, increase interaction with delinquent peers, and increase the probability of being unemployed. In addition to these direct effects, we hypothesize that official intervention will be indirectly related to self-esteem, delinquent peers, and unemployment through participation in prosocial activities. Self-esteem, delinquent peers, and unemployment are, in turn, expected to be directly related to general delinquency and to mediate the relationship between official intervention and general delinquency. We estimate this model in two steps. The first step examines the impact of official intervention on both the withdrawal from prosocial activities and on self-esteem, delinquent peers, and unemployment. The second step examines the hypothesized indirect effect of official intervention on general delinquency through the latter three measures.

Using police records, we measure *official intervention* as the total number of police contacts and/or arrests during Waves 6 and 7. Approximately three-fourths of the males did not experience any official interventions but those that did, experienced one to twelve official interventions.

Our model contains a measure of *prosocial activities*, a five-item measure tapping the concept of withdrawal. *Self-esteem* is a nine-item scale measuring the extent to which an individual agrees or disagrees, on a

Figure 8.3
Theoretical model of the effects of official intervention on subsequent offending

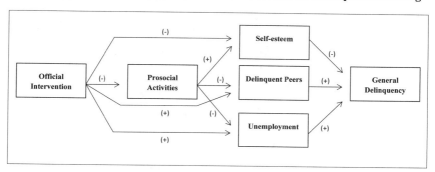

four-point Likert scale, with statements about oneself. We also include a measure of *peer delinquency,* a seven-item scale measuring the proportion of one's peers that engage in delinquent acts.

Unemployment is a measure tapping the percentage of months that the subject, between the ages of nineteen and twenty-one, did not have a job. Respondents were considered to be "employed" if they were working, in the military, or still attending college.

The outcome measure is *general delinquency* which taps the rate of involvement in a broad array of criminal and delinquent behavior, consisting of thirty-two different acts in a number of different domains. For instance, respondents were asked to self-report their involvement in violence (e.g., attack someone with a weapon, involvement in a gang fight), property crime (e.g., damage property, engage in arson), drug sales, and disorderly conduct (e.g., public rowdiness). We measure general delinquency at both Waves 10 and 12. We employ the former measure when examining the mediating effects of self-esteem and peer delinquency measured at Wave 9 and, in order to help preserve temporal order, we employ the latter when examining the mediating effects of the unemployment construct measured during Waves 10 through 12.

We control for respondents' race/ethnicity. Two dichotomous variables were created indicating whether a respondent is *African American* or *Hispanic*; *Whites* served as the reference category. To help rule out the possibility of spurious associations, we also employ general delinquency, self-esteem, involvement in prosocial activities, and peer delinquency at Wave 7 as control variables.

Table 8.1 displays the results of an ordinary least squares (OLS) regression predicting involvement in prosocial activities. In this analysis we are primarily interested in whether official intervention is related to involvement in prosocial activities controlling for a number of other factors including prior participation in prosocial activities, self-esteem, and delinquent peers. We find that official intervention does have the predicted, negative effect. In addition, those with stronger involvement in prosocial activities and higher self-esteem in Wave 7 are significantly more likely to have greater involvement in prosocial activities in Wave 8, but those with higher involvement in general delinquency are less likely to be involved in prosocial activities.

Table 8.2 contains the results from a series of OLS regression models assessing whether official intervention directly or indirectly influences self-esteem, peer delinquency, and unemployment through involvement in prosocial activities (withdrawal). Model 1 estimates the direct effect of official intervention on one's self-esteem. The results indicate that self-esteem at Wave 7 has a very strong statistically significant effect on self-esteem at Wave 8, indicating considerable stability in this construct. Neither official intervention nor other factors influence one's self-esteem at Wave 8, when controlling for prior self-esteem. Model 2 estimates

Table 8.1
OLS regression predicting involvement in prosocial activities
(Robust Standard Errors)

	Prosocial Activities (W8)	
	B	RSE
Constant	0.042	0.223
Black	0.039	0.075
Hispanic	−0.100	0.090
Self-esteem	0.186	0.069*
Prosocial activities (W7)	0.672	0.047*
Peer delinquency	0.053	0.058
General delinquency	−0.002	0.001*
Official intervention	−0.056	0.032#
R^2	.368	
n	577	

*$p \leq .05$; #$p \leq .10$

Table 8.2

OLS regressions predicting non-criminal consequences of official intervention (Robust Standard Errors)

| | Self-esteem | | | | Peer delinquency | | | | Unemployment | | | |
| | (1) | | (2) | | (3) | | (4) | | (5) | | (6) | |
	B	RSE	B	RSE	B	RSE	B	RSE	B	RSE	B	RSE
Constant	1.129	0.117*	1.090	0.120*	0.885	0.200*	0.979	0.205*	0.220	0.099*	0.294	0.099*
Black	0.052	0.036	0.052	0.037	−0.035	0.053	−0.018	0.054	0.138	0.027*	0.147	0.027*
Hispanic	0.004	0.050	0.002	0.051	−0.049	0.075	−0.041	0.075	0.122	0.035*	0.105	0.034
Self-esteem	0.684	0.033*	0.684	0.034*	−0.008	0.059	0.007	0.060	−0.033	0.031	−0.022	0.030
Peer delinquency	−0.032	0.030	−0.030	0.031	0.400	0.067*	0.426	0.067*	−0.016	0.018	−0.015	0.019
General delinquency	−0.001	0.001	−0.001	0.001	−0.001	0.001	−0.001	0.001	0.000	0.000	0.000	0.000
Official intervention	−0.008	0.015	−0.004	0.018	0.068	0.035*	0.041	0.036	0.062	0.011*	0.054	0.014*
Prosocial activities (W8)	—	—	0.021	0.018	—	—	−0.097	0.025*	—	—	−0.063	0.013*
R^2	.425		.430		.173		.188		.117		.140	
N	581		568		551		539		530		519	

$^*p \leq .05; ^\# p \leq .10$

whether involvement in prosocial activities influences self-esteem. The results indicate that involvement in prosocial activities is not a significant exogenous predictor of self-esteem. Due to the possibility that self-esteem may be more fluid during earlier adolescence, we estimated additional models using data from Waves 1 through 3 (not shown). Controlling for race, we found that the effects of official intervention at Wave 2 on self-esteem at Wave 3 were in the expected direction and statistically significant. However, when we controlled for prior self-esteem the association between official intervention and self-esteem was no longer statistically significant. Thus, among our sample of young males, official intervention does not predict self-esteem. However, it is possible that for girls, adults, and/or mental patients being labeled has the hypothesized effect.

Models 3 and 4 report the direct and indirect influences of official intervention on peer delinquency. Specifically, Model 3 demonstrates that official intervention during Waves 6 and 7 has a statistically significant effect on peer delinquency at Wave 9, controlling for peer delinquency at Wave 7 and other relevant variables. Not surprisingly, prior peer delinquency is also a statistically significant predictor of future peer delinquency. Next, we add prosocial activities to the model and find that this variable completely mediates the association between official intervention and delinquent peers (see Model 4). These findings are consistent with an indirect process; that is, the labeled individual first withdraws from conventional groups and then increases associations with deviant others. It is possible that involvement in prosocial activities declines due to exclusion (e.g., violating group rules) which, in turn, causes the juvenile to seek out more accepting peers. Future research should tease out the specific reasons for withdrawal from prosocial groups. Nevertheless, official intervention leads to a subsequent increase in delinquent peers through a reduction in one's involvement in prosocial activities.

Model 5 estimates the direct effects of official intervention on unemployment. Most importantly, those who experience more official interventions are more likely to experience greater unemployment. Finally, Model 6 adds in the involvement in prosocial activities measure to assess whether the effect of official intervention on unemployment is mediated by withdrawal. Unlike the model predicting social network ties (peer delinquency), official intervention retained a statistically significant direct effect on unemployment and the coefficient for official intervention was reduced only slightly. Prosocial activities exhibited a statistically significant effect on unemployment suggesting the path operating through withdrawal is also of substantive interest.

In summary, official intervention failed to have a direct or indirect effect on self-esteem. However, the other outcomes examined provide support for the theoretical propositions put forth by Link and his colleagues (1989). Specifically, official intervention did influence "social network ties" indirectly, through withdrawing from prosocial activities, as well as "earning power," both directly and indirectly. These, in turn, should mediate the effect of official intervention on general delinquency (Bernburg and Krohn, 2003; Bernburg et al., 2006). We briefly explore this possibility below for both social network ties and earning power, as these two constructs appear to be especially relevant to the deviance amplification process.

Given that our general delinquency measures are counts of events and the presence of over-dispersion, we employ a series of negative binomial regression models to examine the mediating effects of the labeling process (see Table 8.3). Model 1 regresses general delinquency at Wave 10 on official interventions during Waves 6 and 7 and control variables. Individuals experiencing more official intervention in late adolescence engage in more general delinquency in early adulthood, controlling for prior delinquency among other variables. Model 2 includes the peer delinquency measure to assess the mediation hypothesis; peer delinquency exhibits a statistically significant effect on general delinquency and renders the coefficient of official intervention non-significant. This is consistent with complete mediation and supportive of theoretical expectations.

Models 3 and 4 examine the direct and indirect effects (through unemployment) of official intervention on general delinquency at Wave 12. Recall, unemployment was measured from Waves 10 through 12 and, consequently, we use general delinquency at Wave 12 for reasons pertaining to temporal order. Similar to the regression model for general delinquency at Wave 10, Model 3 establishes that official intervention has a statistically significant effect on general delinquency at Wave 12. When unemployment is included in the analysis, the coefficient for official intervention is no longer statistically significant (see Model 4). Notably, the coefficient for unemployment exhibits a statistically significant effect on general delinquency. This supports the idea that the influence of a deviant label on subsequent offending behavior operates through one's earning power, in addition to one's social network ties (see Model 2). Collectively, these analyses reinforce the importance of investigating the intermediate processes by which labeling events are suspected to ultimately influence criminal and deviant behavior (see Link et al., 1989; see also Paternoster and Iovanni, 1989).

Table 8.3
Negative binomial regressions predicting general delinquency (Robust Standard Errors)

| | General delinquency (W10) | | | | General delinquency (W12) | | | |
| | (1) | | (2) | | (3) | | (4) | |
	Coef.	RSE	Coef.	RSE	Coef.	RSE	Coef.	RSE
Constant	4.598	1.000	5.253	1.039	1.665	1.265	1.150	1.113
Black	0.618	0.306*	0.482	0.324	0.180	0.302#	0.020	0.326
Hispanic	0.126	0.444	0.037	0.444	0.569	0.480	0.219	0.377
Self-esteem	−0.531	0.314#	−0.849	0.337*	0.480	0.415#	0.605	0.367#
Peer delinquency	0.344	0.150*	0.178	0.174	0.373	0.192*	0.331	0.180#
General delinquency	0.004	0.002#	0.006	0.002*	0.004	0.003#	0.005	0.003
Official intervention	0.260	0.125*	0.045	0.090	0.274	0.116*	0.154	0.101
Peer delinquency (W9)	–	–	0.474	0.179*	–	–	–	–
Unemployment (W10-12)	–	–	–	–	–	–	1.195	0.569*
Alpha	8.376	0.540	8.161	0.541	10.091	0.719	10.047	0.724
Log pseudolikelihood	−1852.8		−1736.4		−1720.5		−1639.1	
N	561		526		549		530	

$^*p \leq .05$; $^\#p \leq .10$

Conclusion

Paternoster and Iovanni (1989), as well as others, chastised the discipline for prematurely dismissing labeling theory as a viable explanation of the effects of official intervention on subsequent delinquent and criminal behavior. The research to date had either focused on the direct effects of official intervention or the indirect effects through some measure of self-esteem. Largely through the efforts of Link (1982; 1987; Link et al., 1989), whose research examined the impact of being labeled mentally ill, and through those of Sampson and Laub (1993, 1997) in the area of crime, researchers began to explore the effects of official intervention on variables like educational participation and achievement, employment status, and delinquent peers; these factors are critical in affecting life chances, and in some instances, the continued participation in crime.

This chapter has focused primarily on research that has come out of the RYDS. In a series of articles and papers reviewed above, Bernburg and associates have examined aspects of Link's modified labeling theory which specifies the intervening and cumulative mechanisms through which the deleterious impact of official intervention is predicted to have an enhancing effect on subsequent criminal behavior. We have found that official intervention is indirectly related to continuing crime through education and employment status (Bernburg and Krohn, 2003) and through deviant peer networks (Bernburg et al., 2006). We also found the problematic effect is evident even at the age of about thirty when educational and career paths should be defined or they are becoming defined (Lopes et al., 2012). Official intervention is either directly or indirectly related to employment, welfare status, and various measures of subsequent crime and drug use.

In addition to reviewing the research that we have done, we presented some preliminary analysis that includes Link's notion that people who are labeled will remove themselves from conventional opportunities because they recognize how others feel about them resulting in lowered self-esteem, increased probability of being unemployed, and increased associations with deviant others. Hypotheses concerning self-esteem were not supported, but those regarding the withdrawal from conventional activities and its impact on deviant peer associations and unemployment were supported. These two non-criminal outcomes, in turn, influenced criminal behavior in early adulthood consistent with theoretical expectations. Although these findings are tentative, they do indicate that continuing to apply Link's modified labeling theory to understand the labeling process and the effects of official intervention on non-criminal and criminal outcomes is warranted. One future direction in our own analysis is to examine the impact of official intervention on the quality of partner relationships.

Our work, along with our assessment of recent research by other scholars, supports Paternoster and Iovanni's (1989) ironic assertion that the labeling perspective was itself prematurely labeled dead. As the evidence suggests, there are problematic effects of experiencing official intervention which encompass both decreased life chances and increased probability of continuing criminal involvement.

References

Adams, M. S., J. D. Johnson, and T. D. Evans. "Racial Differences in Informal Labeling Effects." *Deviant Behavior* 19 (1998): 157–71.

Ageton, S. and D. Elliott. "The Effect of Legal Processing on Delinquent Orientations." *Social Problems* 22 (1974): 87–100.

Bartusch, D. J. and R. L. Matsueda. "Gender, Reflected Appraisals, and Labeling: A Cross-Group Test of an Interactionist Theory of Delinquency." *Social Forces* 75 (1996): 145–76.

Becker, H. S. *Outsiders: Studies in the Sociology of Deviance*. New York: Free Press, 1963.

Benson, M. L. *Crime and the Life Course*. Los Angeles, CA: Roxbury Press, 2002.

Berk, R., A. Campbell, R. Klap, and B. Western. "The Deterrent Effect of Arrest in Incidents of Domestic Violence: A Bayesian Analysis of Four Field Experiments." *American Sociological Review* 57 (1992): 698–708.

Bernburg, J. G. *State Reaction, Life-Course Outcomes, and Structural Disadvantage: A Panel Study of the Impact of Formal Criminal Labeling on the Transition to Adulthood*. Unpublished doctoral dissertation, University at Albany, State University of New York, Albany, NY (UMI no.: 3058971), 2002.

Bernburg, J. G. and M. D. Krohn. "Labeling, Life Chances, and Adult Crime: The Direct and Indirect Effects of Official Intervention in Adolescence on Crime in Early Adulthood." *Criminology* 41 (2003): 1287–317.

Bernburg, J. G., M. D. Krohn, and C. J. Rivera. "Official Labeling, Criminal Embeddedness, and Subsequent Delinquency: A Longitudinal Test of Labeling Theory." *Journal of Research in Crime and Delinquency* 43 (2006): 67–88.

Boshier, R. and D. Johnson. "Does Conviction Affect Employment Opportunities?" *British Journal of Criminology* 14 (1974): 264–68.

Bowditch, C. "Getting Rid of Troublemakers: High School Disciplinary Procedures and the Production of Dropouts." *Social Problems* 40 (1993): 493–509.

Buikhuisen, W. and F. P. H. Dijksterhuis. "Delinquency and Stigmatization." *British Journal of Criminology* 11 (1971): 185–87.

Chiricos, T., K. Barrick, W. Bales, and S. Bontranger. "The Labeling of Convicted Felons and its Consequences for Recidivism." *Criminology* 45 (2007): 547–81.

Cooley, C. H. *Human Nature and the Social Order*. New York: Charles Scribner's Sons, 1902.

Cumming, J. and E. Cumming. "On the Stigma of Mental Illness." *Community Mental Health Journal* 1 (1965): 135–43.

Davies, S. and J. Tanner. "The Long Arm of the Law: Effects of Labeling on Employment." *Sociological Quarterly* 44 (2003): 385–404.

DeLi, S. "Legal Sanctions and Youths' Status Achievement: A Longitudinal Study." *Justice Quarterly* 16 (1999): 377–401.

Elder, G. H. *Life-course dynamics: trajectories and transitions, 1968–1980.* Ithaca, NY: Cornell University Press, 1985.

———. "Time, Human Agency, and Social Change: Perspectives on the Life Course." *Social Psychology Quarterly* 57 (1994): 4–15.

Farrington, D. P. "The Effects of Public Labelling." *British Journal of Criminology* 17 (1977): 112–25.

———. *Integrated Developmental and Life-Course Theories of Offending.* New Brunswick, NJ: Transaction Publishers, 2005.

Farrington, D. P., S. G. Osborn, and D. J. West. "The Persistence of Labeling Effects." *British Journal of Criminology* 18 (1978): 277–84.

Foner, P. S. *History of the Labor Movement in the United States: The Industrial Workers of the World, 1905–1917: Vol. 4.* New York: International Publishers Company, Inc., 1965.

Freeman, R. *Crime and Employment of Disadvantaged Youth.* Cambridge, MA: Harvard University, NBER series, 1991.

Garfinkel, H. "Conditions of Successful Degradation Ceremonies." *American Journal of Sociology* 61 (1956): 420–24.

Goffman, E. *Asylums: Essays on the Social Situation of Mental Patients and Other Inmates.* Garden City, NY: Anchor Books, 1961.

———. *Stigma: Notes in the Management of a Spoiled Identity.* Englewoods Cliffs, NJ: Prentice-Hall, 1963.

Hagan, J. and A. Palloni. "The Social Reproduction of a Criminal Class in Working Class London, Circa 1950–1980." *American Journal of Sociology* 96 (1990): 265–99.

Harris, A. R. "Race, Commitment to Deviance, and Spoiled Identity." *American Sociological Review* 41 (1976): 432–42.

Heimer, K. "Gender, Interaction, and Delinquency: Testing a Theory of Differential Social Control." *Social Psychology Quarterly* 59 (1996): 39–61.

Heimer, K. and R. L. Matsueda. "Role-Taking, Role-Commitment, and Delinquency: A Theory of Differential Social Control." *American Sociological Review* 59 (1994): 365–90.

Hirschi, T. "Labelling Theory and Juvenile Delinquency: An Assessment of the Evidence." In *The Labelling of Deviance: Evaluating a Perspective*, edited by W. Gove, 181–204. New York: Wiley, 1980.

Hjalmarsson, R. "Criminal Justice Involvement and High School Completion." *Journal of Urban Economics* 63 (2008): 613–30.

Irwin, J. *The Warehouse Prison: Disposal of the New Dangerous Class.* Los Angeles, CA: Roxbury Press, 2005.

Jensen, G. F. "Labeling and Identity: Toward a Reconciliation of Divergent Findings." *Criminology* 18 (1980): 121–29.

Johnson, L. M., R. L. Simons, and R. D. Conger. "Criminal Justice System Involvement and Continuity of Youth Crime: A Longitudinal Analysis." *Youth & Society* 36 (2004): 3–29.

Lanctôt, N., S. A. Cernkovich, and P. C. Giordano. "Delinquent Behavior, Official Delinquency, and Gender: Consequences for Adulthood Functioning and Well-Being." *Criminology* 45 (2007): 131–57.

Laub, J. H., and R. J. Sampson. "Unemployment, Marital Discord, and Deviant Behavior: The Long-Term Correlates of Childhood Misbehavior." In *The Generality of Deviance*, edited by T. Hirschi, and M. R. Gottfredson, 235–52. New Brunswick, NJ: Transaction Publishers, 1994.

Lemert, E. M. *Human Deviance, Social Problems, and Social Control.* Englewoods Cliffs, NJ: Prentice-Hall, 1967.
———. *Social Pathology: A Systematic Approach to the Theory of Sociopathic Behavior.* New York: McGraw-Hill, 1951.
Link, B. G. "Mental Patient Status, Work, and Income: An Examination of the Effects of a Psychiatric Label." *American Sociological Review* 47 (1982): 202–15.
———. "Understanding Labeling Effects in the Area of Mental Disorders: An Assessment of the Effects of Expectations of Rejection." *American Sociological Review* 52 (1987): 96–112.
Link, B. G., F. T. Cullen, J. Frank, and J. F. Wozniak. "The Social Rejection of Former Mental Patients: Understanding Why Labels Matter." *American Journal of Sociology* 92 (1987): 1461–500.
Link, B. G., F. T. Cullen, E. Struening, P. E. Shrout, and B. P. Dohrenwend. "A Modified Labeling Theory Approach to Mental Disorders: An Empirical Assessment." *American Sociological Review* 54 (1989): 400–23.
Link, B. G., J. Mirotznik, and F. T. Cullen. "The Effectiveness of Stigma Coping Orientations: Can Negative Consequences of Mental Illness Labeling be Avoided?" *Journal of Health and Social Behavior* 32 (1991): 302–20.
Lopes, G., M. D. Krohn, A. J. Lizotte, N. Schmidt, B. E. Vasquez, and J. G. Bernburg. "Labeling and Cumulative Disadvantage: The Impact of Official Intervention on Life Chances and Crime in Emerging Adulthood." *Crime and Delinquency* 58, no. 3 (2012): 456–88.
Matsueda, R. L. "Reflected Appraisal, Parental Labeling, and Delinquency: Specifying a Symbolic Interactionist Theory." *American Journal of Sociology* 97 (1992): 1577–611.
Matsueda, R. L. and K. Heimer. "A Symbolic Interactionist Theory of Role-Transitions, Role-Commitments, and Delinquency." In *Developmental Theories of Crime and Delinquency*, edited by T. P. Thornberry, 163–213. New Brunswick, NJ: Transaction, 1997.
Mead, G. H. *Mind, Self, and Society: From the Standpoint of a Social Behaviorist.* Ed. C. W. Morris. Chicago, IL: University of Chicago Press, 1934.
Merton, R. "The Matthew Effect in Science: The Reward and Communication Systems of Science are Considered." *Science* 159 (1968): 56–63.
———. "The Matthew Effect in Science, II: Cumulative Advantage and the Symbolism of Intellectual Property." *Isis* 79 (1988): 606–23.
Pager, D. "The Mark of a Criminal Record." *American Journal of Sociology* 108 (2003): 937–75.
Palamara, F., F. T. Cullen, and J. C. Gersten. "The Effect of Police and Mental Health Intervention on Juvenile Deviance: Specifying Contingencies in the Impact of Formal Reaction." *Journal of Health and Social Behavior* 27 (1986): 90–105.
Pate, A. and E. Hamilton. "Formal and Informal Deterrents to Domestic Violence: The Dade County Spouse Assault Experiment." *American Sociological Review* 57 (1992): 691–97.
Paternoster, R. and Iovanni, L. "The Labeling Perspective and Delinquency: An Elaboration of the Theory and Assessment of the Evidence." *Justice Quarterly* 6 (1989): 359–94.
Ray, M. C. and W. Downs. "An Empirical Test of Labeling Theory Using Longitudinal Data." *Journal of Research of Crime and Delinquency* 23 (1986): 169–94.
Sampson, R. J. and J. H. Laub. *Crime in the Making: Pathways and Turning Points through Life.* Cambridge, MA: Harvard University Press, 1993.

————. "A Life-Course Theory of Cumulative Disadvantage and the Stability of Delinquency." In *Developmental Theories of Crime and Delinquency*, edited by T. P. Thornberry, 133–61. New Brunswick, NJ: Transaction, 1997.

Scheff, T. J. *Being Mentally Ill: A Sociological Theory*. Chicago, IL: Aldine Pub. Co., 1966.

Schwartz, R. D. and J. H. Skolnick. "Two Studies of Legal Stigma." *Social Problems* 10 (1962): 133–43.

Sherman, L., D. Smith, J. Schmidt, and D. Rogan. "Crime, Punishment, and Stake in Conformity: Legal and Informal Control of Domestic Violence." *American Sociological Review* 57 (1992): 680–90.

Stewart, E. A., R. L. Simons, R. D. Conger, and L. V. Scaramella. "Beyond the Interactional Relationship between Delinquency and Parenting Practices: The Contribution of Legal Sanctions." *Journal of Research in Crime and Delinquency* 39 (2002): 36–59.

Sweeten, G. "Who will Graduate? Disruptions of High School Education by Arrest and Court Involvement." *Justice Quarterly* 23 (2006): 462–80.

Tannenbaum, F. *Crime and the Community*. New York and London: Columbia University Press, 1938.

————. *The Mexican Agrarian Revolution*. Archon Books, 1929.

————. *A Philosophy of Labor*. New York: Alfred A. Knopf, Inc., 1951.

————. *Slave and Citizen*. New York: Alfred A. Knopf, Inc., 1946.

————. *Wall Shadows: A Study in American Prisons*. New York and London: The Knickerbocker Press, 1922.

Thomas, W. I. "The Unadjusted Girl: With Cases and Standpoint for Behavior Analysis." *Criminal Sciences Monographs* 4 (1923): 1–257.

Thornberry, T. P. and M. D. Krohn. "Applying Interactional Theory to the Explanation of Continuity and Change in Antisocial Behavior." In *Integrated Developmental and Life-Course Theories of Offending*, edited by D. P. Farrington, 183–209. New Brunswick, NJ: Transaction Publishers, 2005.

————. "The Development of Delinquency: An Interactional Perspective." In *Handbook of Law and Social Science: Youth and Justice*, edited by S. O. White, 289–305. New York: Plenum Publishers, 2001.

Tittle, C. "Labeling and Crime: An Empirical Evaluation." In *The Labelling of Deviance: Evaluating a Perspective*, edited by W. Gove, 241–63. New York: Wiley, 1980.

Western, B. and K. Beckett. "How Unregulated is the U.S. Labor Market?" *American Journal of Sociology*, 104 (1999): 1030–60.

9

Long-Term Effects of Conviction and Incarceration on Men in the Cambridge Study in Delinquent Development

Joseph Murray, Arjan Blokland,
David P. Farrington, and Delphine Theobald

Introduction

Labeling theory suggests that punishment by the criminal justice system is counterproductive and causes increases in criminal behavior. Such undesirable effects may be cumulative and long-lasting, and may also affect other spheres of life, such as employment, relationships, and mental health. In this paper, we examine consequences of conviction and incarceration on multiple life outcomes up to age forty-eight years in the Cambridge Study in Delinquent Development (CSDD), a prospective longitudinal survey of over 400 English males studied from age eight. Using regression analyses and propensity score matching, we find persistent and strong associations between juvenile conviction and adult criminal behavior, antisocial personality, and life success. The consequences of juvenile conviction are partly explained by men's antisocial attitudes, involvement with delinquent groups, and unemployment at age eighteen. Undesirable effects of juvenile conviction are stronger for boys who had a convicted parent than boys who did not have a convicted parent. Incarceration increases the risk for early adult antisocial personality and poor life success over and above the effects of conviction without incarceration.

Effects of Conviction and Incarceration on Future Crime

The idea that criminal justice sanctions are counterproductive and actually cause an increase in criminal behavior is commonly attributed to the classic writings of Edwin Lemert (1951, 1967) and other so-called labeling theorists (Tannenbaum, 1938; Garfinkel, 1956; Becker, 1963; Scheff, 1966). Lemert theorized that, after initial experimentation in childhood misbehavior, which he called "primary deviance," social reactions are critical in determining whether further "secondary deviance" develops. For example, if an adolescent is convicted for delinquent behavior, a labeling process may follow in which stigmatization, alteration of personal identity, and increased association with other delinquents cause further criminal behavior. Although labeling theory is not deterministic (and individuals are likely to vary in their reactions to criminal justice sanctions, Sherman, 2013), it suggests that criminal justice processing will tend to increase criminal behavior rather than diminish it. At its height of popularity in the 1970s, labeling theory drew criminology's focus away from examining individual psychopathology as a cause of crime, and highlighted the importance of interactions between young offenders, the criminal justice system, and social responses to deviance for understanding criminal behavior (Paternoster and Iovanni, 1989).

The labeling hypothesis that criminal justice processing has criminogenic effects is often contrasted with predictions from deterrence theory. According to the specific deterrence hypothesis, criminal sanctions are likely to reduce criminal behavior by causing punished offenders to perceive a greater risk of being caught and sanctioned for possible future criminal acts (Paternoster, 1987; Smith and Gartin, 1989; Nagin et al., 2009). As David Huizinga and Kimberly Henry (2008) and Avinash Bhati and Alex Piquero (2007) point out, it is also possible that criminal justice sanctions have no discernable effect on criminal behavior, either because labeling processes and deterrent effects cancel each other out, or because, if a constant criminal propensity is rooted in early childhood factors, later conviction or incarceration would have negligible effects on future criminal behavior. In this context, the proposition that criminal justice processing tends to have criminogenic effects must be empirically tested against competing hypotheses of deterrent or null effects.

Mediators of Labeling Effects

In an important review, Raymond Paternoster and LeeAnn Iovanni (1989) argued for a rejuvenation of labeling theory, and emphasized the need to carefully specify and test mediators of labeling effects. Mediators are links in the causal chain that explain how labeling experiences affect behavioral outcomes, such as future criminal behavior. Ideally, mediators should be measured after the labeling event and it should be tested whether there is an indirect path from labeling to future crime via the mediators. In the labeling literature, two categories of mediators can be distinguished linking criminal justice sanctions and future crime. First, drawing on symbolic interactionism, labeling theorists suggested that criminal justice system involvement causes criminal behavior via stigma, changes in personal identity, altered attitudes and beliefs, and through association with delinquent peers (Becker, 1963; Lemert, 1967; Paternoster and Iovanni, 1989; Matsueda, 1992; Bernburg et al., 2006). Thus, this first category of mediators focuses on internal processes and delinquent associations. In the current study, we examine antisocial attitudes and involvement with delinquent groups as possible mediators of labeling effects.

A second type of mediator that might explain labeling effects is changes in social opportunities, such as access to education and employment (Sampson and Laub, 1997; Bernburg and Krohn, 2003; Bernburg et al., 2006). This idea is consistent with social bonding theory and is a critical element in Robert Sampson and John Laub's theory of cumulative disadvantage (Sampson and Laub, 1997). According to Sampson and Laub, criminal sanctions reduce conventional opportunities such as legitimate employment and, in a snowball fashion, push people into further disadvantage and crime: "Cumulative disadvantage posits that arrest and especially incarceration may spark failure in school, unemployment, and weak community bonds, in turn increasing adult crime" (Laub and Sampson, 2003: 291). In the current study, we examine whether unemployment mediates labeling effects on adult outcomes. Unemployment has been linked to increases in criminal behavior (e.g., Farrington et al., 1986), higher rates of psychiatric disorder (e.g., Fergusson et al., 1997), and problems for families and children (see Ström, 2003 for a review). Thus, if social and economic factors like unemployment mediate labeling effects, it seems likely that multiple life outcomes will be affected, not just criminal behavior. We examine long-term labeling effects both on criminal behavior and other domains of adult life summarized in a life success score.

Moderators of Labeling Effects

It has long been acknowledged that labeling experiences do not have deterministic effects (Becker, 1963; Paternoster and Iovanni, 1989). Criminal conviction and incarceration may increase criminal behavior for some individuals but not for others (Sherman, 2013). Thus, an important challenge for research is to identify the conditions under which labeling experiences have different effects. To investigate this issue, moderators need to be tested. Moderators are variables which predict different effects at different levels of the moderator (Kraemer et al., 2005). For example, if labeling effects are stronger for males than females, then a person's sex is a moderator of labeling effects.

Paternoster and Iovanni (1989) suggested a number of possible moderators of labeling effects, including social class membership, race, degree of self-orientation, and whether the label is made more or less public. They also argued that criminal justice sanctions are likely to have stronger effects for people who have not previously been labeled (see, e.g., Klein, 1986). It is also possible that labeling has stronger effects at an earlier age, when personality and behavioral dispositions are more malleable (Bernburg et al., 2006). We also think it is plausible that criminal convictions have different effects according to the person's previous antisocial behavior. There might be weaker effects for people with early-onset antisocial behavior, which predicts life-course-persistent offending (Moffitt, 1993), and stronger effects for people whose antisocial behavior commences later (e.g., Sweeten, 2006). We test this hypothesis in the current study.

There is good reason to suppose that different types of criminal justice sanction have different labeling effects (Cullen and Jonson, 2013). Among criminal justice sanctions, incarceration may have more undesirable consequences than conviction followed by other types of sentences, such as fines or community service (Killias et al., 2006; Gatti et al., 2009; Nagin et al., 2009; Nieuwbeerta et al., 2009). The potentially stronger effects of incarceration might derive from physical separation of the offender from their family and community, time spent inside with other "deviants" causing offenders to develop or solidify a criminal identity, and strong social reactions to the "mark" of incarceration after release. According to recent systematic reviews and meta-analyses (Killias et al., 2006; Nagin et al., 2009), the evidence points toward an average criminogenic effect of incarceration compared to non-custodial sentences, but results are often non-statistically significant and based on short follow-up periods, rarely over two years. In the current study, we compare effects of incarceration versus conviction without incarceration on outcomes over two decades, up to age forty-eight.

John Hagan and Alberto Palloni (1990) suggested that labeling effects might differ according to a person's family history of criminal justice involvement. They hypothesized that adolescents with convicted parents experience stronger labeling effects than adolescents without convicted parents, and found evidence for this up to age twenty-one in the CSDD. This might occur because adjudicated youth with convicted parents experience harsher judgments about their "deviant character" than other adjudicated youth, and this may increase the chances that they adopt a "deviant identity" and commit further criminal behavior. In the current study, we test whether intergenerational labeling effects endure into adult life.

Previous tests of labeling theory in the Cambridge Study in Delinquent Development (CSDD)

Overview of the CSDD

The CSDD is a prospective longitudinal survey of the development of offending and antisocial behavior in 411 males (Farrington, 2003; Farrington et al., 2006, 2009, 2013). At the time they were first contacted in 1961–62, these males were all living in a working-class inner-city area of South London. The sample was chosen by taking all the boys who were then aged eight to nine and on the registers of six state primary schools within a one-mile radius of a research office that had been established. Hence, the most common year of birth of these males was 1953. The families of the boys were predominantly working-class, two-parent households. Most of the males (87 percent) were white and of British origin. Interviews with the males and key informants, including parents and teachers, have been conducted since the males were eight, and criminal record searches have been conducted on the boys, their parents, and other family members repeatedly through the Study. Most recently, the males in the Study were contacted at age forty-eight, when 93 percent of those in the original sample still alive were interviewed. The Study was directed by Donald West until 1982, and since then it has been directed by David Farrington.

The CSDD is unique in combining many strengths for studying labeling effects (Hagan and Palloni, 1990): (1) it is based on a community sample; (2) the study started before the onset of official offending; (3) it has a prospective longitudinal design; (4) it includes repeated measures of both self-reported crime and criminal records; (5) there is a long follow-up period with high retention rates; and (6) a very rich range of data were collected on the participants and their families from childhood, which can be used to control for confounding variables and to investigate mediators and moderators of labeling effects.

Farrington (1977; Farrington et al., 1978)

Previously in the CSDD, Farrington (1977) investigated whether a first conviction during adolescence caused an increase in delinquent behavior by age eighteen. Fifty-three boys in the Study were first convicted between ages fourteen and eighteen. Their self-reported delinquency increased significantly from before to after conviction. By contrast, among non-convicted boys (individually matched with convicted boys on self-reported delinquency at age fourteen), delinquency actually decreased by age eighteen. Age eighteen delinquency scores were significantly higher for convicted boys than for the matched non-convicted boys, even after accounting for other risk factors. These results were consistent with the labeling hypothesis that official conviction causes an increase in delinquent behavior. Farrington (1977) also compared convicted and non-convicted boys on changes in hostile attitude to the police and peer delinquency scores from before to after first conviction. The results were consistent with the hypothesis that conviction increases hostility to the police, which in turn leads to increased delinquency. However, conviction was not associated with an increase in association with delinquent peers.

In a follow-up study, Farrington et al. (1978) tested whether labeling effects in the CSDD persisted to age twenty-one. They found that self-reported delinquency increased between ages eighteen and twenty-one for those first convicted between these ages. This increase was associated with increases in aggressive attitude during the same period. Also, following a first conviction between ages fourteen and eighteen, higher rates of self-reported delinquency persisted to age twenty-one, whether or not the boy was reconvicted between ages eighteen and twenty-one. Generally, these results suggested a persistence of labeling effects up to age twenty-one. However, boys who were first convicted before age fourteen showed a decrease in self-reported delinquency by age twenty-one, which was interpreted as a possible "wearing off" of earlier labeling effects.

Nagin and Waldfogel (1995)

Daniel Nagin and Joel Waldfogel (1995) investigated the effects of conviction on employment outcomes between ages seventeen and nineteen in the CSDD. The results are significant for labeling theory in showing effects of conviction on variables that might mediate labeling effects. Nagin and Waldfogel compared men who were convicted between ages seventeen and nineteen with non-convicted men who were similar on self-reported delinquency scores at both ages seventeen and nineteen. Although being convicted was associated with greater job instability (a higher total number of jobs, a shorter longest period in any one job, more time unemployed), it was also associated with a higher rate of pay at age nineteen. Nagin and Waldfogel suggested that convicted men had a higher rate of pay because the stigma of conviction pushed them into the spot labor market, where initial pay is higher but career prospects are lower. Thus, while conviction was associated with short-term pay advantages, it also predicted job instability that could cause longer term disadvantage in adult life.

Li (1999)

Drawing on Sampson and Laub's theory of cumulative disadvantage, Spencer De Li (1999) examined direct and indirect effects of juvenile conviction on achievement and self-reported delinquency at ages eighteen to nineteen in the CSDD. "Achievement" referred to a single latent construct including exam results, job status, number of jobs per year, time unemployed, longest period in any one job, and frequency of being dismissed from a job. Measures of childhood antisocial behavior, intelligence, social disadvantage, and parental conviction at ages eight to nine were controlled for as confounding variables. Self-reported delinquency at ages fourteen to fifteen, conviction at ages fourteen to sixteen, and unemployment at ages sixteen to seventeen were examined as possible mediators of the effects of early conviction (ages ten to thirteen). Early conviction was found to both directly and indirectly reduce achievement and indirectly increase delinquency via the mediators in the model. Conviction at ages fourteen to sixteen had weaker effects than earlier conviction, but nonetheless there were significant direct effects on delinquency and indirect effects on achievement at ages eighteen to nineteen. Li (1999: 393) concluded that "legal sanctions escalate involvement in antisocial behavior and diminish . . . life chances in early adulthood."

Hagan and Palloni (1990)

Hagan and Palloni (1990) used data from the CSDD to test the hypothesis of an intergenerational labeling effect. Specifically, they tested whether conviction of a boy had stronger labeling effects if the boy had a parent who had also been convicted. Parental conviction was measured up to age ten, boys' own convictions were measured between ages fourteen and eighteen, and boys' self-reported delinquency between ages sixteen and twenty-two. A wide variety of other measures between ages eight and fifteen were used as control variables, including individual, parenting, family, and peer characteristics, and prior self-reported delinquency. An interaction term (Parental Conviction * Boy's Own Conviction) was used to test whether parental conviction moderated the effects of the boy's own conviction on future offending. Regression models showed unfavorable effects of conviction on self-reported delinquency at ages sixteen to seventeen net of background variables, and a positive interaction effect, consistent with the authors' hypothesis that parental conviction amplified criminogenic labeling effects. Intergenerational labeling effects on self-reported delinquency at later ages were also evident but were more modest.

Murray and Farrington (2005, 2008a, 2008b)

Murray and Farrington (2005, 2008a, 2008b) examined intergenerational effects of parental incarceration on boys in the CSDD. Boys whose parents were incarcerated between birth and age ten were compared with four control groups: boys who never experienced lengthy separation from their parents or parental incarceration, boys separated from parents because of hospitalization or death, boys separated from parents for other reasons, and boys whose parents were incarcerated before the boy's birth but not afterwards. Criminal behavior, mental health problems, and other adverse outcomes were examined up to age forty-eight. Even when controlling for a wide range of childhood risk factors, separation because of parental incarceration predicted undesirable outcomes throughout the life course.

Separation because of parental incarceration (occurring during childhood) had stronger effects than parental incarceration occurring before the boy's birth, suggesting that environmental mechanisms were important. However, because parental incarceration predicted worse outcomes than other forms of parent-child separation, it did not seem to be separation *per se* that caused the effects. Also, effects of parental incarceration were not explained by police or court bias against children of prisoners, because similarly strong effects were observed for self-reported criminal behavior as for officially recorded crime. Interestingly, effects of parental incarceration in the CSDD were stronger than in a well matched study in Sweden (Murray et al., 2007), suggesting that effects of parental incarceration on children may be moderated by the social and penal culture in which it takes place.

Possible Long-Term Effects of Criminal Justice Sanctions

As reviewed in the previous section, prior work in the CSDD suggests that juvenile conviction has criminogenic effects up to age twenty-one, but later life outcomes have not been tested. The theory of cumulative disadvantage suggests that undesirable labeling effects might escalate through adult life and "increasingly 'mortgage' one's future, especially later life chances molded by schooling and employment" (Sampson and Laub, 1997: 147).

Despite the strength of longitudinal research in criminology, surprisingly little evidence exists on long-term consequences of conviction or incarceration (Sampson and Laub, 1997: 139–140; Huizinga and Henry, 2008: 223; Nagin, et al., 2009). Two studies examined outcomes up to age twenty-five (Smith and Gartin, 1989) and twenty-six (Brennan and Mednick, 1994) in large cohorts, but both studies were based on official records only (both showed slight deterrent effects of criminal sanctions on later officially recorded crime). Important recent work, using both official and self-report data in the Rochester Youth Development Study, shows that criminal justice intervention (police contact and juvenile justice involvement) in mid-adolescence increases delinquency up to age twenty-two, via reduced educational attainment and unemployment (Bernburg and Krohn, 2003). More recent analyses of this Study suggest that arrest in adolescence also increases the probability of unemployment, welfare receipt, drug use, and general crime up to age thirty (Krohn et al., 2013).

Scott Davies and Julian Tanner (2003) investigated effects of criminal justice contact and sentencing between ages fifteen and twenty-three on employment outcomes at ages twenty-nine to thirty-seven in the National Longitudinal Survey of Youth. Controlling for prior delinquency and social background variables, conviction and incarceration contributed to the prediction of low occupational status, low income, and unemployment in mid-adulthood.

Using data from the Gluecks' classic study of 500 delinquents and 500 non-delinquents, Sampson and Laub (1993) investigated effects of time incarcerated on job stability and self-reported crime up to age thirty-two. Although there was no direct effect of time served on later criminal behavior (when job stability was controlled), longer incarceration spells predicted more job instability, and this, in turn, predicted higher rates of criminal behavior in adulthood.

Nadine Lanctot et al. (2007) examined the effects of juvenile incarceration in a sample of 210 previously institutionalized offenders and 721 individuals in private households, followed from adolescence to their late twenties. They examined a number of outcomes of life success and well-being in adulthood, including measures of socioeconomic disadvantage, job stability, cohabitation and parenthood, support from relatives and peers, emotional well-being, domestic violence, and adult antisocial behavior. They controlled for self-reported delinquency in adolescence to try to isolate the effects of juvenile incarceration from the effects of criminal propensity. Juvenile incarceration predicted depression, drug-related problems, and many other social difficulties. However, net of juvenile delinquency, incarceration did not predict adult criminal involvement.

The Current Study of Long-Term Labeling Effects in the CSDD

Previous findings from the CSDD are consistent with the existence of labeling effects of conviction up to age twenty-one. Evidence from a few other studies points toward possible undesirable effects of conviction and incarceration on multiple outcomes in early adulthood. We used recently collected data in the CSDD to investigate consequences of conviction and incarceration on crime, antisocial personality, and life success at ages thirty-two and forty-eight. We tested the following five hypotheses about possible long lasting effects of first conviction and incarceration on adult outcomes.

1. First conviction as a juvenile (ages fifteen to eighteen) and as a young adult (ages nineteen to twenty-six) increases the probability of crime, antisocial personality, and poor life success at ages thirty-two and forty-eight.
2. Juvenile conviction has stronger effects than young adult conviction.
3. Incarceration has stronger effects than conviction without incarceration.

4. Long-term labeling effects are substantially mediated by aggressive attitudes, pro-drugs attitudes, antiestablishment attitudes, delinquent group activity, and unemployment.
5. Long-term labeling effects are moderated by having a convicted parent and by having early-onset antisocial behavior.

Measures

Conviction and incarceration were measured throughout the Study in repeated searches of the central Criminal Record Office in London (see Farrington et al., 2006). When the boys were juveniles, these data were supplemented by searches of various local authorities, such as Children's Departments, nearby police, court, and probation offices, and occasionally by information from teachers.

Self-reported criminal behavior was measured at ages fourteen, eighteen, thirty-two, and forty-eight by asking the male subjects of the Study to self-report offenses that they had committed that had not necessarily come to the notice of the police (see Farrington et al., 2006, for details). The reference periods were: ever (fourteen), last three years (eighteen) and last five years (thirty-two and forty-eight). Ten types of offenses were enquired about on most occasions: burglary, theft of motor vehicles, theft from motor vehicles, shoplifting, theft from machines, theft from work (not ages fourteen or eighteen), fraud (not ages fourteen or eighteen), assault, drug use, and vandalism. On each occasion, each criminal act was scored 1–4 for frequency, and the sum of these scores was used as a total self-reported criminal behavior score.

Antisocial personality scores were derived from interviews with the males, parents, and teachers chosen for the Study, and official records at ages ten, fourteen, eighteen, thirty-two, and forty-eight (see Farrington, 1991, for details). The antisocial personality scales were devised from items included in the definitions of conduct disorder, antisocial personality disorder, and psychopathy. For example, at age thirty-two, the antisocial personality scale (referring to the previous five years) comprised: convicted, self-reported delinquency, involved in fights, taken drugs, heavy drinking, poor relationship with parents, poor relationship with wife, divorced or child elsewhere, frequently unemployed, anti-establishment, tattooed, and impulsive.

Life success was measured at ages thirty-two and forty-eight (see Farrington et al., 2006), using combined scales of life outcomes referring to the previous five years. At age thirty-two, items in the scale were:

satisfactory accommodation history, satisfactory cohabitation history, successful with children, satisfactory employment history, not involved in fights, no substances use, no self-reported offenses (other than theft from work or tax fraud), satisfactory mental health, and no convictions in the previous five years. Each man was scored according to the percentage of these nine criteria on which he was considered successful. A similar scale was constructed based on age forty-eight data.

Confounding variables. Numerous aspects of the boys' personalities, behaviors, their parents' characteristics, family characteristics, and their social backgrounds were measured at the beginning of the Study, at ages eight to ten. Many of these have been identified as key risk factors for future antisocial and delinquent behavior (Farrington, 2003). We used the following dichotomous indicators of fifteen risk factors measured at ages eight to ten as control variables in the analyses: antisocial personality, poor child rearing, convicted parent, high daring, large family size, poor junior school leaving results, poor housing conditions, low family income, low IQ, low popularity, high delinquency rate secondary school, low family socioeconomic status, parent-child separation, low parental supervision, troublesome behavior at school, and lack of concentration or restless in class. Details of the measures can be found in prior publications (West and Farrington, 1973, 1977). We also controlled for the self-reported delinquency and antisocial personality scores that were measured most recently before the labeling event (either at age fourteen or at age eighteen).

Mediators. The five mediators examined in this study were all measured in interviews with the male subjects of the Study at age eighteen. *Pro-aggressive attitude* was measured as a summed scale of eleven items, including, for example, "I enjoy watching people get beaten up on T.V." *Pro-drugs attitude* was measured as a summed scale of four items, including "Pot smokers should be left alone by the police." *Antiestablishment attitude* was measured as a summed scale of eleven items such as "This country would be better run by young people" and "Anyone who works hard is stupid." *Delinquent friends* referred to the previous two years, and was coded as follows: (1) not participant in a group involved in vandalism or fighting; (2) involved in group vandalism only; (3) involved in group fighting only; and (4) involved in group fighting and group vandalism. *Unemployment* referred to the number of weeks unemployed in the previous year.

Moderators. Parental criminal convictions were measured by searching for findings of guilt in the Criminal Record Office in London.

A dichotomous variable was used to represent having at least one parent convicted versus neither parent convicted. The age ten antisocial personality scale (described above) was dichotomized into the quarter of the sample with the highest scores versus the remainder.

Analytic techniques

Three key comparisons were made between male subjects of the Study to investigate the effects of juvenile conviction, young adult conviction, and incarceration on adult outcomes:

(1) To estimate effects of juvenile conviction, boys first convicted between ages fifteen and eighteen ($n = 53$) were compared with boys not convicted up to age eighteen ($n = 310$).

(2) To estimate effects of conviction in young adulthood, boys first convicted between ages nineteen and twenty-six ($n = 31$) were compared with boys not convicted up to age twenty-six ($n = 279$).

(3) To estimate effects of incarceration, boys first incarcerated between ages fifteen and twenty-six ($n = 34$) were compared with boys convicted between ages fifteen and twenty-six who were not incarcerated up to age twenty-six ($n = 87$).

Outcomes were compared between each "treated"[1] and comparison group to estimate average labeling effects. Two analytical approaches were used to control for confounding variables: propensity score matching and regression models.

Propensity Score Estimates of Labeling Effects

The greatest challenge for estimating causal effects in nonexperimental studies is that background differences between treated and comparison groups might influence outcomes and bias the results. Traditional matching methods are rarely able to match groups on more than a few variables, but the development of propensity score matching methods (Rosenbaum and Rubin, 1983) offers a powerful tool to create comparison groups that are similar on many confounding variables, and thus draw more confident conclusions about causal effects. Propensity score matching is especially useful when many covariates have been measured that could influence the outcome, as in the CSDD.

For each of the three treatment-comparisons, we calculated propensity scores in four steps. (1) First, confounding variables were selected to calculate propensity scores. Fifteen factors measured at ages eight to ten that were not missing data for more than fifty cases were selected for this purpose (honesty and the father's involvement in the boy's leisure activities were excluded on this criterion). Each of these fifteen risk factors was significantly associated ($p < .10$) with at least one adult outcome and none was completely overlapping ($0.9 < OR < 1.1$) with any of the three treatment-comparison variables. Along with the fifteen risk factors, two other variables were also used to calculate propensity scores: self-reported delinquency and antisocial personality measured in the interview wave before treatment (either at age fourteen or at age eighteen). Thus seventeen variables were used to calculate the propensity scores for each treatment condition. (2) Because logistic regression deletes cases listwise, missing data on risk factors were imputed using the mean score on other risk factors.[2] (3) Logistic regression was used to predict treatment status in each treatment-comparison variable, based on the seventeen background variables identified in step 1. (4) The predicted probabilities from the regression models were saved as propensity scores.

Matching of treated and comparison individuals was done as follows. For each treated individual, up to three comparison individuals were selected with similar propensity scores. The purpose of using more than one matched individual per treated individual is to increase precision (reduce the standard error) of the effect estimate. We used nearest neighbor matching without replacement, with a caliper of 0.05.[3] Some treated individuals had propensity scores that were too different (beyond the caliper of 0.05) from all non-treated individuals, and so could not be included in the analyses. The final numbers of matched treated and comparison cases were: thirty-six and seventy-six in Comparison 1 (conducted to test effects of juvenile conviction); twenty-four and sixty-six in Comparison 2 (conducted to test effects of young adult conviction); and eighteen and thirty-three in Comparison 3 (conducted to test effects of incarceration).

To examine the success of the matching process in creating similar treatment and control groups, Cohen's d was calculated for each of the seventeen variables (risk factors and prior delinquency/antisocial personality) that had been used to calculate propensity scores. Cohen's d is equal to the difference between the mean value for the treated group and the mean value for the comparison group, divided by the pooled standard deviation.[4] Conventionally $d < .20$ indicates successful matching. For the seventeen background variables, none had $d > .20$ for Comparison 1 (mean $d = .06$, sd $= .04$); three had $d > .20$ for Comparison 2 (mean $d = .12$, sd $= .08$), and six had $d > .20$ for Comparison 3 (mean $d = .15$, sd $= .10$). Thus, the matched treatment and comparison groups were very similar in Comparison 1, but some differences were observed in Comparisons 2 and 3.

Treatment effects were estimated by comparing adult outcome scores for the matched treatment and comparison groups. Because of the varying number of comparison individuals per treated individual, treatment effects were calculated using the difference between each treated individual's outcome score and the average of that person's matched comparisons. These differences were then averaged to estimate the overall treatment effect.[5] This average treatment effect (and its confidence interval),[6] was then converted to a *d*-type effect size by dividing it by the standard deviation of the outcome variable in the whole sample.[7]

Regression Estimates of Labeling Effects

Along with propensity score matching, we used regression models to estimate effects of the three treatments. This was done to compare results across the two methods, and because tests of mediators and moderators fit better within a regression framework. Regression models for each outcome included the treatment-comparison variable as the key predictor and the seventeen covariates that were used to calculate propensity scores as control variables. A *d*-type effect size was calculated by dividing the unstandardized B coefficient (which represents the mean difference in outcome scores between treated and comparison individuals, net of controls) by the standard deviation of the outcome for the whole sample. The confidence interval for B was transformed in the same way.

Tests of Indirect Effects

Five variables measured at age eighteen were tested as possible mediators of the effects of juvenile conviction on age thirty-two outcomes. Mediators were tested following the procedures recommended by Kristopher Preacher and Andrew Hayes (2008). Mediator effects are estimated as the product of two path coefficients: one path from the treatment (juvenile conviction) to the mediator, and one path from the mediator to the outcome. We examined multiple mediator models, which estimated the total indirect effect of all five mediators jointly, as well as the effects of each mediator variable separately, while controlling for other mediators and the seventeen background variables. Standard errors and confidence intervals were calculated using bias corrected and accelerated bootstraps with 5,000 samples. The tests were conducted in SPSS using the macro described in Preacher and Hayes (2008). To compare with the main regression results, we standardized the estimated mediator effects by dividing the coefficients for the indirect paths (and their confidence limits) by the standard deviation of the outcome variable.

Tests of Moderators

We tested whether the effects of juvenile conviction on age thirty-two outcomes were moderated by two variables: convicted parent and antisocial personality at ages eight to ten. To test for moderation, interaction terms were computed between the dichotomous moderator variable and the treatment-comparison variable. We entered the interaction term, with each of its main effects, into regression models, while controlling for the same seventeen covariates included in the main analyses. We examined p values of the interaction terms to identify significant moderators of labeling effects.

Results

Average Effects of Criminal Justice Sanctions on Adult Outcomes

Tables 9.1, 9.2, and 9.3 show the results from propensity score matching and regression analyses for the effects of juvenile conviction, young adult conviction, and incarceration on outcomes at ages thirty-two and forty-eight in the CSDD. Although the regression analyses generally show larger effect sizes (*d*) than propensity score matching, results from both the methods are nearly all in the same direction and have similar substantive interpretations.

Table 9.1 shows that men who were first convicted as juveniles (between ages fifteen and eighteen) had higher mean scores for self-reported crime, antisocial personality, and poor life success at both ages thirty-two and forty-eight, compared with matched men who were not convicted by age eighteen. Nearly all differences were significant, according to both propensity score estimates and regression models. These results are consistent with the hypothesis that juvenile conviction contributes to crime and other adverse outcomes in adulthood. Regression results show stronger effects of juvenile conviction on age thirty-two outcomes compared with age forty-eight outcomes, suggesting some wearing off of labeling effects by age forty-eight (propensity score estimates show this only for antisocial personality). On a comparison of different outcomes at age thirty-two, the largest effects of juvenile conviction were found for antisocial personality.

Table 9.2 shows that all but one adult outcomes were, on average, worse for men who were first convicted in young adulthood (between ages

Table 9.1
Effects of juvenile conviction (ages 15–18) on adult outcomes

	Propensity score estimates				Regression estimates	
	Mean convicted	**Mean non-convicted**	**d**	**CI**	**d**	**CI**
Self-reported crime 32	23.7	21.6	.25*	(.01, .49)	.67*	(.35, 1.00)
Self-reported crime 48	22.0	21.4	.32*	(.01, .63)	.37*	(.04, .70)
Antisocial personality 32	36.7	18.6	.31*	(.21, .41)	.83*	(.55, 1.12)
Antisocial personality 48	19.3	15.1	.10	(.00, .21)	.19	(−.12, .51)
Poor life success 32	37.1	23.5	.19*	(.10, .28)	.70*	(.39, 1.01)
Poor life success 48	20.1	15.4	.18*	(.08, .28)	.18	(−.13, .49)

Notes: CI = 95% confidence interval; *$p < .05$

Table 9.2
Effects of young adult conviction (ages 19–26) on adult outcomes

	Propensity score estimates				Regression estimates	
	Mean convicted	**Mean non-convicted**	**d**	**CI**	**d**	**CI**
Self-reported crime 32	22.6	21.7	.26	(−.03, .54)	.30	(.00, .61)
Self-reported crime 48	21.8	21.7	.08	(−.27, .44)	.24	(−.13, .60)
Antisocial personality 32	27.9	18.7	.35*	(.24, .47)	.39*	(.11, .68)
Antisocial personality 48	18.6	16.9	.10	(−.02, .22)	.29	(−.06, .65)
Poor life success 32	29.9	23.6	.25*	(.14, .36)	.27	(−.06, .60)
Poor life success 48	17.3	17.8	−.14	(−.25, −.03)	.11	(−.24, .47)

Notes: CI = 95% confidence interval; *$p < .05$

Table 9.3
Effects of incarceration (ages 15–26) on adult outcomes

	Propensity score estimates				Regression estimates	
	Mean incarcerated	Mean convicted, not incarcerated	*d*	CI	*d*	CI
Self-reported crime 32	25.2	23.4	.37	(–.04, .78)	.30	(–.30, 89)
Self-reported crime 48	22.1	21.9	.05	(–.41, .51)	–.09	(–.69, 50)
Antisocial personality 32	51.4	30.3	.49*	(.34, .64)	.85*	(.28, 1.41)
Antisocial personality 48	27.5	22.4	.11	(–.05, .27)	.32	(–.22, .87)
Poor life success 32	52.2	35.7	.31*	(.17, .46)	.70*	(.15, 1.24)
Poor life success 48	28.2	23.6	.10	(–.05, .25)	.14	(–.41, .69)

Notes: CI = 95% confidence interval; $*p < .05$

nineteen and twenty-six), compared with matched unconvicted men. However, effect sizes (*d*) are generally smaller than those found for juvenile conviction, and only a few are significant. This suggests that first conviction as a young adult does not contribute to adverse outcomes as much as first conviction as a juvenile. Effects of young adult conviction are all larger for age thirty-two outcomes compared with age forty-eight outcomes. At age thirty-two, the largest effects are found for antisocial personality.

Table 9.3 shows that all adult outcomes were, on average, worse for men who were first incarcerated between ages fifteen and twenty-six, compared with matched men who were convicted between ages fifteen and twenty-six but not incarcerated up to age twenty-six. However, only two differences are statistically significant: antisocial personality and poor life success at age thirty-two. Effect sizes are all larger at age thirty-two compared with age forty-eight. The largest effect size for incarceration compared with conviction without incarceration is found for antisocial personality scores at age thirty-two.

Indirect Effects of Juvenile Conviction on Age 32 Outcomes

Next, we investigated possible indirect labeling effects on adult outcomes via men's attitudes, involvement with delinquent friends, and unemployment at age eighteen. We tested whether these variables mediated effects of juvenile conviction on age thirty-two outcomes, for which the largest effect sizes were observed in the previous analyses. Tables 9.4, 9.5, and 9.6 show the results of multiple mediator models for the effects of juvenile conviction on crime, antisocial personality, and poor life success at age thirty-two. For all three outcomes, there was evidence of indirect effects via the five mediating variables. Total indirect effects (d values), across all five mediators, were .10 for crime, .13 for antisocial personality, and .10 for poor life success. While significant, these indirect effects represent only about one-seventh of the total effects of juvenile conviction on adult outcomes (compare with the total effects in regression estimates in Table 9.1). Examining individual mediators, the only variable that had significant effects, while controlling for other mediators and background

Table 9.4
Indirect effects of juvenile conviction on self-reported crime at age 32

	Indirect effect (d)	CI
All five mediating variables	*0.10**	*(0.01, 0.25)*
Aggressive attitude	0.03	(−0.01, 0.11)
Pro-drugs attitude	0.02	(−0.01, 0.09)
Antiestablishment attitude	0.01	(−0.02, 0.10)
Delinquent friends	0.03	(−0.01, 0.14)
Unemployment	0.00	(−0.04, 0.02)

Notes: CI = 95% confidence interval; *p < .05

Table 9.5
Indirect effects of juvenile conviction on antisocial personality at age 32

	Indirect effect (d)	CI
All five mediating variables	*0.13**	*(0.03, 0.28)*
Aggressive attitude	0.02	(−0.01, 0.09)
Pro-drugs attitude	0.05*	(0.00, 0.12)
Antiestablishment attitude	0.04	(0.00, 0.13)
Delinquent friends	0.03	(−0.02, 0.13)
Unemployment	0.00	(−0.02, 0.04)

Notes: CI = 95% confidence interval; *p < .05

Table 9.6
Indirect effects of juvenile conviction on life success at age 32

	Indirect effect (*d*)	CI
All five mediating variables	*0.10**	*(0.01, 0.24)*
Aggressive attitude	0.01	(−0.01, 0.09)
Pro-drugs attitude	0.04*	(0.00, 0.11)
Antiestablishment attitude	0.02	(−0.01, 0.11)
Delinquent friends	0.03	(−0.02, 0.13)
Unemployment	0.00	(−0.03, 0.03)

Notes: CI = 95% confidence interval; *p* < .05

covariates, was a pro-drugs attitude, which mediated effects of juvenile conviction on both antisocial personality and poor life success at age thirty-two.

Moderating Effects of Parental Conviction and Early Antisocial Behavior

Finally, we tested whether the effects of juvenile conviction on age thirty-two outcomes were moderated by two variables: parent convicted and antisocial personality at ages eight to ten. Tests of interaction showed that having a convicted parent significantly moderated the effects of juvenile conviction on all three adult outcomes. Controlling for background covariates, parental conviction predicted significantly larger effects of juvenile conviction on self-reported crime ($p = .012$), antisocial personality ($p = .045$), and poor life success ($p = .011$) at age thirty-two. There was no evidence that childhood antisocial personality moderated effects of juvenile conviction on age thirty-two outcomes: all interaction terms were insignificant.

Discussion

Results from the current study are generally consistent with the labeling hypothesis that criminal justice sanctions have undesirable effects. Juvenile conviction, in particular, predicted increased levels of self-reported criminal behavior, antisocial personality, and poor life success in adulthood, showing a diverse range of possible long-lasting harms of criminal justice sanctioning. The most important findings about labeling effects from the current analyses and previous work in the CSDD can be summarized as follows.

(1) Juvenile conviction predicts increased criminal behavior at ages eighteen, twenty-one, thirty-two, and forty-eight, net of childhood risk factors and prior criminal behavior.
(2) Juvenile conviction increases job instability and hostile attitudes to the police in late adolescence, which might mediate the effects of conviction on criminal behavior in early adulthood.
(3) Juvenile conviction has strongest effects on antisocial personality in adulthood, but also contributes to crime and poor life success.
(4) Pro-drugs attitudes, aggressive attitudes, antiestablishment attitudes, involvement with delinquent groups, and unemployment partly mediate the effects of juvenile conviction on adult outcomes.
(5) Conviction in early adulthood has weaker effects on adult outcomes than juvenile conviction.
(6) Incarceration in early adulthood increases antisocial personality and poor life success at age thirty-two over and above the effects of conviction.
(7) Criminal justice sanctioning as a juvenile and as a young adult has stronger effects on outcomes at age thirty-two than at age forty-eight. Therefore, there is some wearing off of labeling effects during adulthood.
(8) Having a parent convicted exacerbates labeling effects of juvenile conviction on both juvenile delinquency and other undesirable outcomes at age thirty-two.
(9) Parental incarceration predicts increased criminal behavior and other adverse outcomes through the life course.
(10) Despite these findings, which are consistent with predictions of labeling theory, criminal justice sanctions certainly are not the only predictor of crime and other undesirable outcomes in adulthood; many other important risk factors have been identified in the CSDD.

Two of our hypotheses were not supported in the current study. First, we did not find evidence that a history of childhood antisocial behavior moderated the effects of juvenile conviction on adult outcomes. Second, although the men's attitudes, involvement with delinquent groups, and unemployment at age eighteen partly mediated the effects of juvenile conviction on adult outcomes, these indirect effects were not "substantial," as we had expected. Rather, they accounted for about one-seventh of the total effects of juvenile conviction, suggesting that other important mediating mechanisms are at work.

Before discussing the implications of the findings for labeling theory and research, it is important to note the study limitations. The greatest challenge for testing labeling hypotheses in the CSDD, like in any other nonexperimental study, is accurately estimating causal effects. Although every effort was made to account for a rich variety of covariates, it is still possible that the results are be biased because of selection effects or differential history. Even after matching on propensity scores, there was some nonequivalence on background variables for some of the groups compared, and other unmeasured variables that influence the probability of conviction or incarceration might have inflated estimates of labeling effects in the current study. Another limitation is that prospective research over many decades necessarily refers to individuals who grew up in an earlier historical period. Thus, it may not be possible to generalize our findings to current day juvenile populations. Paul Hirschfield (2008) argues that in today's disadvantaged inner-city communities there may be a declining significance of labeling effects, where criminal justice system involvement has become normal and an expected ritual in male adolescence.

Notwithstanding these limitations, the CSDD has provided unique evidence on both medium and long-term consequences of conviction and incarceration, using high quality, prospective data with excellent follow-up rates over four decades. Consistent with labeling theory, and contrary to the specific deterrence thesis, various analyses in the CSDD point toward possible criminogenic effects of criminal justice sanctions. Notably, in the current analyses, labeling experiences also predicted outcomes that were of a different nature from the behavior originally labeled. Thus, conviction for juvenile criminal behavior predicted poor life success in adulthood, which included measures of accommodation history, cohabitation, relationships with children, employment, and mental health, as well as criminal behavior. These findings are consistent with Sampson and Laub's theory of cumulative disadvantage, which focuses on the importance of social structural consequences of criminal justice sanctions, as well as changes in personal identity that labeling theorists have traditionally emphasized. However, we did not observe an escalation of labeling effects throughout adult life. Effects were weaker at age forty-eight than at age thirty-two, suggesting the importance of other endogenous experiences in adult life that are unrelated to earlier criminal justice involvement.

The results on intergenerational labeling effects in the CSDD are particularly intriguing, whereby parental conviction exacerbates undesirable effects of a boy's own conviction on later outcomes. Surprisingly little theoretical attention has been given to intergenerational labeling effects, and it would be desirable to test various hypotheses about the processes involved. For example, it should be tested whether youths with convicted parents are subject to prejudice that they will follow in their parents' footsteps and whether such expectations increase when youths themselves are first convicted. Another possibility is that official bias toward convicted youth is particularly strong for those who have convicted parents, making them even more likely to be arrested, prosecuted, or found guilty for their behavior. A third possibility is that having a convicted parent increases the chances that convicted youth will accept the label of "delinquent," adopt a criminal identity, and commit further crime. We hope that other studies with longitudinal data over multiple generations will investigate this topic further and test some of these hypotheses.

Although juvenile conviction had important consequences for various outcomes in early adulthood in the CSDD, the mediators that we tested did not provide a full explanation for these effects. Thus, new studies should consider a wider range of possible mediators and maximize measurement quality to help identify the most important mechanisms involved. Criminologists might do well to examine the mediators that are postulated to explain the labeling effects of mental illness, including social withdrawal, and changes in self-esteem, social networks, and earning power (see, e.g., Link et al., 1989, 1997).

Overall, the CSDD suggests that criminal justice sanctions increase crime and contribute to a cycle of disadvantage flowing through adulthood and across generations. The results are striking, worrying, and need replication. No other study has examined effects of criminal conviction and incarceration over such a long period of time in a large community sample. Full advantage should be taken of other large longitudinal studies that combine measures of self-reported criminal behavior, official criminal records, and long-term follow-up to test whether these findings generalize to other contexts.

Notes

1. Although this study is not an experiment, we use the term "treated" to refer to being convicted or incarcerated by the criminal justice system.
2. Of course, multiple imputation is generally a better method to impute missing data, but we are not aware that this method can be combined with propensity score matching.
3. The matching algorithm was written in SPSS by Arjan Blokland and Paul Nieuwbeerta.
4. The equation for the pooled standard deviation is $s_{pooled} = \sqrt{\frac{(n_t - 1)s_t^2 + (n_c - 1)s_c^2}{n_t + n_c - 2}}$, where n_t = number in the treated group, n_c = number in the comparison group, s_t = standard deviation of the treated group, s_c = standard deviation of the comparison group.

Because there was a variable number of comparison individuals per treated individual (between one and three), results were weighted by the inverse of the number of comparison individuals for each treated individual.

5. The equation for the average treatment effect (T) is: $T = \frac{1}{N}\Sigma_i^N \left| y_i^t - \left(\frac{1}{n_i}\Sigma_j^{n_i} y_{ij}^c\right)\right|$, where N is the number of treated individuals; i is an index of the ith treated individual; n_i is the number of comparison individuals matched to the ith treated individual; j is an index of the jth comparison individual matched to i; y_i^t is the treated individual's outcome score; y_{ij}^c is the jth comparison individual's outcome score matched to i.

6. The standard error (se) of T is calculated as follows: $se = \frac{1}{N}\left|\Sigma_i^N\left|\sigma_t + \frac{\sigma_c}{n_i}\right|\right|^{1/2}$, where σ_t is the standard deviation of the treated individuals; σ_c is the standard deviation of all matched comparison individuals; and se is the standard error for T. The confidence interval for T is calculated as $CI = T \pm 1.96 * se$

7. The standard deviation for the whole sample was used, rather than the pooled standard deviation across treatment and comparison groups, in order to make results from the propensity scores more comparable with results from regression models.

References

Becker, H. S. *Outsiders: Studies in the Sociology of Deviance*. New York: Free Press, 1963.

Bernburg, J. G. and M. D. Krohn. "Labeling, Life Chances, and Adult Crime: The Direct and Indirect Effects of Official Intervention in Adolescence on Crime in Early Adulthood." *Criminology* 41, no. 4 (2003): 1287–318.

Bernburg, J. G., M. D. Krohn, and C. J. Rivera. "Official Labeling, Criminal Embeddedness, and Subsequent Delinquency: A Longitudinal Test of Labeling Theory." *Journal of Research in Crime and Delinquency* 43, no. 1 (2006): 67–88.

Bhati, A. S. and A. R. Piquero. "Estimating the Impact of Incarceration on Subsequent Offending Trajectories: Deterrent, Criminogenic, or Null Effect?" *Journal of Criminal Law and Criminology* 98, no. 1 (2007): 207–53.

Brennan, P. A. and S. A. Mednick. "Learning Theory Approach to the Deterrence of Criminal Recidivism." *Journal of Abnormal Psychology* 103, no. 3 (1994): 430–40.

Cullen, F. T. and C. L. Jonson. "Labeling Theory and Correctional Rehabilitiation: Beyond Unanticipated Consequences." In *Labeling Theory: Empirical Tests (Advances in Criminological Theory, Volume 18)*, edited by D. P. Farrington and J. Murray. New Brunswick, NJ: Transaction, 2013.

Davies, S. and J. Tanner. "The Long Arm of the Law: Effects of Labeling on Employment." *Sociological Quarterly* 44, no. 3 (2003): 385–404.

Farrington, D. P. "Antisocial Personality from Childhood to Adulthood." *The Psychologist* 4, no. 9 (1991): 389–94.

———. "The Effects of Public Labeling." *British Journal of Criminology* 17, no. 2 (1977): 112–35.

———. "Key Results from the First Forty Years of the Cambridge Study in Delinquent Development." In *Taking Stock of Delinquency: An Overview of Findings from Contemporary Longitudinal Studies*, edited by T. P. Thornberry and M. D. Krohn, 137–83. New York: Kluwer/Plenum, 2003.

Farrington, D. P., J. W. Coid, L. Harnett, D. Jolliffe, N. Soteriou, R. Turner, et al. *Criminal Careers Up to Age 50 and Life Success up to Age 48: New Findings from the Cambridge Study in Delinquent Development*. London: Home Office, 2006. (Research Study No. 299).

Farrington, D. P., J. Coid, and D. J. West. "The Development of Offending from Age 8 to Age 50: Recent Results from the Cambridge Study in Delinquent Development."

Monatsschrift fur Kriminologie und Strafrechtsreform (Journal of Criminology and Penal Reform) 92 (2009): 160–73.

Farrington, D. P., B. Gallagher, L. Morley, R. J. St. Ledger, and D. J. West. "Unemployment, School Leaving, and Crime." *British Journal of Criminology* 26, no. 4 (1986): 335–56.

Farrington, D. P., S. G. Osborn, and D. J. West. "The Persistence of Labeling Effects." *British Journal of Criminology* 18, no. 3 (1978): 277–84.

Farrington, D. P., A. R. Piquero, and W. G. Jennings. *Offending from Childhood to Late Middle Age: Recent Results from the Cambridge Study in Delinquent Development.* New York: Springer, 2013.

Fergusson, D. M., L. J. Horwood, and M. T. Lynskey. "The Effects of Unemployment on Psychiatric Illness During Young Adulthood." *Psychological Medicine* 27, no. 2 (1997): 371–81.

Garfinkel, H. "Conditions of Successful Degradation Ceremonies." *American Journal of Sociology* 61, no. 5 (1956): 420–24.

Gatti, U., R. E. Tremblay, and F. Vitaro. "Iatrogenic Effect of Juvenile Justice." *Journal of Child Psychology and Psychiatry* 50, no. 8 (2009): 991–98.

Hagan, J. and A. Palloni. "The Social Reproduction of a Criminal Class in Working Class London, circa 1950–80." *American Journal of Sociology* 96, no. 2 (1990): 265–99.

Hirschfield, P. J. "The Declining Significance of Delinquent Labels in Disadvantaged Urban Communities." *Sociological Forum* 23, no. 3 (2008): 575–601.

Huizinga, D. and K. L. Henry. "The Effect of Arrest and Justice System Sanctions on Subsequent Behavior: Findings from Longitudinal and Other Studies." In *The Long View of Crime: A Synthesis of Longitudinal Research*, edited by A. M. Liberman, 220–54. New York: Springer, 2008.

Killias, M., P. Villettaz, and I. Zoder. "The Effects of Custodial versus Non-Custodial Sentences on Re-Offending: A Systematic Review of the State of Knowledge." *Campbell Systematic Reviews* (2006): 13. Doi: 10.4073/csr.2006.13.

Klein, M. W. "Labeling Theory and Delinquency Policy: An Experimental Test." *Criminal Justice and Behavior* 13, no. 1, (1986): 47–79.

Kraemer, H. C., K. K. Lowe, and D. J. Kupfer. *To Your Health: How to Understand What Research Tells Us About Risk.* New York: Oxford University Press, 2005.

Krohn, M. D., G. Lopes, and J. T. Ward. "Effects of Official Intervention on Later Offending in the Rochester Youth Development Study." In *Labeling Theory: Empirical Tests (Advances in Criminological Theory, Volume 18)*, edited by D. P. Farrington and J. Murray. New Brunswick, NJ: Transaction, 2013.

Lanctot, N., S. A. Cernkovich, and P. C. Giordano. "Delinquent Behavior, Official Delinquency, and Gender: Consequences for Adulthood Functioning and Well-Being." *Criminology* 45, no. 1 (2007): 131–57.

Laub, J. H. and R. Sampson. *Shared Beginnings, Divergent Lives: Delinquent Boys to Age 70.* Cambridge, MA: Harvard University Press, 2003.

Lemert, E. M. *Human Deviance, Social Problems, and Social Control.* Englewood Cliffs, NJ: Prentice-Hall, 1967.

———. *Social Pathology: A Systematic Approach to the Theory of Sociopathic Behavior.* New York, NY: McGraw-Hill, 1951.

Li, S. "Legal Sanctions and Youths' Status Achievement: A Longitudinal Study." *Justice Quarterly* 16, no. 2, (1999): 377–401.

Link, B. G., F. T. Cullen, E. Struening, P. E. Shrout, and B. P. Dohrenwend. "A Modified Labeling Theory Approach to Mental Disorders: An Empirical Assessment." *American Sociological Review* 54, no. 3 (1989): 400–23.

Link, B. G., E. L. Struening, M. Rahav, J. C. Phelan, and L. Nuttbrock. "On Stigma and its Consequences: Evidence from a Longitudinal Study of Men with Dual Diagnoses of Mental Illness and Substance Abuse." *Journal of Health and Social Behavior* 38 (1997): 177–90.

Matsueda, R. L. "Reflected Appraisals, Parental Labeling, and Delinquency: Specifying a Symbolic Interactionist Theory." *American Journal of Sociology* 97, no. 6 (1992): 1577–611.

Moffitt, T. E. "Adolescence-Limited and Life-Course-Persistent Antisocial Behavior: A Developmental Taxonomy." *Psychological Review* 100, no. 4 (1993): 674–701.

Murray, J. and D. P. Farrington. "The Effects of Parental Imprisonment on Children." In *Crime and Justice: A Review of Research*, edited by M. Tonry, vol. 37, 133–206. Chicago, IL: University of Chicago Press, 2008a.

———. "Parental Imprisonment: Effects on Boys' Antisocial Behaviour and Delinquency Through the Life-Course." *Journal of Child Psychology and Psychiatry* 46, no. 12 (2005): 1269–78.

———. "Parental Imprisonment: Long-Lasting Effects on Boys' Internalizing Problems Through the Life-Course." *Development and Psychopathology* 20, no. 1 (2008b): 273–90.

Murray, J., C.-G. Janson, and D. P. Farrington. "Crime in Adult Offspring of Prisoners: A Cross-National Comparison of Two Longitudinal Samples." *Criminal Justice and Behavior* 34, no. 1 (2007): 133–49.

Nagin, D., F. Cullen, and Cheryl L. Jonson. "Imprisonment and Reoffending." *Crime and Justice* 38, no. 1 (2009): 115–200.

Nagin, D. and J. Waldfogel. "The Effects of Criminality and Conviction on the Labor Market Status of Young British Offenders." *International Review of Law and Economics* 15, no. 1 (1995): 109–26.

Nieuwbeerta, P., D. Nagin, and A. Blokland. "Assessing the Impact of First-Time Imprisonment on Offenders' Subsequent Criminal Career Development: A Matched Samples Comparison." *Journal of Quantitative Criminology* 25, no. 3 (2009): 227–57.

Paternoster, R. "The Deterrent Effect of the Perceived Certainty and Severity of Punishment: A Review of the Evidence and Issues." *Justice Quarterly* 4, no. 2 (1987): 173–217.

Paternoster, R. and L. Iovanni. "The Labeling Perspective and Delinquency: An Elaboration of the Theory and Assessment of the Evidence." *Justice Quarterly* 6, no. 3 (1989): 359–94.

Preacher, K. J. and A. F. Hayes. "Asymptotic and Resampling Strategies for Assessing and Comparing Indirect Effects in Multiple Mediator Models." *Behavior Research Methods* 40, no. 3 (2008): 879–91.

Rosenbaum, P. R. and D. B. Rubin. "The Central Role of the Propensity Score in Observational Studies for Causal Effects." *Biometrika* 70, no. 1 (1983): 41–55.

Sampson, R. J. and J. H. Laub. *Crime in the Making: Pathways and Turning Points Through Life*. Cambridge, MA: Harvard University Press, 1993.

———. "A Life-Course Theory of Cumulative Disadvantage and the Stability of Delinquency." In *Developmental Theories of Crime and Delinquency: Advances in Criminological Theory Volume 7*, edited by T. P. Thornberry, 133–61. New Brunswick: Transaction, 1997.

Scheff, T. J. *Being Mentally Ill: A Sociological Theory*. Chicago, IL: Aldine, 1966.

Sherman, L. W. "Experiments in Criminal Sanctions: Labeling, Defiance, and Restorative Justice." In *Labeling Theory: Empirical Tests (Advances in Criminological Theory Volume 18)*, edited by D. P. Farrington and J. Murray. New Brunswick, NJ: Transaction, 2013.

Smith, D. A. and P. R. Gartin. "Specifying Specific Deterrence: The Influence of Arrest on Future Criminal Activity." *American Sociological Review* 54, no. 1 (1989): 94–106.

Ström, S. "Unemployment and Families: A Review of Research." *The Social Service Review* 77, no. 3 (2003): 399–430.

Sweeten, G. "Who will Graduate? Disruption of High School Education by Arrest and Court Involvement." *Justice Quarterly* 23, no. 4 (2006): 462–80.

Tannenbaum, F. *Crime and the Community*. Boston, MA: Ginn, 1938.

West, D. J. and D. P. Farrington. *Who Becomes Delinquent?* London: Heinemann, 1973.

———. *The Delinquent Way of Life*. London: Heinemann, 1977.

10

The Effects of Conviction and Incarceration on Future Employment Outcomes

Steven Raphael

Introduction

Upon being released from prison, former inmates face a number of challenges in reorienting themselves and reintegrating into non-institutional society. In addition to having to procure housing and official identification, making contact with one's parole officer if placed into the community corrections system, and meeting one's alimentary and health needs, nearly all former inmates must find some form of legitimate employment to affect a successful reentry. While in some instances correctional systems may place released inmates with employers, sometimes through reentry planning and sometimes through work-release programs, post-release employment among former inmates tends to be quite low, and many face serious difficulties in procuring and maintaining employment.

The employment difficulties of former prison inmates can be tied to a number of factors. First are the characteristics of former inmates themselves. Most individuals with felony convictions (whether or not they have served time) have relatively low levels of formal educational attainment, weak employment histories, and often lack many of the soft skills that are valued by employers, especially employers hiring individuals that must interact with customers. Second, the experience of incarceration may render the individual to be of less value to employers for a number of reasons. In addition, a criminal conviction and prior prison spell may mark the individual, in the sense that employers may exhibit reluctance to hire a former prison inmate, whether or not having served time is in any way related to productivity.

Beyond the direct effect of incarceration on the post-release employment prospects of former inmates, a high incidence of incarceration among specific demographic groups may negatively impact members of such groups who have never done time. This would occur when employers use simple physical signals, such as race, gender, and area of residence to formulate probabilistic assessments of one's prior involvement in the criminal justice system. In the presence of such "statistical discrimination," even those who never serve may be adversely impacted by incarceration. To be sure, such a mechanism should be more important in nations where the incarceration rate is particularly high (e.g., the United States).

This chapter discusses the relationship between incarceration and employment. I begin by presenting a simple economic model of employer demand for workers with criminal history records. The model demonstrates how the potential downside of hiring such workers (in terms of liability or the costs to the employer of deviant behavior by the employee) impacts employer hiring decisions at the individual firm level and the equilibrium wage of convicted felons at the level of the market. I then review recent empirical research assessing the impact of having served time or having been convicted of a crime on subsequent employment outcomes.

Criminal Histories, Employer Demand, and the Market Wages Earned by Convicted Felons

There are several reasons why employers may consider information from criminal history records in screening potential employees. First, serving time may reduce one's productivity in the legitimate market. The long-term incarcerated fail to accumulate legitimate work experience, and may experience negative socialization towards norms and behaviors that may be a functional adaptation to the prison environment yet poorly suited to the legitimate workplace.

Second, in the United States, certain occupations are closed to individuals with felony convictions under state and in some cases, federal law (Hahn, 1991; Colgate, 2008). Examples include jobs requiring contact with children, certain health services occupations, and employment with firms providing security services.

Employers may also be concerned about the potential liability associated with hiring a convicted felon. In many U.S. states employers can be held liable for the criminal actions of their employees. As articulated by Shawn Bushway (1996), "employers who know, or should have known, that an employee has had a history of criminal behavior may be liable for the employee's criminal or tortuous acts." Under the theory of negligent hiring, employers may be exposed to punitive damages as well as liability for loss, pain, and suffering (Craig, 1987).[1]

Finally, employers who need to fill positions where employee monitoring is imperfect may place a premium on trustworthiness. To the extent that past criminal activity signals a lack of trustworthiness, employers may take such information into account when screening applicants.[2]

Theoretically, the problems that an applicant with a criminal history record poses to a potential employer can be grouped into issues associated with lower productivity on the job and the potential additional costs that such an employee may generate. To formalize the impact of these considerations on employer hiring behavior and market wages, here I present a modification and extension of the labor demand model developed in Angrist and Acemoglu (2001). Suppose that employers can perfectly distinguish between workers without criminal convictions (the quantity of which employed in any given year we will denote by L_t) and workers with criminal history records (the quantity of which in any given year we will denote by R_t). The employer produces a product for sale (denoted by Q_t) by combining the labor of those who have never been convicted with the labor of those who have been convicted using the production function.

$$Q_t = F(L_t, R_t) \tag{1}$$

We will assume that the marginal product of both types of labor is positive yet diminishing—that is, $F_L, F_R > 0$, $F_{LL}, F_{RR} < 0$, where single subscripts indicate the partial first derivative of the production function and double subscripts indicate the partial second derivatives.[3] Let s_R be the likelihood that type R workers transgress on the job and assume that type L workers never transgress. While in reality workers of either type may offend while employed, the important content of this assumption is that the probability of transgression is, or is perceived to be, higher for those with prior criminal convictions. The cost of an employee's transgression is given by c, and is borne in the period after the transgression (the cost to the employer is assumed to be the cleanup costs incurred in the subsequent period). The cost of the transgression may be thought of as either the cost to the employer of the infraction (e.g., loss through theft or liability) or the costs of firing and replacing the employee. Thus, the expected value of costs associated with such deviant behavior in any given period is $s_R c R_{t-1}$ for employees with prior criminal convictions. Expected costs increase with the transgression probability, the cost of a transgression, and the overall employment levels of convicted felons within the firm.

Assume that the employer has an infinite horizon and discounts future returns with the period discount factor $\beta < 1$, that the employer is risk neutral (i.e., that the employer seeks to maximize the expected value of profits), and that the price of the product produced is one. The employer takes prices as given, facing wage rates w_L and w_R. While from the viewpoint of the employer, the prices are given, we will eventually explore the determinants of equilibrium wages. Under these assumptions, firms will choose employment levels to maximize the discounted present value of profits. This optimization problem can be stated formerly as

$$\max_{L_t, R_t} \Pi = \sum_{t=0}^{\infty} \beta^t \left[F(L_t, R_t) - w_L L_t - w_R R_t - R_{t-1} s_R c \right] \qquad (2)$$

The components of equation (2) are fairly straightforward. For any period t, period profits are given by the value of output ($F(L_t, R_t)$) minus the wage bill ($w_L L_t + w_R R_t$) minus the costs associated with last period's transgressions ($R_{t-1} s_R c$). The value of profits in all future periods indexed by t is discounted to the present value via multiplication by β^t, and then added up.

Following Angrist and Acemoglou (2001), this optimization problem can be simplified by first noting that transgression costs are equal to zero in period zero (since the firm does not exist in the prior period). Taking this into account, the optimization problem can be rewritten as

$$\max_{L_t, R_t} \Pi = \sum_{t=0}^{\infty} \beta^t \left[F(L_t, R_t) - w_L L_t - w_R R_t \right] - \sum_{t=0}^{\infty} \beta^t R_{t-1} s_R c$$

Second, we can assume that rational employers immediately identify the steady-state values of L_t and R_t, defined by the condition $L_t = L_{t-1} = L$. Substituting the steady-state values and solving the infinite series involving β yields the much simplified optimization problem

$$\max_{L, R} \Pi = \frac{1}{1-\beta} \left[F(L_t, R_t) - w_L L_t - w_R R_t \right] - \frac{\beta}{1-\beta} \left[R_{t-1} s_R c \right] \qquad (3)$$

Having defined the objectives of employers and how the labor of convicted felons fits into this objective function, we can now analyze how the particular aspects of the labor of former inmates will impact employer behavior and, at the market level, wages. To foreshadow the theoretical predictions, we will show the following:

- The lower productivity of convicted felons, all else equal, reduces the amount of such labor that employers will hire.
- The higher transgression costs associated with employing convicted felons reduce employer demand for such workers.
- At the level of the market, both lower productivity as well as the components of expected transgression costs suppress the wages of convicted felons. Assuming that labor supply of such workers is responsive to wages, suppressed wages should translate into lower labor force participation, at least at the extensive margin of this market.

The Behavior of Individual Employers

The behavior of employers can be analyzed by deriving the first-order conditions of the optimization problem in equation (3). Differentiating the profit function with respect to L and R, setting these two equations to zero, and simplifying yields the following equations that implicitly define the employer's labor demand functions:

$$F_L = w_L$$
$$F_R = w_R + \beta s_R c \tag{4}$$

These two first-order conditions have an intuitive interpretation. The left side of each gives the marginal product of the two types of labor, while the right side of each equation gives marginal cost. For workers with criminal histories, the marginal cost to employers has two components: the wage paid to the marginal worker as well as the discounted present value of the expected cost from a current period transgression.

These conditions can be used to analyze how the demand for workers with prior criminal convictions depends on the likelihood that these workers will transgress on the job and the cost of such transgressions. Any increase in the marginal cost of hiring someone with a criminal conviction will increase the right-hand side of the second conditions in equation (4). In order to optimize, the employer would have to adjust employment levels to reequate the marginal product of labor to marginal cost. With diminishing marginal product, such an adjustment would require reducing the employment levels of those with criminal records to increase marginal product. Thus, anything that increases the marginal cost of hiring someone with a criminal history (e.g., an increase in c or s_R) will reduce the quantity of said labor demanded by the employer.

These conditions can also be used to highlight the relationship between the lower overall productivity of convicted felons and the hiring outcomes of employers. A slight rearrangement of the two conditions in equation (4) yields the following statement:

$$\frac{F_L}{w_L} = \frac{F_R}{w_R + \beta s_R c} \tag{5}$$

This restatement of the employer's first-order conditions also has an intuitive explanation. Each ratio in equation (5) gives the ratio of the marginal benefit of hiring the last worker to the marginal cost of hiring said worker. In other words, the two ratios give us the "bang-per-buck" from hiring workers with clean criminal history records and workers with felony convictions. An employer who is optimizing will employ workers such that these ratios are equalized across labor groups. If this were not the case, an employer would be able to reorient the composition of its workforce in a manner that would produce more output at lower cost.

Equation (5) can be used to highlight the impact of the lower productivity of convicted felons on hiring levels. Such lower productivity translates into lower values of F_R for all levels of R. With convicted felons having a low-marginal product, maintaining the equality in equation (5) requires keeping the employment level of convicted felons low. Moreover, the greater the adverse impact of serving time on productivity, the lower the employment levels will be. In the extreme, for some employers it may be the case that

$$\frac{F_L}{w_L} > \frac{F_R}{w_R + \beta s_R c} \tag{6}$$

even when the firm employs no convicted felons (i.e., $R = 0$). In such an instance, the employer would never hire a former inmate/convicted felon since the benefit–cost ratio of doing so to the employer would never exceed that for the marginal hire with the clean criminal history record.

This analysis of employer behavior can be summarized by noting that the two first-order conditions in equation (4) implicitly define a functional relationship between the firm's optimal choice of R, the wage rate earned by convicted felons, and the cost components of the expected costs of transgression. This general labor demand function can be expressed as

$$R = R(w_R, s_R, c) \tag{7}$$

where the firm's demand for former inmates/felons is decreasing in all three arguments of the function. In other words, an increase in the likelihood that someone with a criminal history will transgress on the job will reduce employer demand for such workers, as will an increase in the resulting cost in the event of a transgression. Moreover, even if the transgression costs were set to zero, the lower productivity of convicted felons means that the labor demand function in equation (7) is everywhere to the left of the comparable labor demand function for those with clean records. That is to say, holding wages and transgression costs constant, employers will still hire fewer convicted felons relative to those with no criminal histories due to the relatively lower productivity of the former.[4]

Market-Level Analysis

We can extend the analysis to the market level to assess the impact of such consideration on the wages earned by former inmates. Aggregate demand for former inmates/convicted felons is derived by summing the individual firm level demand curves across all firms. Denote the market demand curve for those with criminal history records by the bolded function $\mathbf{R}(w_R, s_R, c)$. Labor supply for this group of individuals is described by the function $S(w_R)$, where we will assume that labor supply increases with increases in wages. The equilibrium wage for former offenders will be that which equates aggregate labor demand and labor supply, or where

$$\mathbf{R}(w_R, s_R, c) = S(w_R) \qquad (8)$$

Of particular interest is how the equilibrium wage paid to former offenders changes in response to changes in s_R and c. Note that these changes can be real, in the sense that former offenders may become more or less likely to transgress on the job, or the costs of such transgression may change due to say government interventions intended to indemnify employers against any liability associated with hiring a former inmate, or these changes may simply be perceived by employers. Equation (8) implicitly defines a relationship between wages and the components of the expected transgression costs associated with hiring a former inmate. Implicitly differentiating equation (8) with respect to either of these parameters can be used to assess how wages will response to changes in these cost components. For example, totally differentiating equation (6) with respect to c yields the expression

$$\frac{\partial \mathbf{R}(w_R, s_R, c)}{\partial w_R}\frac{\partial w_R}{\partial c} + \frac{\partial \mathbf{R}(w_R, s_R, c)}{\partial c} = \frac{\partial S(w_R)}{\partial w_R}\frac{\partial w_R}{\partial c} \qquad (9)$$

Solving equation (9) $\frac{\partial w_R}{\partial c}$ for yields the expression

$$\frac{\partial w_R}{\partial c} = \frac{\dfrac{\partial \mathbf{R}(w_R, s_R, c)}{\partial c}}{\dfrac{\partial S(w_R)}{\partial w_R} - \dfrac{\partial \mathbf{R}(w_R, s_R, c)}{\partial w_R}} < 0 \qquad (10)$$

where we are able to sign this market effect on wages given our knowledge of the signs of the three component partial derivates on the right-hand side of equation (10). A similar derivation of the responsiveness of wages to changes in the probability of transgressing shows that the equilibrium wage rate declines with increases in this likelihood.

This result is again quite intuitive. Additional transgression costs associated with hiring former felons reduce the marginal benefit to employers of hiring such workers. Unless employers are compensated for this additional cost by a reduction in wage costs, they will never hire the more costly, less productive workers. Thus, in equilibrium higher transgressions costs (real or perceived)[5] translate into lower wages for former felons. This in turn should result in a lower employment rate for this group, and possible lower work hours conditional on employment. On the positive side, any intervention intended to reduce the costs of such intervention (e.g., government bonding of former inmates) should increase wages and employment for former offenders.

Empirical Evidence on the Relationship between Prior Incarceration and Future Employment

There has recently been a surge in research in the United States on the impact of having been to prison on one's post-release employment prospects. This new wave of research has been prompted in large part by the very substantial increases in the U.S. incarceration rate. To highlight this development for different sub-populations, Tables 10.1 through 10.3 show how the likelihood of being incarcerated on any given day has changed for U.S. adult males by race, level of educational attainment, and age. The figures in the table are based on tabulations of the 1980 and 2000 Public Use Microdata Samples (PUMSs) of the U.S. Census of Population and Housing. The decennial census enumerates both the institutionalized as well as the non-institutionalized population. Within the institutionalized population, one can separately identify individuals residing in non-military institutions. This category includes inmates of federal and state prisons, local jail inmates, residents of inpatient mental hospitals, and residents of other non-aged institutions. I use residence in a non-military institution as the principal indicator of incarceration. In previous research (Raphael, 2005), I have demonstrated that estimates of the incarcerated population based on residents in non-military group quarters in the census are quite close to incarceration totals from alternative sources.[6]

Each table presents the proportion of the respective population that is engaged in a productive activity (either employed, in school, or in the military), the proportion that is not-institutionalized but idle (not employed, not in school, and not in the military), and the proportion institutionalized. All figures pertain to men who are eighteen to fifty-five years of age. Table 10.1 presents overall estimates for men for four mutually exclusive race/ethnicity groupings. The proportion incarcerated increased for all groups of men between 1980 and 2000. However, the absolute increase is largest for both non-Hispanic black men and Hispanic men. The 2000 census indicates that roughly 9 percent of the adult black male

Table 10.1

Estimates of the proportion of men 18 to 55 engaged in a productive activity, non-institutionalized and idle, and institutionalized by race/ethnicity from the 1980 and 2000 PUMS files

	1980	2000	Change, 2000 to 1980
Non-Hispanic white			
Employed/in school	0.899	0.878	−0.021
Idle	0.093	0.109	0.016
Institutionalized	0.008	0.014	0.006
Non-Hispanic black			
Employed/in school	0.758	0.673	−0.085
Idle	0.206	0.239	0.033
Institutionalized	0.037	0.089	0.052
Non-Hispanic Asian			
Employed/in school	0.918	0.859	−0.059
Idle	0.079	0.135	0.056
Institutionalized	0.003	0.006	0.003
Hispanic			
Employed/in school	0.845	0.744	−0.101
Idle	0.140	0.226	0.086
Institutionalized	0.014	0.030	0.016

Tabulated from the 1980 and 2000 Census PUMSs. Men in the armed forces are included in the "Employed/In School" category.

population was incarcerated on any given day. The comparable figures for other groups are 3 percent for Hispanics, 1.4 percent for whites, and 0.6 percent for Asians.

Table 10.2 reveals that the proportion incarcerated has increased the most for the least educated men, and that this education–incarceration relationship differs substantially across racial groups. Among white men in 2000, those without a high school diploma are more than twice as likely to be institutionalized relative to those with a high school degree, with 4.5 percent of the former and approximately 2 percent of the latter institutionalized in 2000. Moreover, among white males, high school dropouts experienced the largest increase in institutionalization rates between 1980 and 2000 (2.4 percentage point change, compared with a 1.3 percentage

Table 10.2
Estimates of the proportion of men 18 to 55 engaged in a productive activity, non-institutionalized and idle, and institutionalized by race/ethnicity and education from the 1980 and 2000 PUMS files

	Non-Hispanic white		Non-Hispanic black		Non-Hispanic Asian	
	1980	**2000**	**1980**	**2000**	**1980**	**2000**
Less then high school						
Employed/in school	0.794	0.698	0.658	0.430	0.804	0.699
Idle	0.185	0.257	0.285	0.364	0.186	0.278
Institutionalized	0.021	0.045	0.057	0.206	0.010	0.023
High school grad						
Employed/in school	0.895	0.835	0.776	0.630	0.889	0.793
Idle	0.099	0.146	0.197	0.284	0.106	0.195
Institutionalized	0.006	0.019	0.027	0.087	0.005	0.012
Some college						
Employed/in school	0.941	0.911	0.866	0.794	0.952	0.880
Idle	0.054	0.079	0.110	0.156	0.046	0.115
Institutionalized	0.005	0.009	0.024	0.050	0.002	0.005
College Plus						
Employed/in school	0.963	0.947	0.917	0.890	0.958	0.913
Idle	0.035	0.051	0.073	0.096	0.041	0.087
Institutionalized	0.002	0.002	0.011	0.014	0.000	0.000

Tabulated from the 1980 and 2000 Census PUMSs. Men in the armed forced are included in the "Employed/In School" category.

point increase for white high school graduates, and a 0.4 percentage point increase for those with some college education).

These changes as well as the levels are small in comparison to what is observed for black men. Between 1980 and 2000, the proportion of black men with less than a high school degree that is institutionalized on any given day increases from 0.057 to 0.206. For black male high school graduates, the proportion institutionalized increases from 0.027 to 0.087. Even among black men with some college education, the incarceration rate increases by over two percentage points. In fact, the changes observed among this group of black men are comparable in magnitude to the changes observed among white high school dropouts.

By comparison, the changes in institutionalization rates among Asian men are small, as are the changes among Hispanic men. The relatively low-institutionalization rates among Hispanic men are consistent with research by Kristin Butcher and Anne Piehl (2006) demonstrating the relatively low levels of incarceration among recent immigrants (levels that are particularly surprising given the much lower levels of educational attainment).

Table 10.3 parses the data further for the least educated by age. For high school dropouts and those with a high school diploma, the table presents the distribution of each group across the three possible states by race/ethnicity and by three age groups (eighteen to twenty-five, twenty-six to thirty-five, and thirty-six to forty-five years of age). While not true in all instances, the proportion institutionalized is greatest for men between twenty-six and thirty-five within each education/race group. The most startling figures are those for black men in 2000. Among black men, roughly one-third of high school dropouts between twenty-six and thirty-five are incarcerated on a given day, a number comparable to the proportion of this sub-group employed. The comparable figure for black men with a high school degree is approximately 23 percent. More generally, the institutionalization rate increases for all of these sub-groups of less educated young men. However, the patterns for black males are particularly severe.

A careful reading of the patterns in Tables 10.1 through 10.3 reveals a strong inverse relationship between growth in group-specific incarceration rates and changes in the proportion employed. In particular, we observe marked increases in the proportion of men incarcerated on any given day for relatively young, less educated, minority men. Conversely, there are corresponding sizable declines in the proportions of men who are active in a productive activity (defined here as in school, employed, or in the

Table 10.3
Estimates of the proportion of men 18 to 55 engaged in a productive activity, non-institutionalized and idle, and institutionalized by race/ethnicity and education from the 1980 and 2000 PUMS files

| | Less than High school | | | | | |
| | Non-Hispanic white | | Non-Hispanic black | | Non-Hispanic Asian | |
	1980	2000	1980	2000	1980	2000
Ages 18 to 25						
Employed/in school	0.784	0.797	0.604	0.473	0.791	0.794
Idle	0.188	0.161	0.314	0.307	0.192	0.164
Institutionalized	0.028	0.041	0.081	0.221	0.017	0.043
Ages 26 to 35						
Employed/in school	0.783	0.683	0.634	0.343	0.783	0.655
Idle	0.186	0.249	0.281	0.336	0.207	0.311
Institutionalized	0.032	0.069	0.085	0.321	0.010	0.034
Ages 36 to 45						
Employed/in school	0.823	0.666	0.726	0.423	0.845	0.685
Idle	0.161	0.286	0.240	0.387	0.150	0.301
Institutionalized	0.016	0.047	0.034	0.191	0.005	0.013
	High School graduates					
	Non-Hispanic white		Non-Hispanic black		Non-Hispanic Asian	
	1980	2000	1980	2000	1980	2000
Ages 18 to 25						
Employed/in school	0.872	0.843	0.742	0.634	0.871	0.848
Idle	0.121	0.136	0.229	0.281	0.123	0.140
Institutionalized	0.007	0.021	0.029	0.084	0.007	0.012
Ages 26 to 35						
Employed/in school	0.900	0.845	0.780	0.624	0.888	0.769
Idle	0.093	0.131	0.184	0.259	0.104	0.213
Institutionalized	0.007	0.024	0.036	0.117	0.008	0.019
Ages 36 to 45						
Employed/in school	0.926	0.845	0.827	0.635	0.913	0.785
Idle	0.069	0.137	0.156	0.280	0.085	0.208
Institutionalized	0.005	0.018	0.017	0.085	0.001	0.007

Tabulated from the 1980 and 2000 Census PUMSs. Men in the armed forced are included in the "Employed/In School" category.

military). For example, Table 10.2 reveals declines in the proportion of black men that are active between 1980 and 2000 of twenty-three percentage points for high school dropouts, fifteen percentage points for high school graduates, and seven percentage points for those with some college education. These declines are particularly large for the young and less educated minority men depicted in Table 10.3.

Figure 10.1 demonstrates directly the correspondence between the changes in the proportion employed/active and the changes in the proportion incarcerated. The figure plots the ten-year changes in the proportion active for the 1980s and 1990s against the corresponding ten-year changes in the proportion institutionalized for each of the demographic groups defined by the complete interaction of the four race/ethnicity groups and four education attainment groups displayed in Table 10.2 as well as four age groups corresponding to those used in Table 10.3 plus the group of men aged forty-six to fifty-five. There is a clear negative correlation between these two variables. The results from a simple bivariate regression suggest that a one percentage point increase in the proportion incarcerated is associated with a 0.83 percentage point decrease in the proportion employed/active. If one were to interpret this coefficient as a causal effect, it would suggest that the twenty-four percentage point increase in the incarceration rate of male black high school dropouts between twenty-six and thirty-five caused

Figure 10.1
Scatter plot of change in the ten-year changes in the proportion
employed/in school/in the military against the ten-year change
in the proportion institutionalized, 1980 to 2000

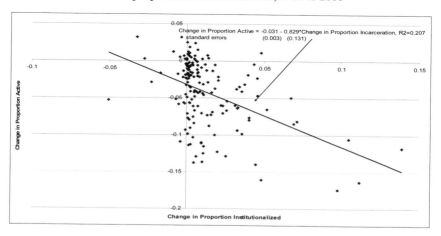

Change in Proportion Active = -0.031 - 0.829*Change in Proportion Incarceration, R2=0.207
standard errors   (0.003) (0.131)

Change in Proportion Institutionalized

an approximate twenty percentage point decline in the employment rate of this group (thus explaining almost 70 percent of the actual decline of twenty-nine percentage points).

What causal pathways may link changes in incarceration rates to the employment outcomes of low-skilled men? First, there is a simple contemporaneous mechanical incapacitation effect of incarceration, in that institutionalized men cannot be employed in the conventional sense. If one were to randomly select a group of men and incarcerate them, the slope coefficient from a regression of the change in employment on the change in incarceration should equal the employment rate for men overall. To be sure, those admitted to prison are hardly a random sample of adult men and are likely to have employment rates substantially below that of the average male. Nonetheless, exogenous increases in incarceration will mechanically reduce the employment rate for those impacted to the extent that some of the newly admitted inmates were employed at the time of arrest.[7,8]

Beyond this contemporaneous effect, incarceration is also likely to have a dynamic lagged impact on the employment prospects of former inmates as well as a contemporaneous impact on the employment outcomes of men who have not been to prison yet come from demographic sub-groups with high incarceration rates. The dynamic effects are derived from the labor demand considerations modeled in the previous section. In particular, the failure to accumulate human capital while incarcerated as well as the stigmatizing effects (sometimes exacerbated by state and federal policy) associated with a prior felony conviction and incarceration may induce employers to curtail their hiring of former inmates. The alternative contemporaneous effect results from employers statistically discriminating against people from high incarceration demographic groups in an attempt to avoid hiring ex-offenders.

Incarceration and the Accumulation of Work Experience

Serving time interrupts one's work career. The extent of this interruption depends on both the expected amount of time served on a typical term as well as the likelihood of serving subsequent prison terms. The average prisoner admitted during the late 1990s on a new commitment faced a maximum sentence of three years and a minimum of one year, with many serving time around the mid-point of this range (Raphael and Stoll, 2005). If this were the only time served for most, then the time interruption of prison would not be that substantial.[9]

However, many people serve multiple terms in prison, either due to the commission of new felonies or due to violation of parole conditions post-release. A large body of criminological research consistently finds that nearly two-thirds of ex-inmates are rearrested within a few years of release from prison (Petersilia, 2003). Moreover, a sizable majority of the rearrested will serve subsequent prison terms. Thus, for many offenders, the typical experience between the ages of eighteen and thirty is characterized by multiple short prison spells with intermittent, and relatively short, spells outside of prison.

In prior longitudinal research on young offenders entering the California state prison system, I documented the degree to which prison interrupts the early potential work careers of young men. I followed a cohort of young men entering the state prison system in 1990 and gauged the amount of time served over the subsequent decade (Raphael, 2005). This analysis is documented in Table 10.4. Panel A shows that the median inmate serves 2.8 years of cumulative time during the 1990s, with the

Table 10.4

Quartile values of the total time served during the 1990s and the time between the date of first admission and date of last release for the 1990 prison cohort between 18 and 25 years of age

Panel A: Distribution of total time served			
	25th Percentile	50th Percentile	75th Percentile
All Inmates	1.44	2.79	4.81
White	1.43	3.09	5.12
Black	1.93	3.53	5.45
Hispanic	1.29	2.23	3.97
Panel B: Distribution of time between the date of first admission and the date of last release			
	25th Percentile	50th Percentile	75th Percentile
All Inmates	1.86	4.99	8.71
White	2.01	6.17	9.11
Black	2.88	6.42	9.16
Hispanic	1.44	3.65	7.62

Tabulation are based on all individuals between the ages of eighteen and twenty-five that entered the California state prison system during 1990 serving the first term of a commitment. Tabulation of the percentiles of the two time distributions are based on all terms served over the subsequent ten years.

median white inmate (3.09 years) and median black inmate (3.53 years) serving more time and the median Hispanic inmate (2.23 years) serving less time.[10] Roughly 25 percent served at least five years during the 1990s while another 25 percent served less than 1.5 years.

However, as a gauge of the extent of the temporal interruption, these figures are misleading. Cumulative time served does not account for the short periods of time between prison spells when inmates may find employment, yet are not able to solidify the employment match with any measurable amount of job tenure. A more appropriate measure of the degree to which incarceration impedes experience accumulation would be the time between the date of admission to prison for the first term served and the date of release from the last term.

Using time lapsed between first admission and final release during the 1990s, the figures in Panel B show that five years elapsed between the first date of admission and the last date of release for the median inmate. For median white, black, and Hispanic inmates, the comparable figures are 6.2, 6.5, and 3.2 years, respectively. For approximately one quarter of inmates, nine years pass between their initial commission to prison and their last release. In other words, one quarter of these inmates spend almost the entire decade cycling in and out of prison.

Spending five years of one's early life (6.5 years for the median black offender) cycling in and out of institutions must impact one's earnings prospects. Clearly, being behind bars and the short spans of time outside of prison prohibits the accumulation of job experiences during a period of one's life when the returns to experience are the greatest.

Does Having Been in Prison Stigmatize Ex-Offenders?

The potential impact of serving time on future labor market prospects extends beyond the failure to accumulate work experience. Employers are averse to hiring former prison inmates and often use formal and informal screening tools to weed ex-offenders out of the applicant pool. Given the high proportion of low-skilled men with prison time on their criminal history records, such employer sentiments and screening practices represent an increasingly important employment barrier, especially for low-skilled African American men.

In all known employer surveys where employers are asked about their willingness to hire ex-offenders, employer responses reveal a strong aversion to hiring applicants with criminal history records (Holzer et al., 2006, 2007; Pager, 2003). For example, Figure 10.2 displays employer responses to a question inquiring about employer willingness to hire ex-offenders from the 1993/1994 Multi-City Study of Urban Inequality. Over 60 percent of employers indicated that they would "probably not" or "definitely not" hire applicants with criminal history records, with "probably not" being the modal response. By contrast, only 8 percent responded similarly when queried about their willingness to hire current and former welfare recipients.

The ability of employers to act on an aversion to ex-offenders, and the nature of the action in terms of hiring and screening behavior, will depend on employer accessibility to criminal history record information. If an employer can and does access criminal history records, the employer may simply screen out applicants based on their actual arrest and conviction records. In the absence of a formal background check, an employer may act on their aversion to hiring ex-offenders using perceived correlates of previous incarceration, such as age, race, or level of educational attainment to attempt to screen out those with criminal histories. In other words, employers may statistically profile applicants and avoid hiring those from demographic groups with high rates of involvement in the criminal justice system.

Such propensity to statistically discriminate is evident in the interaction effect of employers' stated preference regarding their willingness to hire ex-offenders, their screening behavior on this dimension, and

Figure 10.2
Self-reported employer willingness to hire applicants with criminal records

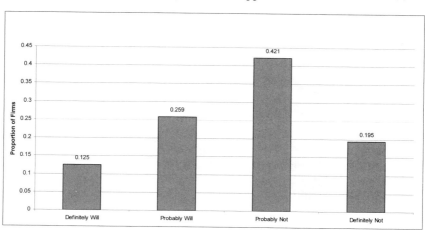

their propensity to hire workers from high incarceration rate groups. This relationship is illustrated in Figure 10.3, which reproduces some of the key findings in Holzer et al. (2006). The figure presents employer survey data collected in 1993/1994 with the y-axis showing the proportion of employers whose recent hire was a black male. Hiring of a black male was predicted by an interaction between employers' self-reported willingness to hire ex-offenders and use of criminal history background checks in screening their potential employees. Among employers who indicate that they are willing to hire ex-offenders, there is no statistically discernable difference in the proportion of recent hires who are black men between those who check and those who do not check criminal backgrounds. Among employers who indicate that they are unwilling to hire ex-offenders, however, checking criminal background is associated with 5.6 percentage point increase in the likelihood that the most recent hire is a black male (statistically significant at the 5 percent level).[11] Thus, among those most averse to hiring former inmates, checking backgrounds actually increases the likelihood that the firm hires black males. This pattern indicates that in the absence of such objective screening methods, employers use more informal screening tools (such as not hiring black males) to weed out potential former inmates. Holzer et al. (2006) find similar patterns with regards to employer willingness to hire other

Figure 10.3
The proportion of employers whose most recent hire was a
black male by their self-stated willingness to hire ex-offenders and
by whether they check criminal backgrounds in screening applicants

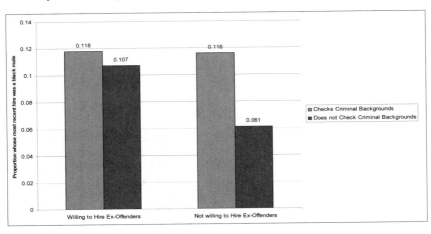

stigmatized groups of workers, such as those with large unaccounted for gaps in their employment histories.

With regards to the direct effect of stigma on former inmates themselves, the audit study by Pager (2003) offers perhaps the clearest evidence of employer aversion to ex-offenders and the stigma associated with having served time in prison. The study uses male auditors matched on observable characteristics including age, education, general appearance, demeanor, and race, to assess the effects of prior prison experience on the likelihood that each auditor is called back for an interview. The author finds consistently sizable negative effects of prior prison experience on the likelihood of being called back by the employer, with callback rates for the auditor with prior prison time one half that of the matched co-auditor.[12]

Existing Research on the Employment Consequences of Incarceration

In conjunction, the effects of stigma combined with the impact of incarceration on human capital accumulation, and perhaps depreciation, suggest that serving time is likely to adversely impact one's employment prospects. Moreover, for men from high incarceration sub-groups, the high rate of involvement with the criminal justice system may have a negative spillover effect to the extent that employers wish to screen out ex-offenders and do so using informal perceived signals of criminality such as race or gaps in one's employment history.

A growing body of empirical research investigates the effects of being convicted and serving time on post-release employment and earnings. In nearly all of these studies, researchers analyze the pre–post-incarceration path of earnings and employment of those who serve time. To be sure, the principal empirical challenge in this research is to define the counterfactual path of earnings and employment for those who go to prison. Defining such a counterfactual path is considerably difficult considering that (1) men tend to go to prison during a time in their lives (early to mid-twenties) when labor force attachment and earnings are changing rapidly, and (2) those who serve time are quite different from those who do not, both on observable and unobservable dimensions.

Researchers have employed a host of strategies to address these methodological challenges. To estimate the effect of previous incarceration on wages, Bruce Western (2002) uses the NLSY79 data to estimate a series of panel regression fixed-effect models where the analysis sample is restricted to those who serve time as well as the additional sub-sample of youth in the NLSY who are at high risk of incarceration as indicated by their self-described involvement in criminal activity. By limiting the study to high-risk youth, Western was able to show that it was not other factors, such as education or income, because all the youth, by being "high risk," shared these attributes to a certain degree. Western finds a sizable relative decline in the hourly wages of formerly incarcerated high-risk youth relative to those who did not serve time.

In previous research (Raphael, 2007), I also employ panel regressions to estimate the effect of a previous incarceration spell on current annual weeks worked, after accounting for current incarceration, the effect of other time-varying covariates, and person-specific fixed effects. The principal empirical innovation in this study is to restrict the analysis sample to youth who eventually serve time. This restriction thus uses youth who serve time later in life as a control group for youth who serve time earlier. I find a significant negative effect of prior incarceration on prior weeks worked on the order of five to six weeks.

Gary Sweeten and Robert Apel (2007) use data from the more recent NLSY97 to estimate the effects of a prior incarceration spell on various employment, educational, and criminal justice outcomes using matching techniques to identify a comparison sample. Specifically, using propensity score matching and a large set of covariates, the authors identify comparison samples for youth who are first incarcerated at sixteen to seventeen years of age and youth who are first incarcerated at eighteen to nineteen years of age and then compare the average outcomes for their treatment and comparison groups for a pre-incarceration year, the year of first incarceration, and the five post-incarceration years. The authors are able to closely match the treated group with good balance on observable covariates and quite comparable pre-incarceration outcomes for the treatment and comparison samples. The authors find sizable effects of a previous incarceration on the probability of employment five years following. The authors also find some evidence that a prior incarceration predicts future criminal activity and poorer post-incarceration educational attainment outcomes relative to the matched comparison sample.

A number of studies have used administrative data on arrest and incarceration matched to administrative earnings records to estimate the effects of involvement in the criminal justice system on employment outcomes. Joel Waldfogel (1994) and Jeffrey Grogger (1995) are among the first to pursue this research strategy. Waldfogel uses data on people who are convicted in federal court and compares pre and post-conviction employment outcomes culled from federal parole records. The author tests for differential effects of actually serving time and of being convicted of a crime involving a breach of trust. The largest earnings penalties occur for those who serve time and those convicted of a "breach" crime. The author also provides evidence that the negative effects of conviction and incarceration on earnings are largest for more educated former inmates.

Grogger (1995) uses California administrative data to study the distributed lagged effect of arrest, conviction, probation, being sentenced to jail, and being sentenced to prison on subsequent earnings and employment using rap sheet information provided by the state attorney general's office and earnings information from state ES-202 records (administrative earnings records used for purposes of administering the unemployment insurance system). Using a series of fixed-effect models, the author finds that arrest has a short-lived negative effect on earnings, while serving a prison sentence has a more pronounced and longer lasting negative effect on earnings. Regarding the latter finding, Grogger cannot assess whether this is a mechanical incapacitation effect of being incarcerated.

A number of recent studies have used state and federal prison administrative records combined with ES-202 earnings records to analyze the pre and post-employment and earnings patterns of prison inmates. For example, Jeffrey Kling (2006) analyzes data for federal prisoners in California and state prisoners in Florida, Haeil Jung (2007) and Rosa Cho and Robert Lalonde (2005) analyze data for state prisoners in Illinois, Becky Pettit and Christopher Lyons (2007) analyze data for prisoners in Washington, while William Sabol (2007) analyzes data for prisoners in Ohio. While these studies differ from one another in terms of the exact questions asked of the data and the methodological approach taken, there are several consistent findings across states.

First, the ES-202 records reveal extremely low levels of labor force participation and earnings among state-prison inmates prior to incarceration (with roughly one-third showing positive quarterly earnings in a given quarter for the two years period preceding incarceration). Kling's (2006) is the only study that compares employment as measured by quarterly earnings records to inmate self-reported employment at the time of arrest. The author reports that while only 33 percent of inmates have positive earnings in the typical pre-incarceration quarter, nearly 65 percent report being employed at the time of arrest. Based on analysis of Current Population Survey data for comparable men, Kling concludes that most of this disparity reflects the fact that inmates are employed in informal jobs where employers are not paying social security taxes or paying into the user interface (UI) system.

Second, nearly all of the studies find that employment increases above pre-incarceration levels immediately following release and then declines to pre-incarceration levels or falls below pre-incarceration levels within a couple of years. The small post-release employment increase is likely driven by the fact that most released prisoners are conditionally released to parole authorities and must meet certain obligations, including employment search or even employment requirements, to remain in the community. To the extent that parole increases employment, or that parole increases the likelihood of being employed in a formal sector job that shows up in quarterly UI records, the post-release increase may be explained by the effect of post-release supervision.

Third, several studies (Cho and Lalonde, 2005; Kling, 2006; Jung, 2007) find that the post-release increase in employment is larger for inmates who serve longer terms. However, Kling (2006) shows that this disparity does not survive controlling for differences in inmates characteristics and program participation differences between inmates serving shorter and longer terms. Particularly important is the difference in the propensity to be involved with a work-release program at the time of the release from prison.

While these studies are suggestive of the impact of conditional supervision on employment, they are generally unable to identify the effects of incarceration on the age earnings and age-employment profiles of those who serve time. The reliance on quarterly UI records renders these results particularly sensitive to any factors that are likely to impact the probability of working for an employer that complies with labor market regulations. It seems reasonable to assume that the employers who participate in work-release programs or who have working relationships with labor market intermediaries that place former inmates have a high degree of compliance with workforce regulation. If this is the case, the pre and post-incarceration employment outcomes as measured by UI earnings records may not be comparable.[13]

In addition, these studies do not identify a comparison group of individuals who do not serve time to whom we could compare the average earnings and employment paths of those who do. Many young men enter prison at a time when labor force attachment is strengthening and earnings are increasing. Failing to account for the slope of the age-earning profile at the time of incarceration seriously distorts inferences regarding the ultimate impacts of incarceration.

A final group of studies uses data from the U.S. census to estimate the partial correlation between the proportion of a given demographic category that is incarcerated and the average employment outcomes of the non-incarcerated among the corresponding group (Raphael, 2005; Raphael and Ronconi, 2006). These studies show that those demographic sub-groups that experience the largest increases in incarceration rates also experience the largest decreases in employment among the non-incarcerated. To the extent that the change in the incarceration rate is correlated with the change in the proportion of the non-incarcerated in the group that has been to prison, these results are suggestive of a negative effect of incarceration. Raphael (2005) shows that changes in the incarceration rates explain a sizable portion of the widening racial disparity in employment rates while Raphael and Ronconi (2006) show the strong covariance between changes in incarceration rates and shifts in the earnings distribution.

Conclusion

A high incarceration rate leaves in its wake a population of former prison inmates who must negotiate the non-institutionalized world. In this chapter, I have laid out a number of mechanisms by which having served time make these negotiations more difficult. Former inmates have under-developed work histories, may have adopted behaviors that are unsuitable for legitimate workplaces, and, above and beyond any impact on actual labor productivity, face stigma among employers when searching for jobs. In many industrialized countries, information on prior criminal history is increasingly available to non-criminal justice entities (e.g., employers), and thus the mark of a criminal record is perhaps more likely to taint one's career prospects today than in the past. Even when information is not available, I have presented evidence suggesting that employers infer previous criminality based on perceived correlates of prior convictions and incarceration.

In certain national contexts, such as the United States where the incarceration rate is particularly high, the incidence of prior incarceration may be sufficiently high such that corrections may be an increasingly important contributor to economic inequality. Certainly, households that experience a parental incarceration suffer an income loss as a result. Moreover, to the extent that serving time is permanently altering one's career profiles, the increasing use of incarceration to punish as well as the increased severity of sentences may be institutionalizing some of the deepest dimensions of inequality, such as those associated with race, class, and the interaction of the two.

Notes

1. Craig (1987) cites several examples where employers were held responsible for the criminal acts of their employees under the theory of negligent hiring, including judgment against the owner of a taxi company and a security services firm for sexual assaults committed by employees. In one cited instance involving a sexual assault committed by an apartment manager, the owner of an apartment complex was found negligent for not taking into account gaps in the manager's work history in the hiring decision.

2. Whether the employer can legally access and consider such information in making hiring decisions is another matter. A 1976 Supreme Court decision ruled arrest and prior conviction records are public given that the initial source of information were public records (Bushway, 1996). Hence, non-criminal justice employees accessing criminal history records do not violate a privacy right. Moreover, who can access records and the extent of information available (e.g., arrests and prior convictions versus prior conviction only) is determined by individual states (U.S. Department of Justice, 1999). The extent to which employers can consider criminal history records is subject to both federal and state guidelines. The Equal Employment Opportunities Commission guidelines prohibit "blanket exclusions" of applicants with criminal records. However, employers can consider criminal histories so long as the severity of the offense is related to the applicant's ability to effectively perform the job and so long as the employer considers the time lapsed since offending in coming to a decision (Bushway, 1996).

3. As written, those with clean histories and those with criminal histories may not be perfect substitutes in production. This might be the case if these two types of labor differ in terms of average productivity.

4. The impact of a change in these parameters on the demand for workers with clean criminal history records is bit more complicated. When optimizing, the employer will use both types of labor up until the point where the ratio of the marginal product of labor to marginal cost is equated across the two labor types. An increase in the costs of employing a felon should increase the proportional employment of those with clean records. In levels, however, the employment level of those with clean records may either increase or decrease in response to increases in the costs of hiring former inmates. The net effect will depend on the degree to which employers can substitute these two alternative types of workers in the production process as well as the magnitude of the scale effect of an increase in labor costs.

5. One might contend that illusory differences in transgression costs should not result in a wage differential if competition for workers among employers is sufficiently fierce. However, I would argue that in actual (as opposed to theoretical) labor markets, search frictions in the process of matching workers to employers are sufficient to preclude competition from undoing a widely held, if erroneous belief.

6. To gauge the validity of using the census data in this manner, in previous research (Raphael, 2005) I compare estimates of the institutionalized population from the census to estimates of the incarcerated populations from other sources by race. While the census estimates are slightly larger than estimates of the incarcerated population from the Bureau of Justice Statistics, the disparities are quite small relative to the overall incarcerated population. The difference likely reflects the very small remaining inpatient population in U.S. mental hospitals.

7. A number of studies demonstrate that roughly one-third to two-thirds of inmates are employed at the time of the arrest leading to their current incarceration (see Kling, 2006; Pettit and Lyons, 2007; Tyler and Kling, 2007; Sabol, 2007).

8. To be sure, causality may also run in the reverse direction—that is, from declining employment prospects, to criminal activity, to incarceration. However, the evidence

on this front is rather weak. First, the decline in wages of the least skilled men between 1980 and 2000 was heavily concentrated in the 1980s, with some low-skilled men regaining lost ground during the 1990s and beyond. However, the increase in incarceration during the 1990s was equal in magnitude to the increase occurring during the 1980s, and the incarceration rate continued to increase between 2000 and 2006. Second, evidence of a behavioral increase in criminal activity is scant, with most research suggesting that the propensity to commit crime actually declined during the 1990s even after accounting for the increase in incarceration.

9.   Of course, I am not saying that a year in prison is not costly. However, a year of absence from the labor market during the beginning of one's career would have only a small effect on accumulated experience.

10. The California inmate population is roughly evenly distributed between whites, Hispanics, and blacks and is overwhelmingly male.

11. The 4.4 percentage point difference relative to firms who are willing to hire black males is statistically significant at the 10 percent level of confidence.

12. Of course, the audit evidence is subject to the critique that the demonstration of the existence of employers who discriminate against former inmates does not necessarily imply a market-level effect of this discrimination. Former inmates can adjust their supply behavior by applying only to those firms willing to hire them. To the extent that the latter set of employers is large relative to the unwilling-to-hire group, the ultimate impact on employment and earnings may be negligible. However, Holzer et al. (2007) find that fairly large proportions of employers express reservations about hiring former inmates. Moreover, in labor market models with search frictions, such unwillingness may reduce the job offer arrival rate of former inmates, resulting in greater unemployment, lower wages when employed (to the extent that former inmates lower their reservation wage), and a higher proportion withdrawing from the workforce.

13. Kornfeld and Bloom (1999) provide a detailed comparison of earnings as measured by quarterly UI records to survey data earnings as measured in the Job Training Partnership Act training experiments and provide estimated program effects using the two sources of data. The authors show that earnings from the UI data are systematically lower than earnings from the survey records. However, relative program effects are similar in magnitude using the two sources of information. The one exception to this rule, however, is for young men with criminal records. The UI data yield larger program effect estimates than the survey records, suggesting that for this particular group, program participation is increasing the likelihood of working for an employer that complies with reporting and tax requirements.

References

Bushway, S. D. "The Impact of a Criminal History Record on Access to Legitimate Employment." Ph.D. diss., Pittsburgh, PA: Carnegie Mellon University, 1996.

Butcher, K. F. and A. M. Piehl. "Why Are Immigrant Incarceration Rates So Low? Evidence on Selective Immigration, Deterrence, and Deportation," Working Paper, New Jersey: Ruckers University, 2006.

Cho, R. and R. Lalonde. *The Impact of Incarceration in State Prison on the Employment Prospects of Women, Harris School Working Paper #5–10*, Chicago, IL: University of Chicago, 2005.

Craig, S. R. "Negligent Hiring: Guilt By Association." *Personnel Administrator,* October (1987) 32–34.

Grogger, J. "The Effect of Arrest on the Employment and Earnings of Young Men," *Quarterly Journal of Economics* 110, no. 1 (1995): 51–71.

Hahn, J. M. "Pre-Employment Information Services: Employers Beware," *Employee Relations Law Journal* 17, no. 1 (1991): 45–69.

Holzer, H. J., S. Raphael, and M. A. Stoll. "The Effect of an Applicant's Criminal History on Employer Hiring Decisions and Screening Practices: Evidence from Los Angeles." In *Barriers to Reentry? The Labor Market for Released Prisoners in Post-Industrial America*, edited by S. Bushway, M. Stoll, and D. Weiman, 117–50. New York, NY: Russell Sage Foundation, 2007.

———. "Perceived Criminality, Criminal Background Checks and the Racial Hiring Practices of Employers," *Journal of Law and Economics* 49, no. 2 (2006): 451–80.

Jung, H. "The Effects of First Incarceration on Male Ex-Offenders' Employment and Earnings." Working Paper, Chicago, IL: University of Chicago, 2007.

Kornfeld, R. and H. Bloom. "Measuring Program Impacts on Earnings and Employment: Do Unemployment Insurance Wage Records Agree with Survey Reports of Individuals," *Journal of Labor Economics* 17, no. 1 (1999): 168–97.

Kling, J. R. "Incarceration Length, Employment, and Earnings," *American Economic Review* 96, no. 3 (2006): 863–76.

Pager, D. "The Mark of a Criminal Record," *American Journal of Sociology* 108, no. 5 (2003) 937–75.

Petersilia, J. *When Prisoners Come Home*, Oxford: Oxford University Press, 2003.

Pettit, B. and C. Lyons. "Status and the Stigma of Incarceration: The Labor Market Effects of Incarceration by Race, Class, and Criminal Involvement." In *Barriers to Reentry? The Labor Market for Released Prisoners in Post-Industrial America*, edited by S. Bushway, M. Stoll and D. Weiman, 206–26. New York, NY: Russell Sage Foundation, 2007.

Raphael, S. "Early Incarceration Spells and the Transition to Adulthood." In *The Price of Independence: The Economics of Early Adulthood*, edited by S. Danziger and C. Rouse, 278–305. New York, NY: Russell Sage Foundation, 2007.

———. "The Socioeconomic Status of Black Males: The Increasing Importance of Incarceration." In *Poverty, the Distribution of Income, and Public Policy*, edited by A. Auerbach, D. Card and J. Quigley, 319–58. New York, NY: Russell Sage Foundation, 2005.

Raphael, S., and L. Ronconi. "Reconciling National and Regional Estimates of the Effects of Immigration on the U.S. Labor Market: The Confounding Effects of Native Male Incarceration Trends," Working Paper. Berkeley, CA: University of California, 2006.

Raphael, S. and M. Stoll. "The Effect of Prison Releases on Regional Crime Rates." In *The Brookings-Wharton Papers on Urban Economic Affairs, Volume 5*, edited by W. G. Gale and J. R. Pack, 207–55. Washington, DC: The Brookings Institution, 2005.

Sabol, W. J. "Local Labor-Market Conditions and Post-Prison Employment Experiences of Offenders released from Ohio State Prisons." In *Barriers to Reentry? The Labor Market for Released Prisoners in Post-Industrial America*, edited by S. Bushway, M. Stoll, and D. Weiman, 257–303. New York, NY: Russell Sage Foundation, 2007.

Sweeten, G. and R. Apel. "Incarceration and the Transition to Adulthood," Working Paper. AZ: Arizona State University, 2007.

Tyler, J. H. and J. R. Kling. "Prison-Based Education and Re-entry into the Mainstream Labor Market." In *Barriers to Reentry? The Labor Market for Released Prisoners in Post-Industrial America*, edited by S. Bushway, M. Stoll, and D. Weiman, 227–56. New York: Russell Sage Foundation, 2007.

Waldfogel, J. "The Effect of Criminal Convictions on Income and the Trust 'Reposed in the Workmen'," *Journal of Human Resources* 29, no. 1 (1994): 62–81.

Western, B. "The Impact of Incarceration on Wage Mobility and Inequality," *American Sociological Review* 67, no. 4 (2002): 526–46.

About the Authors

Kelle Barrick is a Research Criminologist at RTI International, Raleigh-Durham, North Carolina.

Arjan Blokland is a Senior Researcher at the Netherlands Institute for the Study of Crime and Law Enforcement (NSCR) and Professor of Criminology and Criminal Justice in Leiden University, the Netherlands.

Francis T. Cullen is Distinguished Research Professor of Criminal Justice and Sociology, University of Cincinnati, Cincinnati, Ohio.

David P. Farrington is Emeritus Professor of Psychological Criminology and Leverhulme Trust Emeritus Fellow in the Institute of Criminology, Cambridge University, United Kingdom.

Sarah Guckenburg is a Research Associate at WestEd, Woburn, Massachusetts.

Cheryl Lero Jonson is an Assistant Professor in the Department of Criminal Justice, Xavier University, Cincinnati, Ohio.

Marvin D. Krohn is a Professor of Criminology in the University of Florida, Gainesville, Florida.

Giza Lopes is a PhD candidate in the School of Criminal Justice, University at Albany, Albany, New York.

Fred E. Markowitz is an Associate Professor of Sociology in Northern Illinois University, DeKalb, Illinois.

Ross L. Matsueda is Blumstein-Jordan Professor of Sociology in the University of Washington, Seattle, Washington.

Joseph Murray is a Wellcome Trust Research Fellow and Senior Research Associate in the Department of Psychiatry, Cambridge University, United Kingdom.

Anthony Petrosino is a Senior Research Associate at WestEd, Woburn, Massachusetts.

Steven Raphael is a Professor of Public Policy in the Goldman School of Public Policy, University of California, Berkeley, California.

Lawrence W. Sherman is Wolfson Professor of Criminology and Director of the Institute of Criminology, Cambridge University, United Kingdom, and Distinguished University Professor at the University of Maryland, College Park, Maryland.

Delphine Theobald is a Lecturer in Forensic Mental Health at the Institute of Psychiatry, King's College, London, United Kingdom.

Carolyn Turpin-Petrosino is an Associate Professor of Sociology, Anthropology, and Criminal Justice at Bridgewater State College, Bridgewater, Massachusetts.

Jeffrey T. Ward is an Assistant Professor in the Department of Criminal Justice in the University of Texas at San Antonio, Texas.

Index